CHRIST CONSCIOUSNESS

VOICE IS ENERGY, ENERGY CREATES FORM

LINDA IRBY, Ed.D.

Trilogy Christian Publishers
A Wholly Owned Subsidary of Trinity Broadcasting Network
2442 Michelle Drive
Tustin, CA 92780

Cover design by: Cornerstone Creative Solutions

For information, address Trilogy Christian Publishing
Rights Department, 2442 Michelle Drive, Tustin, Ca 92780.
Trilogy Christian Publishing/ TBN and colophon are trademarks of Trinity Broadcasting Network.

For information about special discounts for bulk purchases, please contact Trilogy Christian Publishing.

Manufactured in the United States of America

10 9 8 7 6 5 4 3 2 1

Library of Congress Cataloging-in-Publication Data is available.

ISBN 978-1-63769-340-7 (Print Book)
ISBN 978-1-63769-341-4 (ebook)

DEDICATION

· ·

All glory and praises to God and His only
begotten Son, Jesus Christ.

This book is most humbly dedicated to God (the God of Abraham,
Isaac, and Jacob) and His only begotten Son Jesus Christ, my Lord,
inspiration, and mentor. God and Jesus Christ apparently planned
and orchestrated my religious growth and development, academic
education, work experiences, friendships, and a host of seemingly
hodgepodge travel adventures, exposure to many cultures, and of
course, provided supportive parents, extended family, and friends.

I always pray before starting to research or type this work. My
insecurities about writing for a primarily Christian audience have
intensified my reliance on Jesus. Jesus, of course, is the perfected
intercessor nurturing, protecting, providing specific references, and
giving moral support. All praise and glory to God, Jesus, and the
Holy Trinity! "And it came to pass, when Jesus had ended these sayings, the people were astonished at his doctrine: For he taught them
as one having authority, and not as the scribes" (Matthew 7:28–29).

> Judge not, that ye be not judged. For with what
> judgment ye judge, ye shall be judged: and with
> what measure ye mete, it shall be measured to you
> again. And why beholdest thou the mote that is
> in thy brother's eye, but considerest not the beam
> that is in thine own eye? Or how wilt thou say
> to thy brother, Let me pull out the mote out of
> thine eye; and, behold, a beam is in thine own

eye? Thou hypocrite, first cast out the beam out of thine own eye; and then shalt thou see clearly to cast out the mote out of thy brother's eye. Give not that which is holy unto the dogs, neither cast ye your pearls before swine, lest they trample them under their feet, and turn again and rend you. Ask, and it shall be given you; seek, and ye shall find; knock, and it shall be opened unto you: For every one that asketh receiveth; and he that seeketh findeth; and to him that knocketh it shall be opened. Or what man is there of you, whom if his son ask bread, will he give him a stone? Or if he ask a fish, will he give him a serpent? If ye then, being evil, know how to give good gifts unto your children, how much more shall your Father which is in heaven give good things to them that ask him? Therefore all things whatsoever ye would that men should do to you, do ye even so to them: for this is the law and the prophets. Enter ye in at the strait gate: for wide is the gate, and broad is the way, that leadeth to destruction, and many there be which go in thereat: Because strait is the gate, and narrow is the way, which leadeth unto life, and few there be that find it. Beware of false prophets, which come to you in sheep's clothing, but inwardly they are ravening wolves. Ye shall know them by their fruits. Do men gather grapes of thorns, or figs of thistles? Even so every good tree bringeth forth good fruit; but a corrupt tree bringeth forth evil fruit. A good tree cannot bring forth evil fruit, neither can a corrupt tree bring forth good fruit. Every tree that bringeth not forth good fruit is hewn down, and cast into the fire. Wherefore by their fruits ye shall know them Not every one that saith unto me, Lord, Lord, shall enter into the kingdom of heaven; but he that doeth the will of my Father which is in heaven. Many will say to me in that day, Lord, Lord, have we not prophesied in thy name? and in thy name have cast out devils? and in thy name done many wonderful works? And then will I profess unto them, I never knew you: depart from me, ye that work iniquity. Therefore whosoever heareth these sayings of mine, and doeth them, I will liken him unto a wise man, which built his house upon a rock: And the rain descended, and the floods came, and the winds blew, and beat upon that house; and it fell not: for it was founded upon a rock. And every one that heareth these sayings of mine, and doeth them not, shall be likened unto a foolish man, which built his house upon the sand: And the rain descended, and the floods came, and the winds blew, and beat upon that house; and it fell: and great was the fall of it.

Matthew 7:1–27

CONTENTS

· ·

PREFACE

· ·

"He shall receive the blessing from the LORD,
and righteousness from the God of his salvation"
(Psalms 24:5).

First and foremost, I have to thank Trilogy Publishing in general and specifically Mark Mingle and his staff. Without him and his staff, this book could not have been published. His mentoring and his staff's professional boundless array of knowledge, skills, and abilities they so generously shared is profoundly appreciated.

Pronouns always posed a problem for me, especially in today's widely diverse linguistic preferences. The purpose of this book, in my opinion, needs to flow smoothly. Therefore, for *ease of reading, this work alternates between using the feminine and masculine pronouns when referring to a person whose gender is not known or when under the circumstances of the person's gender is not relevant. This alternation could perhaps be confusing, but overall, it seems easier to read.* There will always be some who will disagree, but regardless of what is done, someone will always disagree. This choice is not meant to offend anyone, just the author's notice about the writing style choice.

This work addresses issues and practices that relate to both our personal lives and our businesses selves. To avoid as often as possible the bulky and difficult-to-read use of slashed nouns (for example, "business/organizations" or "employee/followers") references to individual nouns ("business" and "organization" or "employees" and "followers") are alternated in a similar fashion. I hope that after a few pages, this style choice will allow the text to be both understandable and easy to read and comprehend.

This book has been constructed so that the reader may read the book from beginning to end sequentially, or you may select any section of this book to read independently. However, you are encouraged to read the entire book since the logical progression and scientific development over the past nineteen years, leading to this sequel to the 2002 dissertation's research, will be better understood.

This book acknowledges that catastrophic changes often cause depressions, paranoia, and for most, a "survival of the fittest" action and siege mentality. Changes in reaction to the "new normal" construct more and more physical barriers between individuals. The requirement to wear face masks significantly hinders nonverbal clues and divides and alienates people on a subliminal level. In the particular case of the Coronavirus global pandemic, the requirement for the population to wear face masks and exercise social distancing (requirement to maintain a minimum of six feet between the next closest individual) reinforces isolation even when around another person. Long term, it is particularly contradictory for an individual emotionally to comprehend the oxymoron of being physically isolated while simultaneously surrounded by "untouchable" others. The lingering this damage to our mental health during this two-year juxtaposition will be significant for many. One anticipated result will be significant for some individuals who do not have emotions and then having to express the correct emotion when the masks, literally, come off. But, until then, emotionless people are having a great time, the mask covers their expression less or incorrect expressions to fit the current situation.

To prepare for, react to, and adjust to external changes while being physically isolated as well as mentally demoralized eventually: escalates individuals muted abhorrence to terror and death. Internally motivated change requires self-monitoring the "gap" between our intentions and our behaviors. Self-motivated change can be tricky because once we have gotten used to emotional isolation, there is no reason to care about any gap between our intentions and behaviors, especially if we achieve what we go after. In this "new norm," personal beneficial results determine you "won." Christians, straighten your personal relationship with Jesus, use at all times your discernment initiated by Christ, listen to and obey God's Word, and continue to thank Jesus for covering us with His blood.

DEFINITIONS OF KEY TERMS AND DISCUSSION LIMITATIONS.

Berserk chaos.

The term "berserk chaos" represents multiple changes occurring simultaneously with one or more additional extended catastrophic event(s) unexpectedly. The frantic, total fearfulness manifests; in one or more physiological, psychological, and muscular chronic medical conditions. Often overwhelming hopelessness and the erosion of willpower and apathy reigns in disquieted movements.

Christian tenets

The discussion of Christian tenets is only discussed here in relationship to traditional American work ethics and leadership principles. The scope of discussion is limited to the selected philosophies of John Calvin, Max Weber, and Everett Hagen, all of whom are collectively viewed as (traditional Christians whose tenets are practiced in the United States of America. These selected tenets constitute the "traditional" American work ethic which is considered the "traditional" American business practices. Succinctly put, these combined work ethics comprise the capitalistic, traditional work ethic that expected individuals to choose their vision, work loyally and diligently on the one hand; while on the other hand, these ethics imposed total responsibility on the individual if and when she failed.

Proactive management (of self, followers, and/or projects).

Proactive management goes beyond honesty and sincerity, requiring discipline, balance, dominion, and congruence between core values and actions. These principles are the collection of the leaders (or those to whom administrative authority has been delegated) voice and actions (to include: policies, procedures, laws, ethics, values, negotiated labor agreements, and other work standards) that nourish and sustain a work environment honoring diversity, stimulating productivity, encouraging excellence and aggressively supporting freedom from harassment and discrimination. Competent, purposeful blending and balancing one's personal core values, actively mediating conflicting interpersonal communications, and facilitating productive work systems earmark proactive management principles and best facilitate business profitability.

Christ's Consciousness

Consciousness or awareness is a process of self-reflective information transmission. Christ's Consciousness is all knowledgeable, to include: the cause and effects of in all sciences, healing of every living component, and all emotional interactions to include compassion and love. Christ's Consciousness is the perfect, timeless, steadfast, and righteous discernment of everything. Jesus Christ is God's intercessor for humans. God has the contract with Jesus (through His sacrificial shedding of His blood when crucified), that in His name there is nothing that cannot be achieved. Jesus often spoke in parables when teaching. His goal was to present complex, often compound, and interrelated biological, psychological, physiological, and spiritual motivations, intentions, and behaviors. Along with consciousness occurs an intellectual enlightenment or illumination, which adds a state of moral exaltation, a quickening of one's moral senses, and the appreciation that one is in possession of eternal life.[1]

Community consciousness.

There are two types of community consciousness. The first is God's consciousness, which is (1) omniscience, all-knowing; (2) omnipotence, all-powerful; (3) omnipresence, having direct and immediate knowledge throughout the universe, in all of creation and unoccupied space all the time, simultaneously; and (4) omnibenevolence, possessing perfect and unlimited goodness. The foundation and contention of this work are that Christ's Consciousness conquers catastrophes, change, and chaos.

Core values.

An individual typically has from one to three core values. Core value(s) is a concept, belief, judgment, or thought that defines oneself, including the total of all experiences. The sum of each of our lives, at any given point, shows whether or not significant decisions have purposefully decided based on your unalterable core value or directing what if any changes in your behavior have been made. If, over time your, original core values have remained: impregnable, absorbed, not compromised, or always deliberately infused in your decisions, the essence of your life would be quite unusual! If your core values have never changed, are they different or the same as your community's norm. If you have lived your entire life in this community with extraordinarily little "outside" influences, there is a good chance you and your community's norms will be essentially similar. If, on the other hand, you have experienced two or more communities, there is an increasing chance that some, if not all of your core values may be different (sometimes slightly, sometimes significantly) from your original community.

Core values provide a baseline.

Core values provide a spiritual and emotional boundary to: admit, absorb, deflect and occasionally restructure the balance and fabric of your life. How and what you determine to has to pass through your core value's unalterable turnstile. People, places, speech, and behaviors either "pass or they do not." Occasionally, someone may "jump over their turnstile," ignoring the guaranteed safety precautions. When this happens, the ethical and moral values compass has been disarmed. Sometimes one wants to be defiant, to experience the raw excitement, danger, and freedom—not to determine "deal breakers, correctly discern another's character, reputation, and associations. When defiance has purposefully decided to bypass judgments and "go along to get along," one has in fact selected a new core value system. The applications of your core values are the keys to your survival, sanity, and prosperity. When underestimated, if considered at all, there will be times you discover some this cannot be undone or corrected. Your ability to recognize, to decern has been blindsided, your behavioral principles compromised, and your religious, spiritual tenets bound and gagged. You now contend that basically, we all have the same goals, ambitions, behaviors, and beliefs regarding money, real and personal property, and the stylish trappings of "the good life." Your behaviors and life trajectory will follow your core values.

Creed: to include Affirmative Action guidelines.

There has to be two or more individual that holds the belief or expressed principles for a creed to be "recognized." A "creed" is the written formal statement of governance and values. A creed may include laws, standard codes regarding ethics of care, or minimum performance standards. Religious and/or spiritually inclined creeds typically define their core values, moral or ethical definitions, behaviors, and so forth.

Intent

The internal cognitive (deliberate or subconscious), spoken or written; hopes, dreams, or fears focused on any actual or perceived behavior, physical manifestation, or social collective concern. Intent may or may not become a behavior or action.

Toleration versus Acceptance

Toleration means that you will put up with, perhaps compromise a bit, with different core values. Your core values remain separate and intact. Acceptance means that you will approve of the "other's" core values. You have now conceded that you will completely adapt and behave in accordance with "the others," beliefs, behaviors, and associations. Or, another way of saying this is, according to quantum entanglement theory, Your "core value particles" have interacted sufficiently in such a way with the other's "core values principles" that now neither core values can any longer be individually identified. If and when separation of core values does occur, for whatever reason, each "original core value particle" will always retain some residue of the now "other core values." In other words, each individual will always retain some elements of the other's core values.

Transformational Leadership:

Transforming leadership occurs: when individuals engage with each other so that both leader and follower raise one another to higher levels of motivation, morality, and productivity. Here, in the forming of community and transforming leadership, power bases are linked for mutual support and common purposes. Transformational Leadership reflects the whole integrated person, not just specific skills taught in brief workshops that may or may not fit the core values held by the individual(s). This integrated learning requires a broad educational process that serves to move the leader to a higher stage of moral reasoning and hence to higher levels of principled judgment.

TOLERATION AND ACCEPTANCE ARE NOT EQUAL

You will know what beliefs are your core values because these are the ones that are non-negotiable, and they are something for which you are willing to give anything, including your life, to honor and/or defend. What is interesting about core values is that many of us have no idea specifically what our core values are until we come to a situation for which we will not change our behavior and/or attitude regardless of personal or family peril. Interestingly core values are seldom discussed, even among family members and close friends. Unfortunately, by not discussing core values with those closest to us, misunderstandings and disappointments can occur, causing failures, cracks, and strains, which can demise relationships.

Toleration means that you will put up with some differences, perhaps even compromise a bit. *Acceptance means that you will agree to accept the "others'" core values.* Where some Christians "are tricked, or they rationalize they have not compromised their personal core values because they do not necessarily participate in some or all of the other's core values behaviors. This is a false assumption. Your core values are derived explicitly from your spiritual/religious tenets. You have now conceded and tacitly accepted "another's religious/spiritual tenets. Like any other contract, the following is applicable, you accept:

- whatever is within the "four corners" of the contract;
- whether you understood all the ramifications or not,
- even if you did not "read or discuss" fully,
- once you agree to the contract, you are stuck with it until it elapses (if there is a stipulated length of time for the contract), or
- you negotiate another contract,
- or you "illegally" break the contract.
- *Remember, this contract is spiritual and thus binding both in "the heavens" and on earth.*

So, regarding behaviors that include but are not necessarily limited to "hanging out with friends and associates," remember your behaviors and/or verbal support are at least "tacit," if not, in fact, stating agreeing with "the others," core values. Where I grew up the saying was, "with association, there is assimilation." This is one reason why when some Christians think being "kind" and "tolerating" another's non-Christian behaviors is a ruse (they have actually taken a bite out of the offered apple). These same Christians are surprised when they discover they have been "played" and, in many cases, hated. Sometimes toleration is not possible when it comes up against one's core values. In either case, always remember to pray and ask Jesus for redemption and guidance in these situations. There is a fine line between superficial, limited association, in which one can share God's Word and the redemption available because of Jesus's blood sacrifice to redeem our sins. Work situations must be taken on a case-by-case basis, contingent on the type of work and the mandatory characteristics of the job specifications. If the job is worrisome, then search for another job. We must always remember we are in the world, not of it: "I have given them thy word, and the world hath hated them, because they are not of the world, even as I am not of the world" (John 17:14).

As you can see and appreciate, a whole new set of considerations are necessary when recognizing that at the quantum level, "associations and "interconnectedness" always leave a spiritual residue. After all, if you are a Christian, you do not want to be surprised at the judgment when Jesus states: "And then will I profess unto them, I never knew you: depart from me, ye that work iniquity" (Matthew 7:23).

ACKNOWLEDGEMENTS

BELOVED FAMILY MENTORS

The Reverend Grace Margaret Irby	1892–1985
Grace Margaret Irby Howell R.N.	1923–1987
Reginald Stanley Howell M.D.	1923–1999
Galven Irby LLD.	1921–2017
Virginia Irby B. S.	1931–2015
Ronald Steven Howell B.S.	Alive—yes!

DISSERTATION COMMITTEE

John J. Z. Gardiner Ph.D.	Committee Chair
Gary H. Zarter Ph.D.	Committee Member
Eugene William Wiegman Ph.D.	Committee Member 1929–2020

CHERISHED FAMILY AND FRIENDS

Claudia Adkins
Courtney Adkins
Gerald Adkins
Anthony Ball
Joseph Paul Beaulieu
Ora Chapmen
Michael Hill
Marian Hoffman
Darlene Howell
Spencer Howell
Darrin Howell
Brenden Howell
Cardel Irby Jr.
Craig Irby
Kelly Irby
Veta Irby
Vylda Irby
Merry A Kogut LL.D.
Carolyn Lawson Ed.D.
Shawna Loomis
Paul W. Schmidt M.D.
Nancy Sprowls
Tamara Stewart
Vincent Stewart
James Thomas III
John Wells
James William

BOOK SUMMARY

For I know nothing by myself; yet am I not hereby justified: but he that judgeth me is the Lord. Therefore judge nothing before the time, until the Lord come, who both will bring to light the hidden things of darkness, and will make manifest the counsels of the hearts: and then shall every man have praise of God.

1 Corinthians 4:4–5

Sometimes, most of us think at least once in life that life would be a lot easier if what we wanted, wished for, and dreamed of, would come true. During this dream fabrication, the consideration of other humans does not exist, just our own desires. Selfishness rarely is altruistic, much less operationally prudent, and definitely would come with unanticipated and most probably unwanted consequences. None of these factual details invade self-centered dreaming, and fortunately, reality invades fantasy, and we return to "the real world."

This book is about how our reality "flickers," rarely is "life," a path of smooth, shiny gold. Not only is our path not golden, but the illusion we have of "returning" to our path incorrectly considers "our path" as being our normal life. In reality, our path is fraught with disruptions, detours, and for novelty, outright catastrophic blockages. Is this the normal we anxiously seek? Realistically, the only thing normal about our life's path is: if you do not like something, things will change, and if you do like something, things will change. The only thing that has been is, or will be in our life is change.

This work focuses on how we "deal" or fail to deal with change, catastrophic changes, and berserk chaos. The term "berserk chaos" represents multiple changes occurring simultaneously with one or more additional extended catastrophic event(s) unexpectedly. When one-too-many changes occur, some of us are shredded but still alive, and unfortunately, some of us expire...attempting to cope with the change without changing. This book's premise is that Christians, those individuals who believe in the God of Abraham, Isaac, and Jacob, who is the father of his only begotten son Jesus Christ: is this you? Presumably, we as Christians adjust to changes and chaos less frantically (supposedly) because we have Jesus as our anchor, stabilizer, and cornerstone. The expectation is that even under woeful conditions, The Church and its parishioners individually and collectively bond together. We bond in both prayers and behaviors to support one another, attend to God's Word, and we do the best possible given the circumstances. Why? Because Christians have their system of "rewards, property, and prosperity" vested in eternal life with spiritual peace, conscious awareness, and love everlasting contracted through God's Word in the Holy Bible.

THE PURPOSE OF THIS BOOK IN A NUTSHELL.

This book starts with the premise (based on a 2002 doctoral dissertation), "Leadership Voices™: Values, Proactive Management, and Consciousness," that consciousness is not something to be obtained, but something each of us has and we "just have to" recognize our inextricable and unbreakable connection. I guess another way of putting this is most of the time, we do not pay particular attention to our breathing unless, for some reason, our breath is constricted or has stopped. One of the prominent threads in this research contended that that "voice is energy, energy creates form."

"And the Word was made flesh, and dwelt among us (and we beheld his glory, the glory as of the only begotten of the Father,) full of grace and truth" (John 1:14).

At the time, quantum physicists were developing theories that supported the importance of consciousness (recognition), which was critical in the outcome of one's experiences: for example, Schrodinger's cat.[2] Schrodinger's breakthrough theorized that something exists only as long as it is observed; otherwise, it is simply nonexistent.

This book, nineteen years later, concludes that not only is there "universal consciousness," this consciousness is Christ's Consciousness, existing from the "very beginning, now, and of course, never-ending. In the past intervening years, quantum mechanics has advanced. One significant occurrence was the invention of the Large Hadron Collider (built between 1998 and 2008), the world's largest and highest-energy particle collider. Experiments successfully conducted include the discovery of the Higgs Boson, commonly called the God particle. In my mind's eye, I see God smiling (with a twinkle in His eyes), saying, "of course, I'm God:" and naturally, psychists are ecstatic because they have discovered something new.

Change is an inevitability, and we have witnessed, especially within the U.S., changes (beginning in the late 1950's/1960's) at an exponentially increase in:

- abandonment of civility,
- children indoctrinated to adapt, Aleister Crowley's philosophy, "Do what thou wilt,"
- disintegration of morality,
- expansion of all occult practices,
- increase in deadly violence,
- laws (etc., abortion, catch and release, and elder genocide),
- normalization of occult practices,
- deletion of all Christian values
- satanic rituals at public events,

This book, nineteen years later, picks up where the previous study ended. We now see and hear in general conversations, advertisements the entrepreneurs mainstreaming newly developed, reasonably priced everyday products. Overall, the term conscious awareness has devolved into common conversations with a wide range of diverse "tinkering" with the unfathomable, divine essence of consciousness. To include the following but not necessarily limited to the following:

- a profitable commodity,
- a spiritual badge of prestige,
- anticipated economic spinoffs,
- means to scientific awards,
- military power, and
- one world dominance.

This book reviews the dramatic moral, ethical, and religious/spiritual fundamental changes in the U.S., resulting in a profusion of individuals with mental disorders characterized by a disconnection from reality (of oh so many varieties). The U.S. population has exponentially exploded since the late 1950's–2021 in the search and acceptance of all aspects of the occult practices. These practices range from the seemingly harmless activities of "playing with the pendulum" to worshiping idols with blood rituals. A significant finding of this book once again reminds all Christians that:

1. God is a jealous God.

   "For the LORD thy God is a jealous God among you) lest the anger of the LORD thy God be kindled against thee, and destroy thee from off the face of the earth"
   (Deuteronomy 6:15).

2. Jesus Christ voluntarily gave His life and shed His blood as the blood offering to redeem our sins.

   Who hath believed our report? and to whom is the arm of the LORD revealed? For he shall grow up before him as a tender plant, and as a root out of a dry ground: he hath no form nor comeliness; and when we shall see him, there is no beauty that we should desire him. He is despised and rejected of men; a man of sorrows, and acquainted with grief: and we hid as it were our faces from him; he was despised, and we esteemed him not. Surely he hath borne our griefs, and carried our sorrows: yet we did esteem him stricken, smitten of God, and afflicted. But he was wounded for our transgressions, he was bruised for our iniquities: the chastisement of our peace was upon him; and with his stripes we are healed. All we like sheep have gone astray; we have turned every one to his own way; and the LORD hath laid on him the iniquity of us all. He was oppressed, and he was afflicted, yet he opened not his mouth: he is brought as a lamb to the slaughter, and as a sheep before her shearers is dumb, so he openeth not his mouth. He was taken from prison and from judgment: and who shall declare his generation? for he was cut off out of the land of the living: for the transgression of my people was he stricken. And he made his grave with the wicked, and with the rich in his death; because he had done no violence, neither was any deceit in his mouth.

Isaiah 53: 1–9

3. Jesus Christ is the only way to God and eternal salvation.

Jesus saith unto him, I am the way, the truth, and the life: no man cometh unto the Father, but by me. If ye had known me, ye should have known my Father also: and from henceforth ye know him, and have seen him.

John 14:6–7

A CAUTIONARY TALE NARCISSISTIC AUTONOMY: PREY MEETS PREDATOR.

Christians (should) know identifying their core values are insufficient by itself. Core values need to work "hand-in-hand" with accurate discernment. Discernment (judgment and shrewdness) is critical to:

1) acknowledge the spirt speaking to you is actually Jesus,
2) get an accurate appraisal of one's surroundings, and
3) then make durable decisions.

This skill has always been important. Now many in the U.S. contend, our nation is becoming a mirror version of George Orwell's classic dystopian novel, "Nineteen Eighty-Four." Admittedly, there seem to be lots of similarities, but two distinctive differences should make us pause before declaring the book's ending prophesizes our countries outcome. First, our significantly confused society is by no means "set" yet. Secondly, the characters (protagonist Winston Smith and his girlfriend Julia) are mentally and emotionally eviscerated. Spoiler alert: Winston breaks physically, mentally, and emotionally and chooses the party over his "love" Julia. Just before the novel ends, Winston and Julia meet, and they realize they both betrayed each other under torture. Both now love Big Brother. The most ominous, gut-wrenching despair in this novel is that there is no hope, redemption, no Jesus or Holy Trinity. Happiness and fulfillment in this totalitarian oligarchy are contingent on the degree to which Big Brother and The Party fill every fiber of their skeletal configuration. Pray without ceasing (1 Thessalonians 5:17–23) to ensure that the novel's ending remains Orwell's creative cautionary tale.

> Pray without ceasing. In every thing give thanks: for this is the will of God in Christ Jesus concerning you. Quench not the Spirit. Despise not prophesyings. Prove all things; hold fast that which is good. Abstain from all appearance of evil. And the very God of peace sanctify you

wholly; and I pray God your whole spirit and soul and body be preserved blameless unto the coming of our Lord Jesus Christ.

1 Thessalonians 5:17–23

SELF-EXPLORATORY QUESTIONS INVITE YOU TO ENGAGE.

We have determined core values are the consequence of an individual's conscious awareness. For Christians, that means at a spiritual level, Christ's consciousness is indwelling with your spirit. The importance of our ability to make good decisions, especially during prolonged and unanticipated changes, has greater repercussions over time; than just what occurs for you. Today as individuals, whether or not we like it, we are involved in interconnected systems, and we must not only act communally but also think globally. This truism became glaringly obvious during the global COVID-19 pandemic. As the U.S. became infected we had to drastically curtail our personal liberties.

This book challenges each reader to consider whether or not, sometime in their daily lives, as well as during change and chaotic times, do you look to God's Word, which should be the source of your core values. Our core values should be deliberately considered daily as we make our zillions of small decisions, so when perilous life decisions occur, we are automatedly reliant on God's Word. You are right, this is not easy! This is why we go to Jesus as our intercessor, and we are covered by His blood, and by faith (not works), we are saved.

For by grace are ye saved through faith; and that not of yourselves: it is the gift of God: Not of works, lest any man should boast. We were never promised life would be ease, just that we would be protected, loved, and blessed with life everlasting.

Ephesians 2:8–9

The foundation and contention of this work are that Christ's consciousness conquers change, catastrophic change, and berserk chaos. **This work's intent is to guide each of us through the processes of introspection and self-analysis to:**

1. Extract information gradually, so bit by bit, you amass enough realization to determine if there is a gap between who you think you are…and who you actually are.
2. To correctly assess whether you deliberately incorporate your religious tenets and core values in your daily walk of life.
3. For those who are anything but Christian, have you:
   a. Identified your fundamental statement of belief, your "deal breakers," and your subsequent core values?
   b. Considered which outside influences (youth background, community associations, etc.) contributed to your current statement of belief?
   c. If at one time you were affiliated with a religion/spiritual community, can you succinctly say why you discarded your faith?
   d. Can you identify what guideline(s), if any, that you deliberately access when making decisions?
   e. Do you deliberately modifying your behavior to exhibit your core values?

One does not become a Christian by accident, only by conscious choice. In primary areas of your existence, your day-to-day survival demands interpersonal relationships with others. Your core values significantly influence who you associate with. This a continuing, overlapping, interrelated "circle of life."

BIBLICAL SUPPORT OF TENETS FOUND IN TRANSFORMATIONAL LEADERSHIP.

In both change and chaos, the Transformational Leader's competencies must include the ability to influence others to accomplish the desired outcome. The leader should have the ability to adapt problem-solving styles to the situation, help others invest in inclusive, common core values, goals, and visions. Typically we tend to want both stability and then want change for variety. However, we want "the change" to be convenient, not threatening or compromise our core values. *Our core values are those non-negotiable values we are willing to die for rather than renege.* This is where the power of prayer (beseeching, confused, formal, simple, specific, spontaneous, or thankful), prayed in the name of Jesus Christ, allows Jesus to be both our Servant and Transformational leader.

- "For there is one God, and one mediator between God and men, the man Christ Jesus" (1 Timothy 2:5).
- "I will therefore that men pray every where, lifting up holy hands, without wrath and doubting" (1 Timothy 2:8)

Christians following God's tenets of Servant and Transformational Leadership, mindfully adhering to tenets taught in the Holy Bible, are more resilient, emotionally grounded, and have inner peace. God's Word is:

- eternal (Psalm 119:160 and John 1:14),
- immutable (Numbers 23:19 / 1 Samuel 15:29, / Ps.102:25–27, / Malachi 3:6, / Hebrews 6:17–18, and James 1:17).
- inspired (2 Timothy 3:16),
- infallible (Hebrews 6:16–19),

The questions and difficulties most Christians have are how to incorporate their uncompromised core values, especially during times of stress, change, and traumatic chaos. More specifically, what leadership characteristics enable the best leaders (both Christians and others) to be both flexible visionaries and proactive managers during change that cuts one "down to the bone?" A workbook section is provided for your individual participation in Chapter 9, the last Chapter.

Personal loss forces one to comprehend change's impact directly proportionate with the disruption(s) caused. Anyone can move ahead during times of happiness, but a leader's vision and character, when supported by core values, lead prudently in uncertainty.

Time and change both feeds and drains us in our lives, like rivers ebb and flow. If we are blessed, God will provide people to come to us when it is time, and if we are fortunate, they will leave when it is time. Change reminds us to count our blessings, never filter moments of bliss, and not to count the steps on our journey.

CONTACT INFORMATION:

- Seattle University Academia Profile, (99+) Dr. Linda Irby | Seattle University—Academia.edu
- Access for full 2002 dissertation, "Leadership Voices ™: Values, Proactive Management, and Consciousness. https://www.academia.edu/575575/_Dissertation-Leadership-Voices-Values-Proactive_Management_and_consciousness
- Facebook page: Leadership Voices™: for open discussions, thoughts, and questions. (6) Facebook
- For direct email contact related to (1) 2006, the book "Leadership Voices™: Dealing with Determinedly Difficult People, Bullies, and Predators at Work." (2) Consultation, for a fee, workshops with the dysfunctional work force, (3) General correspondence with me. leadvoices@aol.com
- My educational and work profile, awards, and other publications. https://www.linkedin.com/in/linda-irby-ed-d-20026017

CHAPTER 1

....

Our New Norm Started In 2001

The thing that hath been, it is that which shall be; and that which is done is that which shall be done: and there is no new thing under the sun. Is there any thing whereof it may be said, See, this is new? it hath been already of old time, which was before us. There is no remembrance of former things; neither shall there be any remembrance of things that are to come with those that shall come after.

Ecclesiastes 1:9–11

THIS BOOK'S BACKSTORY.

Despotic regimes, for most, arrive surreptitiously disguised as improvements for the dejected, lonely, differently able, and overlooked. The "party line" is everyone is equal, basic subsistence for all, and of course, "world peace." And then the Iron Curtain drops. In 2002, my dissertation was submitted and accepted, in partial fulfillment of the requirements for the degree of Doctor of Education from Seattle University, Seattle, Washington. The dissertation's title is *Leadership Voices™: Values, Proactive Management, and Consciousness*: UMI Number: 3041363. Since the publication of the dissertation, over the past 19 years, there has been a steady increase of individuals accessing this work, not only in the U.S. but from at least 17 different countries to date. The most used search terms are consciousness, leadership, and Transformational Leadership. Naturally, over the past years, there have been many advancements in research, understanding quantum mechanics (physics), and entanglement theories. Quantum mechanics is a theory that describes the physical properties of nature at the scale of atoms and subatomic particles. Want some help? Watch these YouTube videos:

- "If you don't understand Quantum Physics, try this!" If you do not understand Quantum Physics,[3] https://youtu.be/Usu9xZfabPM
- "Quantum Mechanics: Animation explaining quantum physics" (Schrodinger's Cat)[4] https://youtu.be/iVpXrbZ4bnU

Of course, in the intervening years, quantum physics has exponentially developed. Today is the "age" of quantum sensors that can analyze the full spectrum of radio frequencies. Then there is the nano light, which is a new way to program light on an ultra-small scale. Quantum computing has made its presence known in quite a few fiction novels, considering both the pros and cons of this formally unknown massive computer(s) abilities. And last but not least will be mentioned the continued theoretical physis search for dark matter in the fifth dimension. So, what is the point of this, in a book discussing how to better cope with and change and chaos? *We have seen that it has taken millenniums for quantum physics to scratch the surface of the: magnitude, creation ability, and transference of energy to matter and that God IS alive, sentient, and powerful. Christ's Consciousness is real, entangled, infinite, and has cause and effect.*

LEADERSHIP VOICES™ DISSERTATION IS THE PARADIGM SHIFT TO CHRIST'S CONSCIOUSNESS.

There are several findings in the 2002 publication of the Leadership Voices™ research, that nineteen years later in the year 2021 is emphatically restating the importance of the former ground-breaking work. *First, the concrete importance of the leader's religious/spiritual core values being consistent with her behaviors has never been more important than now.* While the original research focused on individuals in the business environment, this book has expanded the necessity of an individual's authentic, purposeful, and synchronized behaviors with his core values in every aspect of his life. The significant takeaway here is that individuals (not just leaders and managers) must comprehend that her voice is energy, which always creates form. Therefore, "voice is energy, energy creates form;" then and now, and will tomorrow.

First of all, one's words are most powerfully uplifting or demoralizing, determining both one's behavior and self-esteem. One's core values have a direct cause and effect on interpersonal relationships, achievement of goals, the ability to influence others, and contributes to the "tone" of one's environment. Secondly, depending on the individual, one has a choice, either among disciplines or within a discipline (religious or spiritual tenets, management principles, quantum philosophies, sociology, or psychology, etc.), to support the context of what her self-awareness internalizes. This choice, of course, is a cornerstone of her voice (core values). While each discipline jointly and separately arrives at this same conclusion, the paths though parallel, when traveled, will be different. Some decisions will turn out to be permanent, there can be no "do-overs," so each decision is important because one never knows which decision will be irrevocably decisive.

And finally, the dissertation study focused on Christian tenets as practiced within the United States of America. However, other religious and "spiritual beliefs" were hypothesized to be compatible with proactive management principles. This work holds true to this contention that proactive management principles may be compatible beyond individuals who are Christian. It is also continued to be acknowledged that some "leaders" are actually managers.

HOW DID THE MONIKER LEADERSHIP VOICES™ EVOLVE?

The original research focused on identifying the common voices, if any, among core values, proactive management principles, and community consciousness. The term "Leadership Voices™" represents the common elements identified when leadership principles presented in Christian tenets (as practiced within the United States) are compared to proactive management principles. The focus is on Christian tenets as a spiritual source. Obviously, one of the significant strands of the 2002 dissertation centered on Christian tenets.

This work focuses on Christians within the U.S. whose spiritual tenets are based on the Holy Bible, for this book, the King James Version is the Bible used. The Bible is an unlimited, timeless source of comfort, advice, protection, and companionship. I know that walking life's path, I have noted that certain scriptures have greater resonance with me than others, depending on life's circumstances at the time. So I have taken the liberty of providing the scriptures that now provide comfort and guidance to me. The following Table 1 displays twenty-seven selected spiritual scriptures as an example of "Christian spiritual tenets that illuminated my path during these berserk chaotic times. The following scriptures were chosen because they are specifically meaningful to me. The selection is purely personal and given only as an example, should you choose to, or may have already chosen scriptures that have a personal calling to you. What is most important about our choices, at any given time that is our refuge, is that they provide a clue to one's self about the construction and content of our individual core values.

For the sake of presenting this example, I have given each scripture a personally chosen category, which helps me identify how I am drawing my strength and guidance from each. Therefore, the designations listed in the topic column are strictly personal to me. You will notice that I have left the last column blank in case you have a different category that makes them significant to you. Then again, you may have a completely different selection of scriptures. Once again, I say this is a purely personal absorption of God's word. Of course, you may make any other notes in the blank column that you wish. You will also notice that I have designated for each scripture whether or not they are in the Old or New Testament.

Some individuals place great significance on which administration the scripture is under (Old or New), personally, it is a learning guide for me. Jesus brought in a new administration, the significant modification to the "contract with God," in the New Testament, Jesus was given authority and allowed to become the sacrifice for humans to repent our sins. It is my understanding that depending on the Christian denomination, the process and procedure of adhering to each and every rule required in the Old Testament 100 percent of the time seems to be a continuing interdenominational discussion. This discussion is not going to be addressed in this work.

Table 1: Selected scriptures from the KJV Bible.

This table is submitted as an example of scriptures that I personally find to be a "reality check" and soothing. God's Word is worth being still and listening. The Topic designations are mine; they represent how I've categorized them in my mind. The "Reader's Thoughts" are for you to categorize in your mind.

TOPIC	LOCATION		SCRIPTURES I rely on.	READER'S THOUGHTS
	Old/New Testament	Scripture		
Admonishment	Old	Proverbs 6:12–15	A naughty person, a wicked man, walketh with a froward mouth. He winketh with his eyes, he speaketh with his feet, he teacheth with his fingers; Frowardness is in his heart, he deviseth	

			mischief continually; he soweth discord. Therefore shall his calamity come suddenly; suddenly shall he be broken without remedy.	
Admonishment	Old	Proverbs 6:16–19	These six things doth the LORD hate: yea, seven are an abomination unto him: A proud look, a lying tongue, and hands that shed innocent blood, An heart that deviseth wicked imaginations, feet that be swift in running to mischief, A false witness that speaketh lies, and he that soweth discord among brethren.	
Admonishment	New	Matthew 18:8	Wherefore if thy hand or thy foot offend thee, cut them off, and cast *them* from thee: it is better for thee to enter into life halt or maimed, rather than having two hands or two feet to be cast into everlasting fire.	
Admonishment	New	Mark 9:45	And if thy foot offend thee, cut it off: it is better for thee to enter halt into life, than having two feet to be cast into hell, into the fire that never shall be quenched:	

Agreement 2 or 3 together God's Word: Red letter KJV	New	Matthew 18:19–20	Again I say unto you, That if two of you shall agree on earth as touching any thing that they shall ask, it shall be done for them of my Father which is in heaven. For where two or three are gathered together in my name, there am I in the midst of them.	
Agreement 2 or 3 together God's Word: Red letter KJV	New	1 Corinthians 14:29	Let the prophets speak two or three, and let the other judge.	
Apathy	New	Matthew 10:14	And whosoever shall not receive you, nor hear your words, when ye depart out of that house or city, shake off the dust of your feet.	
Apathy	New	Mark 4:15–16	And these are they by the way side, where the word is sown; but when they have heard, Satan cometh immediately, and taketh away the word that was sown in their hearts. And these are they likewise which are sown on stony ground; who when they have heard the word, immediately receive it with gladness;	
Light	New	Luke 1:79	To give light to them that sit in darkness and in the shadow of death, to guide our feet into the way of peace.	

Light	Old	2 Samuel 23:3–4	The God of Israel said, the Rock of Israel spake to me, He that ruleth over men must be just ruling in the fear of God. And he shall be as the light of the morning, when the sun riseth, even a morning without clouds; as the tender grass springing out of the earth by clear shining after rain.	
Protector	Old	Psalm 91:1–16	He that dwelleth in the secret place of the most High shall abide under the shadow of the Almighty. I will say of the LORD, He is my refuge and my fortress: my God; in him will I trust. Surely he shall deliver thee from the snare of the fowler, and from the noisome pestilence. He shall cover thee with his feathers, and under his wings shalt thou trust; his truth shall be thy shield and buckler. *Thou shalt not be afraid for the terror by night; nor for the arrow that flieth by day; Nor for the pestilence that walketh in darkness; nor for the destruction that wasteth at noonday. A thousand shall fall at thy side, and ten thousand at thy right*	

hand; but it shall not come nigh thee. Only with thine eyes shalt thou behold and see the reward of the wicked. Because thou hast made the LORD, which is my refuge, even the most High, thy habitation; *There shall no evil befall thee, neither shall any plague come nigh thy dwelling.* For he shall give his angels charge over thee, to keep thee in all thy ways. They shall bear thee up in their hands, lest thou dash thy foot against a stone. Thou shalt tread upon the lion and adder: the young lion and the dragon shalt thou trample under feet. Because he hath set his love upon me, therefore will I deliver him: I will set him on high, because he hath know my name. He shall call upon me, and I will answer him; I will be with him in trouble; I will deliver him, and honour him. With long life will I satisfy him, and shew him my salvation.

Protector	Old	Ezekiel 2:1–2	And he said unto me, Son of man, stand upon thy feet, and I will speak unto thee. And the spirit entered into me when he spake unto me, and set me upon my feet, that I heard him that spake unto me.	
Protector	Old	Ezekiel 3:24	Then the spirit entered into me, and set me upon my feet, and spake with me, and said unto me, Go, shut thyself within thine house.	
Provider	Old	Nehemiah 9:21	Yea, forty years didst thou sustain them in the wilderness, *so that* they lacked nothing; their clothes waxed not old, and their feet swelled not	
Provider	Old	Psalms 40:2	He brought me up also out of an horrible pit, out of the miry clay, and set my feet upon a rock, *and* established my goings.	
Resurrection	New	1 Corinthians 15:20–28	But now is Christ risen from the dead, and become the firstfruits of them that slept. Forsince by man came death, by man came also the resurrection of the dead. For as in Adam all die, even so in Christ shall all be made alive. But every man in his own order; Christ the firstfruits;	

			afterward they that are Christ's at his coming. Then cometh the end when he shall have delivered. For he must reign, till he hath put all enemies under his feet. The last enemy that shall be destroyed is death. For he hath put all things under his feet. But when he saith all things are put under him, it is manifest that he is expected, which did put all things under him. And when all things shall be subdued unto him, then shall the Son also himself be subject unto him that put all things under him, that God may be all in all.	
Resurrection	New	Luke 24:39	Behold my hands and my feet, that it is I myself: handle me, and see; for a spirit hath not flesh and bones, as ye see me have.	
Resurrection	New	Revelation 11:11–12	And after three days and a half the Spirit of life from God entered into them, and they stood upon their feet; and great fear fell upon them which saw them. And they herd a great voice from heaven saying unto them, Come up hither. And they ascended up to heaven in a cloud and their enemies beheld them.;	

Retribution	New	Romans 12:18–19	If it be possible, as much as lieth in you, live peaceably with all men. Dearly beloved, avenge not yourselves, but rather give place unto wrath: for it is written, Vengeance is mine; I will repay, saith the Lord.	
Retribution	New	Romans 16:20	And the God of peace shall bruise Satan under your feet shortly. The grace of our Lord Jesus Christ *be* with you. Amen.	
Retribution	Old	Deuteronomy 32:35–36	To me belongeth vengeance, and recompence; their foot shall slide in *due* time: for the day of their calamity *is* at hand, and the things that shall come upon them make haste. For the LORD shall judge his people, and repent himself for his servants, when he seeth that *their* power is gone, and *there is* none shut up, or left.	
Retribution	Old	Nahum 1:3	The LORD *is* slow to anger, and great in power, and will not at all acquit *the wicked*: the LORD hath his way in the whirlwind and in the storm, and the clouds *are* the dust of his feet.	

Truth God's Word: Red letter KJV	New	John 17:17	Sanctify them through thy truth: thy word is truth.	
Truth	Old	Psalm 119:160	Thy word *is* true *from* the beginning: and every one of thy righteous judgments *endureth* for ever.	
Truth	Old	Proverbs 30:5–6	Every word of God is pure: he is a shield unto them that put their trust in him. Add thou not unto his words, lest he reprove thee, and thou be found a liar.	
Witness	New	2 Corinthians 13:1	This *is* the third *time* I am coming to you. In the mouth of two or three witnesses shall every word be established.	
Witness God's Word: Red letter KJV	New	Matthew 18:16	But if he will not hear *thee, then* take with thee one or two more, that in the mouth of two or three witnesses every word may be established.	
Witness	New	1 Timothy 5:19	Against an elder receive not an accusation, but before two or three witnesses.	

The previous table only submits Christian scriptures. For those who have different sacred documents with the equivalent of scriptures, to you, I acknowledged and appreciated that other religions and "spiritual scriptures/writings/oral histories" may also be compatible with proactive management principles. This distinction emphasizing management principles is necessary because Christians adhere to the tenet that Jesus Christ is the only his name, his sacrifice on Calvary, and each individual's sanctification is given to us by God's grace, not our works.

> Even when we were dead in sins, hath quickened us together with Christ, (by grace ye are saved;) And hath raised us up together, and made us sit together in heavenly places in Christ Jesus: That in the ages to come he might shew the exceeding riches of his grace in his kindness toward us through Christ Jesus. For by grace are ye saved through faith; and that not of yourselves: it is the gift of God: Not of works, lest any man should boast.
>
> Ephesians 2:5–9 KJV

Dissertation research findings: "Values, Proactive Management, and Consciousness."

The result of the dissertation survey questions, after analysis of composite responses, were significant and led to these findings:

1. A transformational leader's voice cannot be greater than the sum of each employee's voice; leadership is a fluid consciousness that mentors, motivates, and summons the work community to produce, with excellence;
2. Transformational leaders' spiritual or religious affiliations underscore their visions and ethics of care; apprehending their personal and collective voices, congealing collaborative consciousness, and exciting through insight;
3. Leadership Voices™ are the synchronized energetic vibrations of the work community, incorporating diverse personal core values orchestrated by proactive management principles;

4. Proactive management goes beyond honesty and sincerity, requiring discipline, balance, dominion, and congruence between core values and actions;

5. *Transformational leaders must comprehend that they, and those to whom they delegate administrative authority, create their core values in the work environment."*

It is the contention of this 2021 book that these five findings of the published 2002 dissertation have the same or significantly similar importance in the year 2021 when focused on personal and interpersonal relationships. The year 2021 will have significant issues, noted in the dissertation's study, impacting all U.S. citizens today in one way or another. Nationwide, many businesses that closed forever, and those that have managed to keep open, from small businesses (ten or fewer employees) to large businesses (500 or more employees), have emotional scars that are more traumatic than whether or not their business survived. There were many simultaneous calamities occurring than a failed business (example: economic for basic human needs, illness, and death due to the global pandemic COVID-19 and all its mutations, and care of dependent family youth and elderly), to name just a few issues. The next logical steps are addressing the implications relating to personal core values and affiliations. Whether an elected, appointed, or volunteer leader—everyone leads sometimes. No individual can be a better leader than they are a person.

Why this book now?

Why this book now? In my opinion, there is no better opening to this section than the statemen, "These are the times that try men's souls…" This statement was printed by Thomas Paine's December 19, 1776, published "The American Crisis." He is also a noted and revered American patriot and author of "Common Sense."

Throughout the years, I have been able to track the sustained increasing interests and accessing the dissertation abstract and/or the full dissertation, published in 2002. Over the years, individuals from at least seventeen different countries, not including the USA, apparently have found this study. I have been notified my work has been cited as a reference. Among the most used search terms have been conscious awareness, Transformational Leadership, consciousness. This information is important because, as we have witnessed within the U.S., the steady degrading of civility, individual moral, heightened experimental hedonistic creativity, opportunistic political assumptions, and a continuously crystalizing dual layered caste system; the have-and-have-nots.

Chapter 5: What Facilitated Normalization of Occult Practices explores several significant catalysts occurring in the nineteen years between 2002 and 2021. Over the years, we have all been through significant changes, catastrophic changes, and outright strident chaos. So, this book is definitely timely.

In 2008, we Americans experienced the "Great Recession," which caused the collapse of many economic institutions, had a significant impact on the information service technologies and the real estate industry. We will consider the traumatic national "wake up" as a result of the 9–11 triple mega destruction of American lives and business and continuity later in this chapter.

Simply put, we as a nation have witnessed the diabolical obliteration of:

- active enforcement of "voluntary' isolation and tactile deprivation."
- an acceleration of snatching away every vestige of individual "God-given" and Constitutional rights;
- disenfranchisement of our US Constitution, and Bill of Rights,
- immunity, freedom of religion,
- intolerance of Christian religion, tenets, and practices,
- political distain and gaslighting of the voting public,
- the ability to sustain self and family,
- the decimation of the US "middle class,"
- the individual's ability to work,
- the liberalization of our collective morals,

- the mockery and distain toward civic civility,
- the supplanting of freedom of association;
- toleration of terrorism even while increasingly invasive and wicked.

The vast majority of today's Americans have witnessed and experienced a range of traumatic occurrences since 9–11 (in 2001), to the first infected individual with the Coronavirus global pandemic (2020), first arriving in Washington State. In between these two pivotal dates, we have seen the escalation of the senseless mass killings by foreign- and native-born terrorists intent on inducing and sustaining fear, paranoia, and pure evil. The defiance within a large number of today's youth: drug use, open satisfaction with satanic practices and idols, and depressed self-mortification are the best bellwether of the decay of American dreams and civility. It is time to not just ask what happened, but ask, how do we reverse this downward spiral? Today, if the same or similar survey taken in 1995 for the 2002 study is taken, will the same values still provide sufficient protection, grounding, and spiritual uplifting by clinging fast to God's Word? Is there sufficient substance and spiritual uplifting to provide the guidance and equilibrium to totally rely on God during today's catastrophically chaotic times? The 1995 study found that God's truth, unwavering love, and guidance for any and every need, protection, and salvation were absolutely solid and valid then. Today, a majority of people under the age of forty, can they even comprehend what core values are? Can they explain why they "believe" in ghosts, extraterrestrial beings, magic instead of God? *God is steadfast, infinite, and true. Thus today's deliberate infusion of Christ's Consciousness, core values, and intentional conduct is indeed the antidote to the contagious poisoning administered by malicious change, concurrent calamities, and unfettered chaos.* So, you are invited to work through this book with me to see if this work may be of personal value to you or someone you know.

What is a social norm?

Every religion, family, community, and country has prevailing social standards, customs, and laws. Formal and informal groups have charters, articles, and guidelines. Educational institutions have learning models, goals, and standardized outcomes requirements. All governments and businesses have identified (to some extent) the methods, means, and kinds of work. Each business, public or private, has identified at least one deliverable service (reason for existence), expectation of service, fiscal bottom line for operations, and some type of procedural enforcement and repercussions for failure to meet minimum standards (personnel policies and/or procedures).

Collectively, each of us lives under an assortment of norms (customs and rules) that make the fabric of our lives. Most of us have been startled to discover that our "American norms" (some say dreams) have been snatched, hijacked, betrayed, leaving us feeling eviscerated economically, emotionally exhausted, psychologically weary, and overall anxious, troubled, and frightened. The prevailing overhanging question these days are, how did we come to live in this ever-changing hallucinogenic kaleidoscope? And then, for most, if their basic needs are met and they have a social peer group, they relax and once again become mesmerized by the kaleidoscope's beautiful colors and patterns. Only the disenfranchised are annoyingly repetitive in their complaining about the loss of income, homes, healthcare, and assorted other basic concerns. Increasingly it seems the word and corresponding behavior of "compassion" have been removed from the dictionary and human memory.

Tuesday, September 11, 2001–"Our second day of infamy."

The year 2002 was one year after the horrific, traumatizing day, September 11, 2001 (9–11). On this day, most Americans abruptly faced a collective spiritual terror that has forever scared our souls with healing-resistant vulnerability. Both attacks, 9–11 and Pearl

Harbor, are both seared, evil, and unforgettable attacks in our collective minds. The nation of Japan bombed our harbor on Oahu Island, Hawaii, on December 7, 1941. This was the first time our nation stood still. President Roosevelt, as he addressed our nation in the aftermath of this unprovoked attack, declared December 7, 1941, as a Day of Infamy.

The terrorist's intent to instill terror on 9/11 was superbly achieved by three separate but coordinated attacks dispersed on American turf. That day United Airlines, Flights 11 and 175 deliberately crashed into the North and South New York Trade Center Twin Towers, decimating them both. Hijacked American Airlines Flight 77 crashed into the Pentagon in Washington D.C. The last of the day's three terroristic acts concluded when hijacked United Airlines Flight 93, with all passengers on board, crashed in a field in Shanksville, Pennsylvania. These three coordinated acts, for the first time in American history, in one day, introduced Americans to international terrorism on our own soil, and our lives have since been permanently changed.

As the world's nations technologically developed, we have become increasingly interrelated in real time. Therefore, 9/11's assassins attack affected the global community as well. The global stock markets dropped, and our overall economic stability significantly suffered for many years after this unthinkable and barbaric act. For the third time in history, the New York Stock Exchange experienced prolonged closure, and gold and oil prices spiked upwards. Finally, the 9–11 terroristic attacks led directly to the U.S. war in Afghanistan. Fear accommodated the development of the (Federal) Department of Homeland Security and its overreaching internal U.S. "surveillance."

Our U.S. Constitution and Bill of Rights, for the first time to Americans in general realized, restrictions on our rights enumerated in both documents. We were told these restrictions were necessary impediments to our Constitutional and God-given rights. We needed these invasions into our God-given rights and "inalienable rights;" to avert other acts of terrorism and to capture those that intent was to harm and destroy both citizens and real property. Thus we U.S. citizens acquiesced to incrementally escalating internal (U.S.) surveillance, stringent travel restrictions, technological communications monitored, ostensibly to protect and prevent treasonous and seditious acts.

Over time, internal surveillance has become the norm of the internet, cellular correspondence, drone surveillance, Remote Viewing (R.V.), sometimes called non-local pre-and-post observations, and the ever-increasing electronic implanted bar chips and/or bio-identification required for goods and service, and now proposed for individuals. These new methods of simultaneous GPS personal tracking systems and identification initially accepted along with "smart" phones, televisions, home appliances, and many other methods is now considered by a significant number of people as being personally invasive and have striped our "inalienable rights." The network of interconnected surveillance possibilities and the portability of surveillance devices is ominously pervasive and will continue to be intrusive in the future.

When in pandemonium's "topsy-turvy's" grasp, prioritization and a plan are needed.

Over time as various threats and actual occurrences from both foreign and U.S. citizens increased, our nation became progressively paranoid (and rightfully so). A laser-like focused discussion of the necessary "give and take" of safety versus security and personal boundless freedoms is beyond the scope of this book. It is a balancing act that will always be an important discussion within our Nation. It is sufficient to say, on top of innumerable, competing, and significant changes, catastrophic chaos typically claims first priority. Chapter 2: Change, Catastrophic Change, and Berserk Chaos; considers the distinguishing difference (if any) between significantly emotional distressful situations and an individual's strident resistance to change? Does it matter whether or not we can distinguish which type of emotional scourging we have befallen? Is it not enough that we are in shreds? For compassionate and probing sociologists, economic researchers, medical responders in every field, and religious and spiritual leaders: perhaps, but the focus will be on reassembling the individual scars and all. For those of us going through these tumultuous times, heck no, the distinction is not even a consideration—we are too busy trying to survive. When change occurs, there will be collateral damage. Unfortunately, the damaged will have sustained psychological damage, and it appears that this catastrophic crisis is not interested in accommodating the wounded. Our best chances of rebuilding our spirit, our social-economic grounding, and our civility toward each other contingent on the remaining individuals who:

- knew their religious/spiritual tenets,
- based their core values on those tenets,
- and their behaviors were in direct alignment with their religious/spiritual tenets.

Hopefully, in the not too distant future, we will rebalance our nation to include a once lost vocabulary that includes: God, compassion, due process, inalienable rights, inclusion, and national pride.

CHAPTER 2

. . . .

Change, Catastrophic Change, And Berserk Chaos

> Arise, shine; for thy light is come, and the glory
> of the LORD is risen upon thee. For, behold, the
> darkness shall cover the earth, and gross darkness
> the people: but the LORD shall arise upon thee,
> and his glory shall be seen upon thee. And the
> Gentiles shall come to thy light, and kings to the
> brightness of thy rising.
>
> Isaiah 60:1–3

THE PROCESS OF CHANGE WILL NOT ACCOMMODATE A VACUUM

Here we will take a closer looked at three types of changes:

1) "ordinary changes,
2) catastrophic change, and
3) berserk chaos.

What becomes clear is that some type of change is always occurring. If the change at any given time is not desired, stressful, or mind-numbing, "It will change." If the change occurring is something you are anticipating, are thrilled about, or stimulated by, "It will change." So, whatever state you are in, on sooner or later, "It will change." In life, the only thing guaranteed is death. Thus we can conclude since a change of some type is always occurring; for a variety of reasons, we have gotten used to "ordinary change, thus often ignored, therefore we are shocked to face catastrophic change and berserk chaos. *There seems to be a predisposition for humans to diminish change unless and until the change is impossible to be denied and/or resisted.*

Often in retrospect, we have tolerated numerous occults proliferating our society by generally ignoring them; until they infringe on our lifestyle. These assorted occult tenets have challenged, and in some cases, replaced Christian tenets. Occult saturation has eviscerated American laws, thus once unbelievable lawless behaviors are now common. Over time American core values, religious/spiritual ground rules in law and order, education within K-12, and the diabolical tenacity driving political/legal power have changed. This chapter looks at the very real, tangible effects change has, even though the act of change may stir short-lived enjoyable pleasure. Often as change becomes uncomfortable, with unanticipated or undesired consequences, change is rapidly considered to be either catastrophic or berserk. Americans have experienced this transition of fickle, erratic changes, specifically the consequences of awakening to facing the gap between "what one assumes and what actually is."

When "core values" are considered a wish list, and "consciousness is a social cliché: civil disobedience, psychopathic, narcissistic and authoritarian behaviors prevail. At this stage, life hovers in the berserk category. Currently, the majority of Americans seem to have accepted the following, but not necessarily limited to, what were formerly intolerable acts:

- Abortions on demand,
- Child emancipation, and/or trafficking,
- Christian tenets, diluted and/or distained,

- Dissatisfaction with life, anxiety, depression, fear, and apprehension,
- Gratification immediate, self-centered, and/or hedonistic,
- Murder as a problem solution, diversion,
- Occult tenets: fascination, practice, power, and/or intimidation,
- Pedophilia, and normalizing minor sexual behaviors,
- Violent civil disobedience, anarchy, and/or revolt.

The tremendous changes in American culture were significantly impacted in the 1960s and the 1970s: by technology, medical procedures which extended life expectancy as well as an anticipated, improved quality of life. And of course, changes in our social structure were radically challenged to include but not limited to:

- Access to enhanced, "real-time" reporting of news included radio and television, bringing the "action" reported in the news into one's home.
- Civil Rights: racism, sexism, spouse abuse, children's rights (among others),
- Drugs became illegal in food products and for recreational use. Simultaneously, new chemically produced drugs were introduced in society.
- Life longevity was enhanced as well as the improved quality of life. People started living longer than projected "after retirement."
- Quality of life, to include an individual's right to death with dignity.
- War, the cost, technology, logistics, type of weapons, alliances, and strategies substantially changed. The age of terrorism became an art form and had no "codes of ethics."

Each of these changes fertilized the growth of our youth, working-class, public and private businesses, and social interactions to ensure an inalienable fundamental self-gratifying "black hole."[5]. Fear of change and the unknown often tempts one to search for security, personal power, and recognition that one's existence is of value. The promises of the "New Age" movement was exactly what our disenfranchised citizens and the increasingly encroaching One World Government needed to promise ordinary individuals the following:

- ability to "know more" than others,
- access to a better life,
- equalize opportunities,
- individuals can achieve god status,
- influence surreptitiously, and
- "Do what though wilt.

Now the pervasive question is, can this catastrophic overhauling of American values, political uniqueness, and prosperity be modulated? It is unrealistic to think we can return to "the way we were." But have we a society passed the point of a "do-over with modifications?"

WHAT DISTINGUISHES" REGULAR CHAOS," FROM CATASTROPHIC CHANGE?

This book is about change and the Christian's ability to rely on God's word during times of chaos and catastrophic change. Catastrophic change may not have a universal definition. However, there is universal agreement that a catastrophe is typically an unanticipated situation, and has occurrences that call for revised thinking and behaviors that exceed one's normal discernment or problem-solving techniques. During these times, many people who ordinarily do not consider "calling for help" from God will call upon a deity or supernatural power to aid or release them from the devastating situations. *God's steadfast word goes further than just providing prayer as a "crutch." The Church collectively and individually" is protected, advised, provided for, and assured that retribution when appropriate will be dispensed by God himself.*

If it be possible, as much as lieth in you, live peaceably with all men. Dearly beloved, avenge not yourselves, but rather give place unto wrath: for it is written, Vengeance is mine; I will repay, saith the Lord.

Romans 12:18–19

Christians who have a personal relationship with Jesus Christ have an unwavering faith that Jesus is our intercessor. When growing up, we had a colloquial expression: "God may not come early, He will never be late, He is always on time. You can take that to the bank." For those of us who have a personal relationship with Jesus, we tend to look to Him for leadership in times of anguish, need, and emotional and mental support, as well as sharing our joys and happiness. Jesus is both a Servant Leader as well as a Transformational Leader. A Transformational Leader recognizes that religious/spiritual tenets:

(1) form core values which are the gyroscope, providing protection,
(2) acknowledging visions,
(3) facilitate good decision making, and
(4) provides both protective and productive environments amidst changes.

Safety during a catastrophic change is a subjective term. However, "safety" in these situations often means an individual has an unwavering determination to envision the best possible outcome based on the current situation. The individual recognizes that sometimes it is necessary to take small steps, but each step of advancement is recognized and served as motivation to take the "next step" and then the next. So, what can one say to a person who is hurting, facing the trials of change, is confused, and needs help? *Sometimes the best thing you can do for a friend that is going through the chaos in her life is to keep your mouth shut, witness for them, pray with and for them and give them a seriously authentic hug.* Often reassurance and recognition that someone is *"going through"* a situation confirm for them they have both a friend and a way can be figured out. This would also be a good time to pray before departing from each other.

Change and catastrophic change.

There are three essential types of change, each with markers designating what type of "change" you find yourself facing. The prevalence, degree of frenzy, disorientation, and length of occurrence distinguish the first two markers, change, and catastrophic change. Catastrophic change also contains elements of evil, depravation, and abject hopelessness. As a nation, we first experienced the confusion and the pain of having our (individual and collective) soul shattered, scorched, and shredded. Some to this day have the scars of emotionally mortified soul wounds. During those traumatic and tumultuous times on September 11, 2001, we were electronically witnessing three coordinated acts of terrorism:

1) the destruction of the two Trade Center Towers in New York,
2) the attack on the Pentagon in Washington D.C., and
3) the terrorist's deliberate crashing of United Flight 93 in a field near Shanksville, Pennsylvania.

Unfortunately, as each year distances the immediacy of the pain and horror, some may have forgotten or diluted the evil of these terroristic acts. If so, the residue from this evil, horrific, and unanticipated maniacal slaughter of the innocent have etched our psychic and striped away layers of our individual and collective humanity. However, the majority of us had our first rude awakening, which sharpened our skepticism that:

• Evil never normalizes.
• Evil always escalates.
• Evil always courts fear, chaos, and iniquity.
• Evil is a catalyst capable of appearing anywhere.
• Evil never leaves, it may take a vacation, but it comes back.

The only antidote to evil is the name of Jesus Christ, calling on him to bind and remove the obstruction(s). What we bind on earth is bound in heaven.

"Verily I say unto you, Whatsoever ye shall bind on earth shall be bound in heaven: and whatsoever ye shall loose on earth shall be loosed in heaven" (Matthew 18:18).

When the majority of Americans acknowledged and defended our Christian-based tenets, our Constitution had strength because we had the strength, guidance, and protection afforded by the Word of God in His Holy Bible. The God of the Holy Bible was, is, and will remain the God of Abraham, Isaac, and Jacob; there is none other. Jesus Christ is God's only begotten Son, authorized by God to be our intercessor to God. Jesus shed His blood on the Cross of Calvary to atone for our sins. The Body of Christ refers to our spiritual warfare against evil," as putting on the whole Body of Armor:

> Finally, my brethren, be strong in the Lord, and in the power of his might. Put on the whole armor of God, that ye may be able to stand against the wiles of the devil. For we wrestle not against flesh and blood, but against principalities, against powers, and against the rules of the darkness of this world, against spiritual wickedness in high places. Wherefore take unto you the whole armor of God, that ye may be able to withstand in the evil day, and having done all, to stand. Stand therefore, having your loins girt about with truth, and having on the breastplate of righteousness. And your feet shod with the preparation of the gospel of peace. Above all, taking the shield of faith, wherewith ye shall be able to quench all the fiery darts of the wicked. And take the helmet of salvation, the sword of the Spirit, which is the word of God: Praying always with all prayer and supplication in the Spirit and watching thereunto with all perseverance and supplication for

all saints; Peace be to the brethren, and love with faith, from God the Father and the Lord Jesus Christ."

Ephesians 6:10–18, 24

"Grace be with all them that love our Lord Jesus Christ in sincerity. Amen" Ephesians 6:24

Chaos, the third type of change agent.

Chaos, the third and ultimate havoc maker, is the degree to which any combination of a civilization's mores, primal emotional responses, and basic human fears are blurred, reversed, or given neutral and tolerant definitions. Following are thirteen selected oxymorons to consider:

1. Anger vs. Serene
2. Envy vs. Satisfaction
3. Evil vs. Good
4. Fear vs. Safety
5. Gluttony vs. Self-control
6. Greed vs. Generosity
7. Immorality vs. Morality
8. Lust vs. Aversion
9. Pride vs. Humility
10. Scarcity vs. Abundance
11. Sloth vs. Energetic
12. Tradition vs. Innovation
13. War vs. Peace.

Sometimes, chaos occurs as a "natural" result of a combination of situations and/or occurrences. Sometimes chaos is strategically planned, sometimes over years, decades, and centuries by an individual, a group of individuals, or an organized group with a "chain of succession" to facilitate a desired chaotic event(s). Following are a selected set of examples:

- norms (in education, health and wellness, and technology),
- structures (laws, public or private businesses, and spiritual relevancy),
- government, or even social interactions within a civilization.
- Individuals example: Margaret Mead, a cultural anthropologist 1901–1978, following are three of her longstanding quotes:[6]
    1) "Never doubt that a small group of thoughtful, committed citizens can change the world. Indeed, it's the only thing that ever has.
    2) What people say, what people do, and what they say they do are entirely different things.
    3) One of the oldest human needs is having someone to wonder where you are when you don't come home at night."

Witnessing and discussing change and chaos?

Life evolving under "survival of the fittest" inhibits our observation, and what we do observe stands a good chance of being bias. We are not independent agents fighting for ourselves against all others. There is no hostile world out there plotting our demise. There is no "out there." We are utterly intertwined right here on earth. We are constantly negotiating conditions for life. We singly and collectively co-determine the conditions of one another's existence. No one forges ahead independently, molding the world to her presence with the rest of humanity "catches as catch can." The systems we create are closed systems, chosen together, even if we are unaware. Unaware, typically, the response from The U.S. Senate and/or the House of Representatives have a standard reply, you knew or should have known since all legislation, if brought to the floor for a vote, is published giving notice of upcoming voting. A case in point is the

Equality Act (H.R. 5,) which passed the House, Thursday, February 25, 2021, and will go to the Senate for a vote. See YouTube video Flash point, and the Equality Act passes the House. This video concisely lists four issues and thoroughly explains why Christians need to know why this bill is an imminently important video published February 25, 2021). https://youtu.be/UV63ebFBoe4 Flashpoint's video lists concisely four issues and thoroughly explains why Christians need to know about the bill, as follows.

- It endangers the church.
- It encourages the suppression of religious freedom.
- It will obliterate women's rights.
- It will affect your kids.

Awareness of one's freedom to choose gives choice a unique approach to problem-solving. Thoughts, also called imagery or described as visions, are the language of the subconscious. One always moves in the direction of her thoughts. Consciously or not, the visualization process is like using electricity—understanding how electricity works is unnecessary to get results: but it is helpful if one understands. An individual's visionary "power" is always present, even if ignored. Therefore, only direction and flexibility to adjust to unanticipated occurrences are required. Sometimes change is so exhilarating, shocking, or ominous that the most important action one takes is to be a witness.

Being a witness means you have to personally observe (hear, taste, feel, etc.) or in some other way, have a first-hand, real-time experience of an event, think of an "on the scene reporter." Also implicit in the act of witnessing is the "testifying" to the fact that you were there. What distinguishes "witnessing" from ordinary living is the "event" being observed. Sometimes we know immediately that a particular event is significant, and details must/should be remembered as clearly as possible. Events may be happy, sad, and sometimes an event by its very nature is catastrophic (examples: natural disasters, unmanageable acts of cruelty, man's first steps on the moon). Testifying as witnessing an event can include but not be limited to:

FORMAL:
- community values and traditions,
- court setting,
- fine arts, in music, drama, etc.
- land disputes and wars,
- natural and political upheavals, and
- writing books,

INFORMAL:
- community values and traditions,
- labor issues,
- narratives regarding population migrations,
- oral storytelling, and
- religious/spiritual events.

The combination of witnessing and testifying to event documents the occurrence of the event and the participants. It also details the timeline, the sequences of interactions (sights, sounds, actions, and so forth) leading up to "the event." *Finally, witnessing preserves the event for others throughout generations to "remember."* The more witnesses to any event, the greater the collective and diverse perspective, thus the richer the texture. Sometimes the more divergent the witnesses and their testimony, the longer the collective memory revisits the past event and struggles with the event's "lessons."

LEADERSHIP DURING CHAOTIC TIMES MATTERS

The more a memory is witnessed among a group of people with common characteristics, the greater the probability this event will become some type of baseline to compare and contrast current and future interactions. All human culture is based in whole or in part on witnessing and testimony. Stories handed down within families contain witnessed events and serve as "justifications" for family values, fiscal guidelines, and of course, social conformity or rejections. Corporate "war stories" and the retelling of historical political/social stories between co-workers continue or facilitates changes within work organizations. Next to basic human interactions and our need to be physically touched (appropriately, of course), the telling and listening to "stories" is what makes us who we are; and to a great extent, determines our core values, shapes our characters, and helps us envision our future goals. All of these collective witnessed memories have a direct impact on the governance people will elect, tolerate, or overthrow.

Most importantly, succinctly put, the trauma of witnessing significant emotional occurrences dull and disrupt our energetic connection with God's consciousness and our ability to hear and obey God's Word. The goal of "hearing God" is:

- First, to hear and recognize God's voice distinctly from all others.
- Secondly, to hear and obey the direction when spoken to by God.

The sanction for not recognizing God's voice is that you will be misdirected (subject to have tainted spiritual tenets and corrupted understanding or disbelief in God's Word. Another unfortunate outcome is that you will miss the direction to put on your whole Body of Armor: or you will either put on the part of the armor, or a defective but complete armor. Or decide to skip the armor altogether and, if possible, ignore, hide, or become a traitor and assist the threat. This failure to hear and/or obey God's Word has, in your awareness, often an imperceptible, but always a negative outcome for your eternal life. *The tragic and most disheartening revelation for you is when, too late, you have discovered you compromised your eternal soul due to a hardened heart.*

Humanity, as we know it, would cease to exist if all the preceding markers/premonitions of change were ignored. We can sustain and sometimes make monumental strives from brief bouts in chaos. However, without leadership to envision, motivate, and direct followers, civilization unravels. Sooner or later, a leader will evolve or take over. Good leaders in this chaotic situation need to provide for the followers a holistically balanced plan that encourages life-sustaining intercommunications and maintains some degree of responsive predictability.

Your body is your first warning signal that something is going terribly wrong as you notice any one or more of the following: your sleep patterns alter, your anxiety level increases, your level of fatigue is remarkable, and your sense of cynicism and fatalism increases. You are preoccupied with money, or the lack of it, along with your fretting about basic health care and scarcity of ordinary survival resources. Your disassociation from community wellbeing is only surpassed by your distrust of your national and local leaders. You resent needing "big businesses" as employers and providers of goods and services, but you seek their approval and employment. You want your children to "do better" than you, but it is increasingly becoming clear that they may not do at least as well as you have. You noticed shifts in employment: your work environment is fear-driven, continued employment seems tenuous at best, and it seems daily you suffer panic attacks caused by your work environment. If unemployed, you are experiencing the shunning of former friends and associates who are still employed; networking provides no viable job leads, and basic survival resources are vanishing.

While the symptoms of a decaying and seriously inadequate society are being increasingly recognized by people, what to do about this situation is not so apparent. The extremes of any society are always unhappy: either too many restrictions on business or too much assistance to "the masses." Discontentment accompanied by accusations, are most vehement when leadership is inadequate and basic survival resources are scarce. When this occurs, fear prevails, and hoarding occurs with the remaining resources. Fear escalates to chaos as scarce items are either nonexistent or are obtainable to the most powerful only. Many leaders have envisioned a balanced society—and political scientists have called these "visions" a variety of names: utopia, nirvana, socialism, communism, or unachievable.

In summation, we have often heard the terms "chaos," "change," and of course, "adaptability" tossed around. However, when we are personally in the middle of the drama, large or small, what is euphemistically called "chaos," when personally experienced is "the miseries." Whether or not you survive, the quality of your survival and your ability to "recover" from chaos is primarily contingent on four things:

1. your core values (what do you consider "winning, breaking even, or fair"),

2. your self-discipline (what are you willing to do, sacrifice, or tolerate),

3. your options, practical or innovative (are you willing to do something entirely different, for instance, pick another goal; in other words, are you willing to keep your core values while considering a unique way of considering a compromise to maintain your core values and achieve your goals)?

4. Have you considered and are you willing to become the needed Transformational Leader for this "hour of need?"

CHAPTER 3

Conscious Awareness, What Is This?

"Then shall they know that I am the LORD, when I have laid the land most desolate because of all their abominations which they have committed" (Ezekiel 33:29).

ENERGY AND QUANTUM CONSCIOUSNESS.

Trust me, I am not a quantum mechanics physicist or any kind of physicist. Therefore the following discussions on this topic will be very basic. This section will have quite a few endnotes (located at the end of this book), so you can see which of the noted physicist at the time explained the topics discussed. Additionally, the Reference section at the end of this work will have all the citations of each author and their work for you to read for yourself. At the time, circa 1995–2002, there were not that many Christian researchers that turned to physics to try and understand the connection, if any, between consciousness and quantum physics.

Today (2021), there are several Christian ministers (examples: John MacArthur, Chuck Missler, and Charles Lawson) who have made the connection between many Bible scriptures and the "increasing findings" of quantum physics that show significant correlations.

Pastor Lawson has a presentation on YouTube[7] that discusses, from a Christian's point of view, several concerns we should be aware of and monitoring The European Council for Nuclear Research (CERN). Their scientists are mystified that many Bible descriptions are identical to what various experiments have suggested. For instance, ancient Christians had knowledge about different levels of the universes? Quantum experiments allude to different universes and levels, which they cannot fully explain "particles," how or why they work.

QUANTUM MECHANICS AND THE LARGE HADRON COLLIDER.

The CERN Large Hadron Collider (LHC) is located within the European Organization for Nuclear Research facilities on the Franco-Swiss border near Geneva, Switzerland. This is the world's most powerful particle accelerator and consists of a 27-kilometer (17 miles) ring of superconducting magnets with a number of accelerating structures to boost the energy particles along the way. It is located in a tunnel, 100 meters (or 328 feet) underground, and the collider's circumference runs under both France and Switzerland. The CERN facility was founded after World War II as a way to reunite and rebuild science in war-torn Europe.[8] Now scientists from six continents and 100 countries conduct experiments.

According to the online article EarthSky, ten years of Large Hadron Collider (LHC) Discoveries[9], the standard theory of particle physics was developed in the early 1970s. This theory described fundamental particles and their interactions. Later the Standard Model was found to be incomplete, which led to the development of the Large Hadron Collider. It was contended that the research obtained by experiments conducted with the collider might find the answers to the following questions:

1.   Could experiments lead to a unification theory of fundamental forces?

2. Answers to the questions, what are dark matter and dark energy?
3. Why is there far more matter than antimatter in the universe?
4. How does the quark-gluon plasma give rise to the particles that constitute the matter of our Universe?

A significant research finding occurred on July 4, 2012, the discovery of the Higgs Boson or "God particle[10]" was announced. The next anticipated spectacular discovery will be to understand the nature of the most basic building blocks of the universe and how they interact with each other. In other words, scientists want to be able to duplicate the Big Bang that created life while contained in the LHC tubes underground. (I cannot help it; I have to interject a personal opinion here...*really*? Why would you try to duplicate the initial formation of the entire universe (requiring lots and lots of space) enclosed in a pipe...and think that will not be a problem? Oh right, they are trying to duplicate "The Big Bang"...this time an earth extinction event? But what do I know? I am not a physicist.)

Because of the immense but unknown actual power and/or consequences of the experiment, if the test(s) succeeds, there have been several concerns, within the physicist community, regarding safety when energy particles are collided. Of course, there are many who contend there is no reason for concern about safety issues relating to the "atom-smashing." However, naturally, there are other equally qualified physicists who vehemently disagree with continued "atom-smashing" experiments, two of which are, but not necessarily limited to, Stephen Hawking (theoretical physicist and cosmologist), another is Neil deGrasse Tyson (astrophysicist). The primary concern is that there is no certainty what the results will be when the experiments succeed in replicating the Big Bang, the beginning of life. The fear is that this explosion will be a global life extension event. Only time will tell.

If your learning style includes visual and audio stimulation, you might be interested in watching the YouTube video: "Scientist and the Elite Try to Hide What Really Happened at CERN,

Demonic Entities, Extra Dimensions. Speakers: Pastors Chuck Missler and Charles Lawson.[11]" (4) Scientist and the Elite Try to Hide What Really Happened at CERN, Demonic Entities, Extra Dimensions—YouTube

Naturally, there have been discoveries, some of which have become publicized, since 2002. Some of the discoveries are still at the theoretical level, and some applications in "real life" are currently being tested. A synopsis of three selected discoveries published are:

1. Black Holes.
   o The following information is taken from: "What are Black Holes?" By Nola Taylor Redd July 11, 2019[12]
      "Black Holes are extremely dense, with such strong gravitational attraction that even light cannot escape their grasp if it comes near enough. Albert Einstein first predicted the existence of black holes in 1916 with his general theory of relativity. The first physical black hole ever discovered was spotted in 1971. Then, in 2019 the Event Horizon Telescope (EHT) collaboration released the first image ever recorded of a black hole. So far, astronomers have identified three types of black holes: (a) stellar black holes, (b) supermassive black holes, and (c) intermediate black holes. Small black holes populate the universe, but supermassive black holes, dominate. These enormous black holes are millions or even billions of times as massive as the sun but are about the same size in diameter. Such black holes are thought to lie at the center of pretty much every galaxy, including the Milky Way."

2. "Microscopic Smart Dust'" sensors are set to revolutionize a range of sectors—The New Economy By Courtney Goldsmith | Monday, June 3rd, 2019
      "In 1997, the researcher Kristofer Pister coined the term 'smart dust' to describe these millimeter-sized devices. Pister and his colleagues at the University of California,

Berkeley, aimed to create a network of sensors made up of tiny wireless computer systems called 'motes.' Acting as microscopic eyes, ears, and arms, these motes could rove around the world collecting all kinds of data: visual, thermal, chemical, and biological. In theory, smart dust could revolutionize industries by reaching places scientists never thought possible. Networks of tiny sensors known as 'smart dust' are on the cusp of reinventing the Internet of Things. These devices will unlock unprecedented levels of data collection, but their development unearths important security questions. Not only could smart dust dive into oil wells, it could also sit on the wings of a butterfly to monitor migration patterns or be deployed inside the human body to oversee the recovery process of broken bones or damaged organs. Before smart dust can radically change the way businesses around the world operate, researchers must first create microsystems that work."

3. "Programmable Matter." Elliot Hawkes, Byoungkwon (Kwon) An, Nadia Benbernou, Hiroto Tanaka, Sangbae Kim, Erik D. Demaine, Daniela Rus, Robert J. Wood. Proceedings of the National Academy of Sciences 2010.

    o   Programmable matter is a material whose properties can be programmed to achieve specific shapes or stiffness upon command. This concept requires constituent elements to interact and rearrange intelligently in order to meet the goal. This article considers achieving programmable sheets that can form themselves in different shapes autonomously by folding. Past approaches to creating transforming machines have been limited by the small feature sizes, a large number of components, and the associated complexity of communication among the units. Scientists seek to mitigate these difficulties through the unique concept of self-folding origami with universal crease patterns. This approach exploits a single sheet composed of interconnected triangular sections. The sheet is able to fold into a set of predetermined shapes using embedded actuation. To implement this self-folding origami concept requires the development of a scalable end-to-end planning and fabrication process. Given a set of desired objects, the system computes an optimized design for a single sheet and multiple controllers to achieve each of the desired objects. The material, called programmable matter by folding, is an example of a system capable of achieving multiple shapes for multiple functions.

- o View their video, "AutoDesk" Programmable Matter by Folding (autodesk.com)
- o HIGHLY RECOMMENDED: You tube (49) Robot Origami: Robot self-folds, walks and completes tasks—YouTube

2012 TO 2021, SELECTED NOTABLE RESEARCH OBSERVATIONS AT CERN'S LHC.

Significant publicized scientific observations with the LHC have occurred over the past eight years? The following is a brief overview of events.[13] July 4, 2012, in Melbourne, the ATLAS and CMS experiments presented the preliminary results in the "search" for the Higgs Particle (The God particle). The next step is to determine the precise nature of the particle and its significance for our understanding of the universe.

July 13, 2015, the discovery of a class of particles known as pentaquarks. "pentaquark is not just any new particle. It represents a way to aggregate quarks[14], the fundamental constituents of ordinary protons and neutrons, in a pattern that has never been observed before. Studying its properties may allow a better understanding of how ordinary matter (protons and neutrons) are constituted. This finding links back to a 1964 discovery by Murray Gell-Mann (awarded the Nobel Prize in physics in 1969. He proposed a category of particles known as baryons that, when charged, formed quark-antiquark pairs. Antiquarks are quarks of antimatter. A second significant finding is that repetitive and similar studies of pentaquarks all point to the same conclusion. The next step is to analyze how quarks are bound together within the pentaquarks. For those interested in following CERN, their Facebook link is (3) CERN | Facebook

Simply put, when two quantum entities, A and B, briefly interact, then move apart, the quantum theory continues to regard them as a single entity. *If one takes seriously this feature, called quantum inseparability, then all objects that have once interacted are in some sense still connected*[15]. Quantum theory was devised in the late 1920s to deal with the atom. Quantum theory's development has surpassed its inventor's most remote expectations!

Initially considered merely a tool of measurement, quantum physics evolved from primarily a measurement "tool" to a reflection of the fundamental unity of "all." No entity is so exotic that it escapes quantum rules. Quantum theory does not describe entities; it represents them—one description fits all[16]. Consciousness is the second necessary environment of human society, the first being the individual itself.[17] Consciousness is a concept linking the body, psyche, instinct, and image.[18] All consciousness is of an indirect nature and interprets what is perceived.[19]

There are three forms or grades of consciousness: the Simple Consciousness, the Self-consciousness, and the Cosmic Consciousness. With Cosmic Consciousness being a higher form of realization, both subjective and objective. Cosmic consciousness is cognizant of the cosmos, life, and the order of the universe. Along with cosmic consciousness, intellectual enlightenment or illumination occurs: extending to a state of moral exaltation, producing an indescribable feeling of elation, joyousness, and a quickening of moral senses. With awareness, there is a sense of immortality and eternal life—not a conviction that one shall have this, but the consciousness that one already has it.[20] So, why would I care about this on a day-to-day basis?

THE IMPORTANCE OF DISTINGUISHING "ONE THING FROM ANOTHER THING."

Consciousness involves transforming imagery into deciding something and then taking action.[21] The need to link two or more "things" implies a differentiation of one "thing" from another "thing." The term "other" without something else is meaningless.

In any discussions about "self" and/or "selves," we obviously need to be able to distinguish the difference between "us and them." Yes, this also involves interdisciplinary contributions from psychology, which contributes to the "correct implication" that being able to determine a difference, includes having a chance of being unique—or not from all—or only some part of one's soul. Since there are several variables, what this means is that there are—or may be, "still some other part(s)" not covered. So one's psyche presumably makes up the "rest" of "oneself." But in order for any of this to be true, we have to be conscious. So, essentially, the dual meaning of the word "other" is:

1. if the "rest" is added to an existing part,
   o   a wholeness, a may be achieved;
2. but if there is a "rest" that is "left/omitted,"
   o   then a separation, a division results.[22]

Yes, this sounds self-evident, but in quantum mechanics, this is a big deal! Why, because it identifies the singular and collective voices of consciousness and community. How this translates to the rest of us wishing to build, sustain, and work together as a community is discussed in Chapter 4: Building of Community. It is important to remember that Jung[23] never presented an explicit or systematic theory of the "other" as such, although his implication of the "other's" meaning is implicit throughout his entire works. There is an increasing concurrence, from various disciplines, that the "self" as an awareness continuously "struggles" with the paradox of the need for both individuality and inclusiveness from and with "others."

This "struggle" of the "self" for wholeness from the "other" is explained from a quantum mechanics perspective as follows:

1. From a unified field, individual notions of "self" arise. First, something appears for which there is no known antecedent. The ensuing universal, age-old questions of:
   a) Where does the "self" that is organizing originate?
   b) Why does it attempt to separate itself from the unified field?
   c) Why does this movement toward differentiation even start?
2. Life co-evolves; there are no separate individuals.[24] The co-evolutionary process of life cannot support isolation; even our boundaries create an environment for others. We separate ourselves, but we also create the conditions for one another's life. One self-asserting being creates itself, and its presence creates conditions for others to take form.[25]

These questions, as well as many others, are currently unanswered. Sages and scientists both simply state that this is where the world as we know it originates.[26] Everything that follows from this act of "appearance" seeks differentiation. This process of "self" and differentiation is paradoxical. To exist, the "self" must create a boundary. Yet "self" cannot survive behind the boundary it creates. If the "self" does not remember its connectedness, then the "self" ceases to exist.[27]

The interdisciplinary discussion: quantum mechanics and psychology.

In the original 2002 research, consciousness, at that time, manifests itself at various levels: the two primary forms are practical and expansive. Consciousness and/or awareness can be ascribed to both individuals and collective entities or groups.[28] Consciousness may also be considered as a super-individual relational network that binds ideas, beliefs, concepts, and comprehensive blocks of ideology, doctrines, creeds, theories, and traditions.[29] Discussion of quantum consciousness theory in the late 1920s explained the properties of the atom. Current understanding of the atom and its properties has surpassed the founding theorists' expectations.

This is so important it justifies repeating: initially, quantum theory was considered merely a tool to be primarily used to assist in measurements. Over time it evolved into a significant and primal paradigm reflecting the fundamental unity of "all." No entity is so exotic that it escapes quantum rules. Quantum theory does not describe entities; it represents them—one description fits all![30] However, as of November 14, 2019, a paper published in Science Advances shows that two different observers are entitled to their own facts. Because nature itself, apparently nature itself can actually be subjective. Without mentioning "Schroder's cat," the article concedes that the second you observe a quantum system, it picks a specific location or state. Here is the link to the article: November 14, 2019. Quantum physics: our study suggests objective reality does not exist. https://theconversation.com/quantum-psysics-our-study-suggests-objective-reality-doesn't-exist-125805

So, for our purposes (since we are not quantum physicists), we will stick with Dr. Wolinsky's 1993, a 12-year study of "self-observation," culminated in his book, "Quantum Consciousness."[31] His work asserted that in the act of self-observation, "the witness not only witnesses and is mindful of what passes through his mind and body, but is also the creative source of what is being witnessed." Dr. Wolinsky concurs with Heisenberg's Uncertainty Principle that our mental state consists of basic forms of energy and that our reality is observer created. Self-observation (the observer of ones-self) and that which is created (thoughts, feelings, sensations, beliefs, etc.) are fundamentally identical. Dr. Wolinsky's assertions are consistent with Dr. David Bohm's (a theoretical physicist) theories that time contributes unorthodox ideas. These "ideas" contended that the interdisciplinary theories of quantum theory, neuropsychology, and philosophy are entangled. Dr. Bohm contended that there is an "explicit order" and an "implicit order."

- The explicit order is the world as we typically perceive it;
    - the implicit order is the unbroken wholeness that connects us all.
- At the quantum level, objects, particles, people, and emotions are made
    - subatomically, the first part of this statement is made of the same substance.
- At the quantum (subatomic) level, the composition of what we experience as space and what we experience as physical matter is identical.
- The conclusion: there is no difference between space (emptiness) and physical matter.

In Einstein's words, "Everything is emptiness and form is condensed emptiness.[32]" Dr. Heisenberg's Uncertainty Principle demonstrated that the observer creates that which she observes. The implication is that thought and the observer-of-thought are not two separate phenomena.[33] However, there are some physicists that contend that the Uncertainty Principle has been proved false. In other words, the contention is that quantum uncertainty may not always be in the eye of the beholder. A new experiment has shown that measuring a quantum system does not necessarily introduce uncertainty.[34]

Discussion of community consciousness and social consciousness must be treated as one of the distinguishing attributes of social systems. Social systems are peculiar in that their entities, processes, and relationships that emerge are formed by the actions of their members. And these actions, in turn, are predicted in the voice of community members. In other words, social systems are "image directed." Which is what we figured out without being physicists.

The bottom line: social systems are entities for which the knowledge of "itself" (the system) is a significant part of its own dynamics, which in turn changes the system.[35] Consciousness, whether individual, collective, or social, emanates from a single source: "a pool of resources, concepts, symbols, codes, and frames" for interpretations (as we have seen, the agreement is optional/uncertain).

CONSCIOUSNESS AND INTERDISCIPLINARY ENTANGLEMENT EVOLUTION.

One's level of consciousness either keeps one blind to possible constraints and/or opportunities or allows one's eyes to open to all possibilities. One's level of consciousness either supplies inadequate tools for grasping reality or allows one the possibility of debunking illusions by offering factual, analytical alternatives: either of these possibilities are a natural condition.[36] Community consciousness, a gargantuan force, is a living regenerative "pool" from which individuals construct their paradigms: All living systems have the ability to self-produce. Because a living system produces itself, deciding what it will be and how it will operate, it enjoys enormous freedom. It is free to create itself as it desires. At the beginning, this creative expression is not bounded by any external constraints. Life makes itself up by exercising its freedom, by experimenting with different forms, and by asserting different meanings. The freedom to discern and to choose lies at the heart of life. *We are free to notice what we will. We each create our own worlds by what we choose to notice.* We create a world of distinctions that makes sense to us. We then "see" the world through this self we have created. Information from the external world is a minor influence. We connect who we are with selected amounts of new information to enact our particular version of reality. Because information from the outside plays such a small role in our perceptions, we can never direct a living system. We can only disturb it. Thus the psychiatrist's joke: How many psychiatrists does it take to change a light bulb? Answer: one, but he has to really want to. My dad, a psychiatrist, told me this joke and got really tickled about it.

As external agents, we provide only small impulses of information. We can nudge, titillate, or provoke one another into some new ways of seeing. However, we can never give anyone an instruction and expect him to follow it precisely. We can never assume that anyone else sees the world as we do[37]. With wide concurrence, interdisciplinary scholars and leaders assert that community consciousness:

- Is a collective reservoir of psychic possibilities.[38]
- Is aroused by awareness or recognition.[39]
- Is often considered to be intuition.[40]
- Requires one to "appreciate" her awareness or growth,"[41]
- The manifestation of form from energy (accomplishes goals) requiring both reflection and internal congruence.[42]
- Manifesting form from energy requires discernment and synthesis of concepts and ideas. Then the manifested representative "forms" symbolizes the collective good or concerns.[43]

Individuals can develop their awareness of community consciousness through training. Experiential training is most effective when it is repeated and practiced. One's increasing awareness is enhanced when immediately followed by an instruction that is both functional and includes some type of moral principle that incorporates one's core values and behaviors. The outcome of one's awareness of community consciousness is a healthy, competent, effective, and congruent community.[44] Training must specify both one's core values being congruent with the primary features of the communities collective consciousness to be:

- A valid energy of "belief."
- A reality or experience common to all.
- A "point" conceived and shared by all.
- A "clarity" that is inherently congruent.
- A "clarity" conceived identically by all.
- A coercive certainty that "is" knowledge.
- A recognition of universal interrelatedness.

A community is more than the sum of its parts; it is a living organism in its own right. Leaders should focus on the community as a whole, not on individual needs and characteristics. Failure to focus on the community as a whole impedes development of the community. Generally, leaders should restrict their interventions to interpretations of community behavior instead of addressing the behavior of individuals.[45] Here is another paradox. To exist, the self must create a boundary. Yet, no self can survive behind the boundary it creates. If it does not remember its connectedness, the self will expire.[46] Yes, so far, this has been said already several times, but it is definitely worth repeating again. When discussing community, some individuals may believe they can exist and succeed in isolation. *The fact is, when an individual fails to contribute to others, he becomes irrelevant.* If his self-expression is not meaningful to others, the individual will go unnoticed or be rejected.[47]

Seemingly paradoxically, when she opens herself to others, she not only forms the link to others, but she also opens herself to greater creative expression. On the other hand, when she retains autonomy, she develops her own personal sense of collective "aloneness," It is in this state of "aloneness" that each of us discovers new meaning and is able to transform.[48] But, only if you want to. Within this continuous cycle of personal autonomy and inclusiveness, each of us struggles with "self" and "others," as collectively we build communities that are reflections of this struggle.

LEADERSHIP VOICES™ 2002, RESEARCH FINDINGS REGARDING CONSCIOUSNESS.

Beginning in Genesis, it is clear that God is a spirit. When God creates man, He breathes life into him. The implication is that man now has both "a body constructed from the earth, and his" life essence is spirit." See the following Table 2. Selected scriptures supporting man is a spiritual lifeforce.

Table 2. Selected scriptures, supporting man is a spiritual lifeforce.
Note: Man is a spiritual life force encased in an earthly organic body. This Table focuses only on the spiritual life force of man.

In the beginning God created the heaven and the earth. And the earth was without form, and void; and darkness was upon the face of the deep. And the Spirit of God moved upon the face of the waters. And God said, Let there be light: and there was light. Genesis 1:1–3	OLD TESTAMENT
"And the LORD God formed man of the dust of the ground, and breathed into his nostrils the breath of life; and man became a living soul" (Genesis 2:7,).	OLD TESTAMENT
"The Spirit of God hath made me, and the breath of the Almighty hath given me life" (Job 33:4).	OLD TESTAMENT
For there is not a word in my tongue, but, lo, O LORD, thou knowest it altogether. Thou hast beset me behind and before, and laid thine hand upon me. Such knowledge is too wonderful for me; it is high, I cannot attain unto it. I will praise thee; for I am fearfully and wonderfully made: marvellous are thy works; and that my soul knoweth right well. Psalms 139:4–6, 14 (KNV)	OLD TESTAMENT
And he that searcheth the hearts knoweth what is the mind of the Spirit because he maketh intercession for the saints according to the will of God. For whom he did foreknow, he also did predestinate to be conformed to the image of his Son, that he might be the firstborn among many brethren. Romans 8:27, 29	NEW TESTAMENT

"And have put on the new man, which is renewed in knowledge after the image of him that created him" (Colossians 3:10).	NEW TESTAMENT
"Therewith bless we God, even the Father; and therewith curse we men, which are made after the similitude of God" (James 3:9).	NEW TESTAMENT

After the fall, man is still both body and spirit, but now with limitations. Man always has had free will, so by now, man has the choice to recognize that his spirit is open for intimate communications with God, through Jesus, if and when desired. Or, man can refuse to acknowledge his spiritual life force and concentrate on fulfilling his carnal physical body. Man's choice to choose his awareness of his irrevocable spiritual connection to God through Jesus is usually an open option. There are exceptions, of course. If an individual dies first, then he is stuck with whatever option he was currently living with. Or, under some circumstances, God will determine that an individual has a hardened heart. Or sometimes, God Himself will harden an individual's heart to fulfill his purpose.

> And the LORD said unto Moses, When thou goest to return into Egypt, see that thou do all those wonders before Pharaoh, which I have put in thine hand: but I will harden his heart, that he shall not let the people go.
>
> Exodus 4:21

The relevance of the leader's consciousness and voice with regard to leadership effectiveness and productivity was shown to be significant; in the Leadership Voices™ 2002 research findings.[49] Energy and quantum consciousness: defines and discusses the similarities and differences between interconnectedness and community. What is quantum consciousness, and why are we discussing this here? (1) Consciousness, vision, and voice simultaneously create form and community. (2) Interdisciplinary research critiques the various meanings attributed to:

- one's (energy) voice,
- self-awareness,
- self-talk,
- reality,
- intention (culminating in the),
- creation of form from voice.

Many times the Bible has recorded that, first, the spoken word, then the materialization of whatever was activated appeared. It is given that there are many ways that energy can be transferred. In this particular discussion, we will focus on the transfer of energy/will/creation by one's voice. Recently science has become aware and able (significantly but not completely) that through quantum physics, there are energetic transfers between and amongst living creations. It is important to underscore that God and Jesus Christ both exercised the formation of matter to manifest in several different ways: for instance, sometimes there are verbal instructions with manifestation occurring immediately after the pronouncement to "become/occur." Sometimes, the verbal utterances are prophetic, and manifestations occur in the future, exactly as had been pronounced. Finally, sometimes, the verbal statement is subtle but clear, with the manifestations occurring as cerebral ruminations, encouragement, spontaneous insights, or discernments. Any one of these divinely initiated energetic transfers, if headed, rouses the recipient to some type of action. This section will review a sampling of "voice is energy, energy creates form," represented in the selected following biblical scriptures from both the Old and New Testaments:

Old Testament: Examples of voice creating form: all
citations are from the King James Version.

Naturally, in the Old Testament, communication is always between man and God. Of course, we see that God's first "creation" is the universe, which, of course, includes the earth. Then the earth is configured to include all the elements that support life. All of this, according to God's Word, was spoken into existence.

- "And God said, Let there be light: and there was light" (Genesis 1:3).
- "And God said, Let there be lights in the firmament of the heaven to divide the day from the night; and let them be for signs, and for seasons, and for days, and years" (Genesis 1:14).
- And God said, *Let us make man in our image, after our likeness*: and let them have dominion over the fish of the sea, and over the fowl of the air, and over the cattle, and over all the earth, and over every creeping thing that creepeth upon the earth.

Genesis 1:26

- And God blessed them, and God said unto them, Be fruitful, and multiply, and replenish the earth, and subdue it: and have dominion over the fish of the sea, and over the fowl of the air, and over every living thing that moveth upon the earth.

Genesis 1:28

- "And the LORD God said, It is not good that the man should be alone; I will make him an help meet for him" (Genesis 2:18).
- *And I will establish my covenant with you;* neither shall all flesh be cut off any more by the waters of a flood; neither shall there any more be a flood to destroy the earth. And God said, This is the token of the covenant which I make between me and you and every living creature that is with you, for perpetual generations: *I do set my bow in the cloud, and it shall be for a token of a covenant between me and the earth.* And it shall come to pass, when I bring a cloud over the earth, that the bow shall be seen in the cloud: And I

will remember my covenant, which is between me and you and every living creature of all flesh; and the waters shall no more become a flood to destroy all flesh. *And the bow shall be in the cloud; and I will look upon it, that I may remember the everlasting covenant between God and every living creature of all flesh that is upon the earth.*

Genesis 9:11–16

- And the LORD said, Behold, the people is one, and they have all one language; and this they begin to do: and now nothing will be restrained from them, which they have imagined to do.

Genesis 11:6

New Testament: Examples of voice creating form:
all citations are from the King James Version.

In this selection of creating form from voice, the focus here is only the use of Jesus' spoken word to create form. The point of this statement is a reminder that Jesus: used all of his human senses (visual, auditory, smell, taste, tactile, sensations from muscles and joints, and sense of balance and thinking). Can a human actually begin to comprehend His total awesomeness? The following selected scriptures selection demonstrate several different ways voice commands were directed to activate manifestation in different ways, to include the following:

1) verbal instruction to activate immediately after pronouncement,
2) sometimes prophetic activation in a future time,
3) sometimes, clear verbal directives are subtle and allows the individual an opportunity to experience encouragement, "spontaneous insights, and or allows time for reflections or analysis. All of these divinely initiated energetic voice transfers manifests form.

- Again, the devil taketh him up into an exceeding high mountain, and sheweth him all the kingdoms of the world, and the glory of them; And saith unto him, All these things will I give thee if thou wilt fall down and worship me. Then saith Jesus unto him, Get thee hence, Satan: for it is written, Thou shalt worship the Lord thy God, and him only shalt thou serve. Then the devil leaveth him, and, behold, angels came and ministered unto him.

Matthew 4:8–11

- "And Jesus said unto the centurion, Go thy way; and as thou hast believed, so be it done unto thee. And his servant was healed in the selfsame hour" (Matthew 8:13).
- "And Jesus knew their thoughts, and said unto them, Every kingdom divided against itself is brought to desolation; and every city or house divided against itself shall not stand" (Matthew 12:25).
- "And he called the multitude, and said unto them, Hear, and understand" (Matthew 15:10).
- "And while they abode in Galilee, Jesus said unto them, The Son of man shall be betrayed into the hands of men" (Matthew 17:22).
- "And said, Verily I say unto you, Except ye be converted, and become as little children, ye shall not enter into the kingdom of heaven" (Matthew 18:3).
- "And the Word was made flesh, and dwelt among us (and we beheld his glory, the glory as of the only begotton of the Father,) full of grace and truth" (John 1:14 KJV.).
- "For we know him that hath said, Vengeance belongeth unto me, I will recompense, saith the Lord. And again, The Lord shall judge his people" (Hebrews 10:30).
- "Let your conversation be without covetousness; and be content with such things as ye have: for he hath

said, I will never leave thee, nor forsake thee" (Hebrews 13:5).

- "And he said unto me, It is done. I am Alpha and Omega, the beginning and the end. I will give unto him that is athirst of the fountain of the water of life freely" (Revelation 21:6).

There is also other evidence that both God and Jesus Christ's words created form, and this was most dramatically displayed when the dead/sleeping were raised/awakened. What is also phenomenal is that His voice's ability to raise the dead was also accomplished, as described in the Bible, by some of the disciples. Also noticeable, there does not appear to be any instance recorded that any of God's angelic angels raised an individual from the dead. Please note, there were some scriptures that stated a disciple was able to raise the dead with a touch or being touched. The following examples have been selected, specifically to demonstrate occasions when voice alone created manifestations, healings, and other types of "forms." The following selected examples is a sampling of The Bible specifically shows voice creates form.

Jesus and various devotees verbally commanding the dead to rise.

Elijah speaking:

- And she said unto Elijah, What have I to do with thee, O thou man of God? art thou come unto me to call my sin to remembrance, and to slay my son? And he said unto her, Give me thy son. And he took him out of her bosom, and carried him up into a loft, where he abode, and laid him upon his own bed. And he cried unto the LORD, and said, O LORD my God, hast thou also brought evil upon the widow with whom I sojourn, by slaying her son? And he stretched himself upon the child three times, and cried unto the LORD, and said, O LORD my God, I pray thee, let this child's soul come into him again. And the LORD heard the voice of Elijah; and the soul of the child came into him again, and he revived. And Elijah took the child, and brought him down out of the chamber into the house, and delivered him unto his mother: and Elijah said, See, thy son liveth.

King 17:18–23

Jesus speaking:

- And it came to pass the day after, that he went into a city called Nain; and many of his disciples went with him, and much people. Now when he came nigh to the gate of the city, behold, there was a dead man carried out, the only son of his mother, and she was a widow: and much people of the city was with her. And when the Lord saw her, he had compassion on her, and said unto her, Weep not. And he came and touched the bier: and they that bare him stood still. And he said, Young man, I say unto thee, Arise. And he that was dead sat up, and began to speak. And he delivered him to his mother.And there came a fear on all: and they glorified God, saying, That a great prophet is risen up among us; and, That God hath visited his people. And this rumour of him went forth throughout all Judæa, and throughout all the region round about.

Luke 7:11–17 (KJB)

Jesus speaking:

- While he yet spake, there cometh one from the ruler of the synagogue's house, saying to him, Thy daughter is dead; trouble not the Master. But when Jesus heard it, he answered him, saying, Fear not: believe only, and she shall be made whole. And when he came into the house, he suffered no man to go in, save Peter, and James, and John, and the father and the mother of the maiden. And all wept, and bewailed her: but he said, Weep not; she is not dead, but sleepeth. And they laughed him to scorn, knowing that she was dead. And he put them all out, and took her by the hand, and called, saying, Maid, arise. And her spirit came again, and she arose straightway: and he commanded to give her meat. And her parents were astonished: but he charged them that they should tell no man what was done.

Luke 8: 49–56

Jesus speaking:

- Now a certain man was sick, named Lazarus, of Bethany, the town of Mary and her sister Martha. It was that Mary which anointed the Lord with ointment, and wiped his feet with her hair, whose brother Lazarus was sick. Therefore his sisters sent unto him, saying, Lord, behold, he whom thou lovest is sick. When Jesus heard that, he said, This sickness is not unto death, but for the glory of God, that the Son of God might be glorified thereby. Now Jesus loved Martha, and her sister, and Lazarus. When he had heard therefore that he was sick, he abode two days still in the same place where he was. Then after that saith he to his disciples, Let us go into Judæa again. His disciples say unto him, Master, the Jews of late sought to stone thee; and goest thou thither again? Jesus answered, Are there not twelve hours in the day? If any man walk in the day, he stumbleth not, because he seeth the light of this world. But if a man walk in the night, he stumbleth, because there is no light in him. These things said he: and after that he saith unto them, Our friend Lazarus sleepeth; but I go, that I may awake him out of sleep. Then said his disciples, Lord, if he sleep, he shall do well. Howbeit Jesus spake of his death: but they thought that he had spoken of taking of rest in sleep. Then said Jesus unto them plainly, Lazarus is dead. And I am glad for your sakes that I was not there, to the intent ye may believe; nevertheless let us go unto him. Then said Thomas, which is called Didymus, unto his fellow disciples, Let us also go, that we may die with him. Then when Jesus came, he found that he had lain in the grave four days already. Now Bethany was nigh unto Jerusalem, about fifteen furlongs off: And many of the Jews came to Martha and Mary, to comfort them concerning their brother. Then Martha, as soon as she heard that Jesus was coming, went and met him: but Mary sat still in the house. Then said Martha unto Jesus, Lord, if thou hadst been here, my brother had not died. *But I know that even now, whatsoever thou wilt ask of God, God will give it thee.* Jesus saith unto her, Thy brother shall rise again. Martha saith unto him, I know that he shall rise again in the resurrection at the last day. *Jesus said unto her, I am the resurrection, and the life: he that believeth in me, though he were dead, yet shall he live: And whosoever liveth and believeth in me shall never die. Believest thou this?* She saith unto him, Yea, Lord: I believe that thou art the Christ, the Son of God, which should come into the world. And when she had so said, she went her way, and called Mary her sister secretly, saying, The Master is come, and calleth for thee. As soon as she heard that, she arose quickly, and came unto him. Now Jesus was not yet come into the town, but was in that place where Martha met him. The Jews then which were with her in the house, and comforted her, when they saw Mary, that she rose up hastily and went out, followed her, saying, She goeth unto the grave to weep there. Then when Mary was come where Jesus was, and saw him, she fell down at his feet, saying unto him, Lord, if thou hadst been here, my brother had not died. When Jesus therefore saw her weeping, and the Jews also weeping which came with her, he groaned in the spirit, and was troubled, And said, Where have ye laid him? They said unto him, Lord, come and see. *Jesus wept.* Then said the Jews, Behold how he loved him! And some of them said, Could not this man, which opened the eyes of the blind, have caused that even this man should not have died? Jesus therefore again groaning in himself cometh to the grave. It was a cave, and a stone lay upon it. Jesus said, Take ye away the stone. Martha, the sister of him that was dead, saith unto him, Lord, by this time he stinketh: for he hath been dead four days. Jesus saith unto her, Said I not unto thee, that, if thou wouldest believe, thou shouldest see the glory of God? Then they took away the stone from the place where the dead was laid. *And Jesus lifted up his eyes, and said, Father, I thank thee that thou hast heard me. And I knew that thou hearest me always: but because of the people which stand by I said it, that they may believe that thou hast sent me. And when he thus had spoken, he cried with a loud voice, Lazarus, come forth.* And he that was dead came forth, bound hand and foot with graveclothes: and his face was bound about with a napkin. Jesus saith unto them, Loose him, and let him go. Then many of the Jews which came to Mary, and had seen the things which Jesus did, believed on him. But some of them went their ways to the Pharisees, and told them what things Jesus had done.

John 11:1–45

Jesus prophesied,

- In the end of the sabbath, as it began to dawn toward the first day of the week, came Mary Magdalene and the other Mary to see the sepulchre. And, behold, there was a great earthquake: for the angel of the Lord descended from heaven, and came and rolled back the stone from the door, and sat upon it. His countenance was like lightning, and his raiment white as snow: And for fear of him the keepers did shake, and became as dead men. And the angel answered and said unto the women, Fear not ye: for I know that ye seek Jesus, which was crucified. He is not here: for he is risen, as he said. Come, see the place where the Lord lay. And go quickly, and tell his disciples that he is risen from the dead; and, behold, he goeth before you into Galilee; there shall ye see him: lo, I have told you. And they departed quickly from the sepulchre with fear and great joy; and did run to bring his disciples word. And as they went to tell his disciples, behold, Jesus met them, saying, All hail. And they came and held him by the feet, and worshipped him. Then said Jesus unto them, Be not afraid: go tell my brethren that they go into Galilee, and there shall they see me.

Matthew 28:1–10

Jesus speaking, focus on verse 18.

- Then the eleven disciples went away into Galilee, into a mountain where Jesus had appointed them. And when they saw him, they worshipped him: but some doubted. *And Jesus came and spake unto them, saying, All power is given unto me in heaven and in earth.* Go ye therefore, and teach all nations, baptizing them in the name of the Father, and of the Son, and of the Holy Ghost: Teaching them to observe all things whatsoever I have commanded you: and, lo, I am with you alway, even unto the end of the world. Amen.

Matthew 28:16–20

Peter speaking:

- Now there was at Joppa a certain disciple named Tabitha, which by interpretation is called Dorcas: this woman was full of good works and almsdeeds which she did. And it came to pass in those days, that she was sick, and died: whom when they had washed, they laid her in an upper chamber. And forasmuch as Lydda was nigh to Joppa, and the disciples had heard that Peter was there, they sent unto him two men, desiring him that he would not delay to come to them. Then Peter arose and went with them. When he was come, they brought him into the upper chamber:

and all the widows stood by him weeping, and shewing the coats and garments which Dorcas made, while she was with them. But Peter put them all forth, and kneeled down, and prayed; and turning him to the body said, Tabitha, arise. And she opened her eyes: and when she saw Peter, she sat up. And he gave her his hand, and lifted her up, and when he had called the saints and widows, presented her alive. And it was known throughout all Joppa; and many believed in the Lord.

Acts 39:26–42

NONLOCAL REAL-TIME "KNOWING:" OR STEALTH SURVEILLANCE.

Most of us, at one time or another, have had the experience when you had a "hunch," a "gut feeling," an acute observation of something that normally would have gone unnoticed. Depending on our personal value system, some of us dismiss any such correct incident as serendipity, coincidence, or even luck. Our unique personal degree of skepticism, of unexplained, unsolicited, and spontaneous attentiveness to an event, a place, or otherwise formally unknown information, entirely depends on what, if anything, we have noticed. Some of us have always be aware that there are times we "feel" a family member or close friend is in need, distress, or sometimes extremely happy. However, recent research has shown that all humans have the capacity to access/recognize non-local real-time knowing if we just acknowledge this insight exists. All humans have the innate ability to access God's consciousness. Often people fail to understand more than recognition is necessary. One needs to do something with this information. The first thing one needs to do is to test "the message" to ensure that you have accessed God's consciousness and not a purposeful ill-intended destructive conscious communication.

Sometimes individuals evade God entirely, choosing instead to categorize conscious awareness as any of the following variety of other names, to include but are not necessarily limited to the following:

- Ancestral guidance,
- Channeling deceased/aliens,
- Distance Viewing,
- Distance Vision Zones,
- Distant Vision,
- Knowing,
- Non-local viewing (RV),
- Remote influencing, and
- Teleportation (often experienced with knowing).

Please note that R.V. practitioners contend that this capability is not spiritual or psychic. The contention is that every individual has this capability. Some, of course, are more accurate than others. No "sixth sense" is required, just focused intent, following a specific protocol, will access the collective consciousness, and the target will be identified. The more complex the target, the more sessions are required. In complex targets, there may be multi-layers that must be accessed in sequential order to answer the "question." The collective consciousness is timeless, covering all time; more approaching a circular continuity, not necessarily a linear sequential timeline. Collective consciousness also is not space time-sensitive; any place and any time can be accessed if one knows and follows the correct protocol. The U.S. Army established a program in 1978 at Fort Mead, Maryland, under the Defense Intelligence Agency to investigate the potential for psychic phenomena in military and domestic intelligence applications. Dr. H. E. Puythoff, an engineer and parapsychologist, had co-founded the company SRI International, To the Stars" with Tom Delonge in 2010. In 1991, the U.S. Army established the Stargate Project to investigate the potential for psychic phenomena in military and domestic intelligence. This project was overseen by the three primary founders: Dr. Harold Puythoff, Ingo Swann, and Russel Targ established specific training for selected military personnel. At this time, Russia and China were suspected of also having similar defenses and information gathering programs researching non-local "seeing" and influencing. As knowledge of some of these programs leaked into the public domain, affluent corporate businesses and investors hired individuals with exceptional accuracy as business consultants. Around the 1990s, possibly a little earlier, some spiritual groups (for instance, J.Z. Knight's spiritual seeking included R.V. (perhaps under a different name but still R.V.).

The bottom line, as far as this work is concerned: there are as many applications to use non-local knowing as there are individuals using this capability. Many individuals have used these techniques to play and win successive lottery games, foretelling probable dangerous health issues and locations that are best geographical sanctuaries in case of natural or man-made catastrophe. Sometimes a news article will appear that states an R.V. practitioner helped solve a murder case, find a lost person or their body, or even actually predicted some disaster. The most difficult part of R.V. accuracy is pinning down a specific time/date; take particular care if someone factually states they can "pin down the time." Either they are playing "hit or miss," or they are indwelled. Either way, if you keep dabbling in this "art," the more you invite personal involvement with spirits you had not intended to host.

What most individuals engaging in these various paths to "master" R.V., fail to realize; is that it is much easier, psychically safer, and definitely always accurate information if one just asks God. There are also zero negative repercussions with prolonged access to God's collective consciousness: not so with most of the other ways to access the collective consciousness. Anyone can access a collective consciousness; the trap is what consciousness have you connected. Christians do not have to search for the collective consciousness, we just have to pray and pay attention to God's answer.

One word of advice, if you decide to take courses (or if you have already started) in R.V., make sure you pray for protection each and every time you start the protocol process while learning. However, it is best if you just stop R.V. Each viewing success can lead to R.V. addiction, and over time fluctuating consciousness slippage, sometimes migraines, and/or body tremors. In addition to any physical, mental dysfunctions, periodically entirely wrong information will be gathered. Sometimes two or more individuals viewing the same target increases the probability of information accuracy. *All R.V. viewers risk over prolonged time the indwelling of uninvited other dimension residents.* The most successful R.V. practitioners also include "out-of-body experiences (teleportation) when locating information once the target has been identified. If you have already tried any form of non-local viewing and have chosen to no longer practice: make sure you have at least two to three prayer warriors to bind and cast out any anomaly that is not God's affiliates. Note, this is also the perfect time to repent, ask for God to come into your life, and permanently refrain from any more R.V. experiences.

For the Christian, R.V., under any name, is considered an abomination in both the Old Testament (Deuteronomy and 2 Chronicles) and the New Testament (Romans). This is because the practitioners accessing the Akashic Records, ancestors, and all other protocols; purposefully ignore and disregard God's omnipotence (being all-powerful), omniscience (being all-knowing), and omnipresence (being all-present*). Practicing R.V. snubs God, your actions have shown that just about anything and everything is put before acknowledging God as being the one and only God—and conscious awareness is His.*

> And God spake all these words, saying, I am the LORD thy God, which have brought thee out of the land of Egypt, out of the house of bondage. Thou shalt have no other gods before me. Thou shalt not make unto thee any graven image, or any likeness of any thing that is in heaven above, or that is in the earth beneath, or that is in the water under the earth: Thou shalt not bow down thyself to them, nor serve them: for I the LORD thy God am a jealous God, visiting the iniquity of the fathers upon the children unto the third and fourth generation of them that hate me; And shewing mercy unto thousands of them that love

me, and keep my commandments. *Thou shalt not take the name of the LORD thy God in vain; for the LORD will not hold him guiltless that taketh his name in vain.* Remember the sabbath day, to keep it holy. Six days shalt thou labour, and do all thy work: But the seventh day is the sabbath of the LORD thy God: in it thou shalt not do any work, thou, nor thy son, nor thy daughter, thy manservant, nor thy maidservant, nor thy cattle, nor thy stranger that is within thy gates: For in six days the LORD made heaven and earth, the sea, and all that in them is, and rested the seventh day: wherefore the LORD blessed the sabbath day, and hallowed it. Honour thy father and thy mother: that thy days may be long upon the land which the LORD thy God giveth thee. Thou shalt not kill. Thou shalt not commit adultery. Thou shalt not steal. Thou shalt not bear false witness against thy neighbour. Thou shalt not covet thy neighbour's house, thou shalt not covet thy neighbour's wife, nor his manservant, nor his maidservant, nor his ox, nor his ass, nor any thing that is thy neighbour's. And all the people saw the thunderings, and the lightnings, and the noise of the trumpet, and the mountain smoking: and when the people saw it, they removed, and stood afar off. And they said unto Moses, Speak thou with us, and we will hear: but let not God speak with us, lest we die. *And Moses said unto the people, Fear not: for God is come to prove you, and that his fear may be before your faces, that ye sin not. And the people stood afar off, and Moses drew near unto the thick darkness where God was.*

Exodus 20:1–21

God's admonishment against practicing non-local real-time knowing/influencing.

The foundation and contentions of this work are that Christ's Consciousness conquers catastrophes, change, and chaos. The selected following three scriptures, two from the Old Testament (Deuteronomy and 2 Chronicles) and one from the New Testament (Romans), underscore God's consistent distain for this abominable behavior for any type, under any name of non-local real-time "knowing." God's Word is steadfast and does not contradict itself.

- There shall not be found among you any one that maketh his son or his daughter to pass through the fire, or that useth divination, or an observer of times, or an enchanter, or a witch, *Or a charmer, or a consulter with familiar spirits, or a wizard, or a necromancer.* For all that do these things are an abomination unto the LORD: and because of these abominations the LORD thy God doth drive them out from before thee. Thou shalt be perfect with the LORD thy God. For these nations, which thou shalt possess, hearkened unto observers of times, and unto diviners: but as for thee, the LORD thy God hath not suffered thee so to do.
  Deuteronomy 18:10–14

- And he caused his children to pass through the fire in the valley of the son of Hinnom: also he observed times, and used enchantments, and used witchcraft, *and dealt with a familiar spirit, and with wizards: he wrought much evil in the sight of the LORD, to provoke him to anger.*
  2 Chronicles 33:6

- For therein is the righteousness of God revealed from faith to faith: as it is written, The just shall live by faith. For the wrath of God is revealed from heaven against all ungodliness and unrighteousness of men, who hold the truth in unrighteousness; Because that which may be known of God is manifest in them; for God hath shewed it unto them. *For the invisible things of him from the creation of the world are clearly seen, being understood by the things that are made, even his eternal power and Godhead; so that they are without excuse:* Because that, when they knew God, they glorified him not as God, neither were thankful; but became vain in their imaginations, and their foolish heart was darkened. Professing themselves to be wise, they became fools, And changed the glory of the uncorruptible God into an image made like to corruptible man, and to birds, and fourfooted beasts, and creeping things. *Wherefore God also gave them up to uncleanness through the lusts of their own hearts, to dishonour their own bodies between themselves: Who changed the truth of God into a lie, and worshipped and served the creature more than the Creator, who is blessed for ever. Amen.* For this cause God gave them up unto vile affections: for even their women did change the natural use into that which is against nature: And likewise also the men, leaving the natural use of the woman, burned in their lust one toward another; men with men working that which is unseemly, and receiving in themselves that recompence of their error which was meet. And even as they did not like to retain God in their knowledge, God gave them over to a reprobate mind, to do those things which are not convenient; Being filled with all unrighteousness, fornication, wickedness, covetousness, maliciousness; full of envy, murder, debate, deceit, malignity; whisperers, Backbiters, haters of God, despiteful, proud, boasters, inventors of evil things, disobedient to parents, Without understanding, covenant breakers, without natural affection, implacable, unmerciful: Who knowing the judgment of God, that they which commit such things are worthy of death, not only do the same, but have pleasure in them that do them.

Romans 1:17–32

Knowing something exists does not necessarily mean you will try it. But, in today's environment, it is important to know that there are a significant number of "ordinary" people you think you know, and there are those that you come in contact with and may not know. Many of these ordinary individuals use R.V. and influence on a regular "stealth" basis. These "regular people" remote view to obtain some type of "power over" individuals, achieve an edge regarding business strategies and profits, tinkering with "mother nature," and masterminding global dominance, among other things. Fortunately for the rest of us, these practitioners never know when the information/influencing will be false or fail. *After all, only God is 100 percent accurate 100 percent of the time. If there is something you really want to know, then when two or three of you are in agreement according to his will, he assuredly will answer your prayer request. He will also protect you. There is something about the name Jesus, as our intercessor, when asked will protect, guide, and keep your mind and body at peace and functioning as designed.* A foray into the unknown spirit world is both hazardous and unnecessary on an individual basis.

TO KNOW, NONLOCALLY IN REAL TIME IS A VERB, CONSCIOUSLY AWARE IS A BEHAVIOR.

Willpower, most of the time, sustains us through dismal, unimaginable trials. But then again, sometimes, one's resolve seems to have taken on a life of its own. The will needs training, like responding when needed and exhibiting determination, sometimes it is a disciplinarian making sure you stick to achieving your long-term deferred gratifications. One's will also should have the capacity to be focused and not deterred by the opinions of others, lack of finances, or other perceived blockages. Finally, willpower has to be consistent with one's core values and definitely more altruistic than malevolent to achieve short- and long-range goals. Accurate discernment and willpower are necessary because, with some challenges, there are no "do-overs." Thus a wrong decision or insufficient willpower may leave an individual decimated, sometimes beyond recovery.

The descent into one's personal hell (okay, depravity for those who do not believe in hell) tends to lead one to rely on their favorite personal weakness: examples: cantankerousness, depression, drugs, addictions, debauchery, and so forth. Those who have not over time trained or straightened their willpower will lack the sufficient strength, flexibility, and stamina needed in times of strife. Most likely, it never occurred to her that the constant, intentional identification and application of her core value for each decision made is spiritual training. Thus when a particularly gnarly situation occurs, her willpower "actually shows up" and has the power to endure to the end. A Christian that obeys God's Word regularly has the internal fortitude to rely on God's Word, protection, and guidance; being assured that she is fully suited with the Full Armor of God, Ephesians 6:10–18.

Many individuals think there are significant advantages to know future occurrences, the personal thoughts of others, and the ability to access hidden documents and other tangible items. Therefore, there are many individuals who practice nonlocal real-time knowing to achieve an advantage by stealth. In this instance, practiced secrecy and craftiness fortifies and invites negativity and false information, therefore, incomplete or wrong outcomes are likely. It has previously been said that if you want 100 percent accuracy and projected planning that has the best of all possible outcomes, then all you have to do is ask God, in Jesus' name, according to His will, for what you want.

Accurate discernment and focused determination always surpass doubt, self-pity, jealousy, and trickery. *The strength of "willpower" is contingent on practiced access to Christ's Consciousness, consistent prayer, and practiced obedience to God's Word.* One cannot give or rely on what one does not have. Finding out during a battle is the wrong time and place to find out you are unarmed and the only soldier.

CHRIST'S CONSCIOUSNESS, LEADERSHIP, AND BUILDING COMMUNITY.

Christ's Consciousness is being mindful, inquisitive, chronicling, and analyzing. This process of outward observation and inward self-reflective review facilitates learning new information, assessing data, and coming to either a conclusion(s) or reasonable inferences. Sometimes there is insufficient time to completely weigh all options, align options with your core values, and then act. When the capability to consider and analyze is time-limited, for whatever reason, then you will have to make the best decision based on the information you have. In whichever case, one's discernment, consciously aware, makes a better decision than "just winging it." Along with consciousness, when you have some familiarity listening to and obeying, Christ's Consciousness always enlightens and explains what to do and when. Sometimes "why," you should have taken that specific action later becomes clear. In time you realize, the timing of taking action was essential because that allowed the best possible outcome to occur. Not only did you realize the best possible outcome occurred, you also experienced joy, gratitude, and a state of moral exaltation. The quickening of your moral senses, along with an appreciation that you have not forfeited retainment of your eternal life: this is unparalleled victory. *Within Christ's Conscious awareness, one typically perceives the world as a mystery, and in this state, visionaries abound.*

Your core values establish boundaries that significantly influence your ability to adapt to change. With self-training and practice purposefully consulting your core values when making all decisions, will over time become automatic, and your decisions will be in alignment with your core values. The options you have for making choices should equal the number of decisions that are deliberately considered and align with your core values. If not, this could lead to second-guessing oneself after a decision has been made or outright regretfulness regarding your decision. For each decision you make, you must consider the situation at hand, desired outcome, and, naturally, the probability that you will achieve your desired goal.

While many of your decisions are made at a subconscious level, often, you are very aware of your decision-making concerns. How you process this barrage of societal "do's" and restraints permeates each of your internal values. Many things compete for your compliance: family, friends, work, status, and financial impact, to name just a few factors that you balance. Therefore, when attempting to effect a change in your behaviors and possibly your beliefs, there will be many external pressures that will attempt to persuade you to remain the same. Not everyone wants to see you grow, change, achieve, and have inner peace and joy.

For Christians with a personal relationship with God and His son Jesus Christ, this relationship is sacred. The Father, Son, and Holy Spirit; when we invite them to dwell within enables

- ability to repent sins
- achieve salvation
- discernment to hear
- obey his word
- real-time protection

No type of change or chaos can bedevil a Christian adorned with the Full Armor of God: Ephesians 6:10–18. If one lives, sooner or later, unfathomable disasters, disappointments, illnesses, deaths, and other assorted calamities will weary one's soul. However, the bitterness of these calamities is tempered, confronted, and overcome by the grace, strength, healing, and infusion of God's love and mercy. "For I am the Lord, I change not; therefore ye sons of Jacob are not consumed" (Malachi 3:6).

CHAPTER 4

· ·

Building Of Community

> I will stand upon my watch, and set me upon the
> tower, and will watch to see what he will say unto
> me, and what I shall answer when I am reproved.
> And the LORD answered me, and said, Write
> the vision, and make it plain upon tables, that he
> may run that readeth it. For the vision is yet for
> an appointed time, but at the end it shall speak,
> and not lie: though it tarry, wait for it; because it
> will surely come, it will not tarry.
> Habakkuk 2:1–3

When facing the transition to a "new normal," one must realize and accept that the "old normal" is already defunct. Resisted or not, the "new normal" abruptness of changes depends on the forces requiring the change. It is also helpful in order to reduce fear, to clearly articulate what changes are necessary, and the procedures for change. The individuals directing the process of change should be clearly identified, have authority, and have open procedures accommodating two-way communication. The need to underscore the inclusion, in some way, of individuals involved in the change is necessary to facilitate an authentic sense of security and belonging. Unfortunately this did not happen in the abrupt, forced changes associated with the Coronavirus global epidemic, and psychologically we are deeply confused, even scared.

This sense of belonging is the foundation for building a community. A community must have at least two individuals. It is helpful if these individuals have some prior acquaintance, compatible core values, sense of governance, and a common goal. Once constructed, a community becomes more than the sum of its parts, the individual members. A community may be a family, a clan, a small group, or a town, a city, and in some cases, a nation. The larger the number comprising the community, the more difficult the leadership becomes. A community does not necessarily require that all members have the same (or even tolerable) core values. The complexities of the community leader(s) developing, maintaining, and growing their communities are beyond the scope of this work. But let us just say that many communities and/or their leaders go through changes rapidly, and many disperse. However, if one is unfortunate enough to be in a "new norm" change that is led by a tyrannical leader, then; get out if you can and, if not, pray without ceasing.

> And we beseech you, brethren, to know them which labour among you, and are over you in the Lord, and admonish you; And to esteem them very highly in love for their work's sake. And be at peace among yourselves. Now we exhort you, brethren, warn them that are unruly, comfort the feebleminded, support the weak, be patient toward all men. See that none render evil for evil unto any man; but ever follow that which is good, both among yourselves, and to all men. Rejoice evermore. *Pray without ceasing. In every thing give thanks: for this is the will of God in Christ Jesus concerning you.* Quench not the Spirit. Despise not prophesyings. Prove all things; hold fast that which is good. Abstain from all appearance of evil. And the very God of peace sanctify you wholly; and I pray God your whole spirit and

soul and body be preserved blameless unto the coming of our Lord Jesus Christ. Faithful is he that calleth you, who also will do it. Brethren, pray for us.

1 Thessalonians 5:12–25

No one said this would be easy. On the other hand, if an opportunity arises that you can escape, or some other type of nonviolent, "evil for evil" transactional activity presents itself, then, by all means, get out! The tyrannical despot does not "get away with it" in God's sight. Remember He said vengeance is His.

Recompense to no man evil for evil. Provide things honest in the sight of all men. If it be possible, as much as lieth in you, live peaceably with all men. Dearly beloved, avenge not yourselves, but rather give place unto wrath: for it is written, Vengeance is mine; I will repay, saith the Lord.

Romans 12: 17–19

WHAT IS A COMMUNITY? WHY IS IT IMPORTANT?

A community must have at least two individuals who come together to enhance their ability to survive and/or for social reasons have decided to live or work together. Once constructed, a community becomes more than the sum of its parts, the individual members. The leader of the community should have the best interest of the community as the goal. The "best person" for the leadership position may, in fact, change contingent on the goals, objective, process, obstacles, and resources available. The distinguishing characteristic of a "community" versus a "group" is that a community is: inclusive, committed, conscious, realistic, and cultivates each participant to encourage a collective spirit. A "group," in contrast, is a collection of two or more autonomous individuals who may or may not know each other or care about harmony or collective goals. In a community, there must be an opportunity for each person to be recognized, contribute, and feel safe. Each person should be willing and able to lead at some point, either the entire community or some project, depending on the situation. Forcing someone to be "the leader" frequently turns out miserably, and if this individual does remain the leader, typically they become a dictator, or worse.

A community cannot be cohesive if the members do not have a vested interest in the long- and short-range goals. Members also must have a willingness to compromise in a way that each individual knows their voice has been heard and considered. Therefore, the "best person" for the leadership position may, in fact, change contingent on the goals, objective, process, obstacles, and resources available. The distinguishing characteristics of a "community" versus a "group" are that a community is inclusive, committed, conscious, realistic, and cultivates (from each participant), and then exudes a collective spirit to all members. It is often the case that in this type of community, there is an "informal" leader who supports the formal leader and helps assuage the community members. A "group," in contrast, is a collection of two or more autonomous individuals who may or may not know each other or care about harmony or collective goals. Within a community, each member has an opportunity to personally be recognized, contribute, and feel acknowledged. Each person should realize that depending on the situation, they might be the leader.

This discussion of community is important to consider here because within the U.S., at best, we have many interchangeable members between a vast number of fractured groups. *Groups of people tend to personally carry their own fears, apprehensions, unique needs, and definitions of winning. Individual group members tend to be more self-centered, prone to force and/or bully other group members, and tend to have a more dictatorial leadership style.* The ever-increasing technology enables group participation by any individual to be geographically separate from each other but still consider themselves to be a "group." Only when a group starts identifying one or more common goals, processes to achieve the desired goals, and starts establishing long-range goals and objectives does it start to transform into a community. There is a tendency that communities operating during major social, economic, and moral changes; have a better chance of forming long-term alliances than groups.

REPETITIVE STORIES CREATE CELLULAR MEMORY.

For those of us lucky enough to have been born and raised in a familial community, we have memories of the community elders. Now, whether or not "your elders" consisted of some aged, wise, and cherished person, or the withered, cranky, and mad shunned "crag or old goat," we have all experienced them. In addition, when fate is malicious, each of us has had to hear an elder's stories for the four millionth time. Whether the story was about climate or economic hardships, great war sacrifices, educational standards, or changes in morality and technology ruining society; we can almost repeat these stories word for word.

Other than teaching each of us patience, respect for the elderly, and of course, bonding with others in our social circle that has also been "entrapped" by these elders, what purpose do these stories serve? These are oral histories, yes, this is exactly what they are oral histories. Unfortunately, oral histories are becoming a lost art, and valuable historical documentation is being forever lost. Currently, oral cultural histories of an entire people are typically only found among indigenous people remaining in the world. All cultures use to have these oral historians, and some are lucky someone steps up as the "historian" and writes down these stories; for those communities that still respect these elders, they provide our primal, traditional grounding.

Have you ever noticed how often, in times of stress, indecision, or when searching for anecdotal parables to express or explain something important, you reference either the elders or their stories? You know, when relating one of these gems, you have made a connection with your audience because immediately they too will relate one of their stories. This sharing of stories is the foundation for all primary and secondary relationships, the essential glue for the building of families and business relationships, and an essential element in the building and sustaining of trust.

As humans, we all share this connection through stories, regardless of race, ethnicity, or national origins, we bring our stories with us and share our stories with others. Stories forge friendships, foster clans, continue feuds, entrench traditions, and permeate religions. Those of us who have never been to the "old country" long to "go home." Some of us make the journey home "in the memory" of a loved one. And others have achieved extraordinary accomplishments based on the stories and dreams of our elders. Pride, both personal and communal, has its roots in shared stories and sanctioned community norms.

Listen carefully the next time a story is repeated for the hundredth time, what you will hear is the emotion that needs to be repeated until you understand why this story is so important to the storyteller. Some emotional need was not met, some slight was endured one time too many, some injustice needs to be acknowledged, some sorrow soothed. Most joyful stories are not continually repeated. The stories most repeated are the painful stories that have contributed to the weathering of the soul over time. The lines on the face, the cracking voice, and the bent bodies are all the manifestations of these mournful stories—transferred as a gift to the listener as custodian of the hard lives about which "old folks talked" to the next generation. *People cannot "let go" of hurt until the story has been told and acknowledged. One incident creates a story, but the life of the story, once created, is capable of living without regard to location or time.*

STORIES REAL OR NOT WEAVE FUTURE EXPERIENCES.

Time is an interesting concept, and each person has his unique acceptance or denial of time. Time is typically observed or felt, and when observed, one generally leans to time being perceived as either linear or circular. For those linear and sequential thinkers, there is the past, the present, and the future. On the other hand, for those absorbing time's circular connections, there are interconnected conscious awareness, Déjà vu, and prophetic second sight. Thankfully, most people have some combination of linear sequential and circular thinking; and this mixture is often applied to situations. The problem often encountered in times of crisis is the inaccurate judgment of the primary issue; thus leaving us insecure, hypersensitive, or just overwhelmed. Some decisions are final, with no "do-overs." The finality of the decision when made, for some, paralyzes the individual. Sometimes, the choice is to imagine an emotional sanctuary, seeking comfort thus ignore everything. Our will/spirit automatically seeks to guard what is left of our tenacity and life force.

Now, more likely than not, if those stories we retell were tangibly documented, say on a video with sound, some might vehemently protest that what is being shown, in whole or in part, is "not really the way it happened." Documented accounts of behaviors cannot convey feelings or intentions, so observers can only conjecture, based on her filters motives and emotional imprinting. We all have some family stories which we could share from our youth. We all know people that we shared significant experiences with. Sometimes our stories, when shared with someone who was also present at the event, show a different perspective of the shared event. If you think about it, there is not one person that you shared your childhood experiences that have an identical value system or prioritization of wishes, hopes, and dreams with you. No wonder the further you get away from "your kind of people," the more you just do not "get" the way folks think.

Now, think of going to work in a diverse workforce or living in a multicultural community. If you just do not pass out from fright with this thought; you most certainly get a headache some days from interacting with "those" people. Have you ever asked the question of how you came to live, work in this "foreign" environment? Either for some reason, you ignored the homogenized environment (which did not include you); or you remained and the diverse horde of folks "moved in" all around you. Now you are overwhelmed, afraid, distrustful, and desperately wish either you could leave this environment or "they" would leave. Given enough fermentation, something is going to erupt.

PRIMAL INSTINCTS MEETS POLITICAL CORRECTNESS.

Humans need to be nurtured, mentally engaged, and challenged to develop and sustain emotional connections, creativity, and recognize accomplishments. Everyone needs to be touched by a caring and loving friend or relative at some time, and preferably often to anchor feelings of belonging and security. This is important because the human mind is incapable of "thinking" a feeling. You can think about a feeling, but you cannot think a feeling. You either feel secure, or you do not. Feeling secure, or not, is one of our primal instinct regulators that influences in some way whether we succeed or fail in our pursuit of happiness. Two other elements inextricably intertwined with our feelings of survival are power and money. Power, arguably, is the ability to influence another to do or refrain from doing what you desire. Power also presumes you have currency, either money or some other valuable exchange commodity. Desire then is the motivation for currency, whether economic, emotional, or physical. Desire may be instinctual or learned and often difficult to control or redirect. Power, however, is usually never satisfied; the quest is always for more.

Most people have some degree of power among their associations and occasionally get to exercise their influence. Most of us have established a range of desires and some degree of ambition to achieve the highest level of "creature comforts "possible. Creature comforts above the minimum necessary for survival will always, at some time, require interaction and exchange with others. The currency of exchange to acquire, maintain, or dispose of goods and services may be tangible (for instance, money, precious metals, gems, or land) or intangible (for instance, emotional support, love, loyalty, or exchange of intellectual properties). Now survival and acquisition of creature comforts tend to produce a range of actions and reactions between and amongst others.

Sometimes our interactions in pursuit of our real or personal property result in amazing synchronicity and productivity with others. Sometimes, our personal exchanges are unthinkably antagonistic and even cruel. An individual's goal(s) begin as an intangible thought. Achievement of one's goal(s) then requires imagination, some planning, and action to obtain the tangible goal. The point is if you have ten or more people within your community, the probability that at least forty percent of the population are having a similar contest with their desires and the reality of achieving their goals. This means that at some time, your desire will be an obstacle to what someone else wants. And, sometimes, your desires will be detained or blocked while someone else achieves their desire.

The building of a community means that on these occasions, the leadership and followers will rely heavily on the trust and mutual concern that, at some point in the near future, all desires will be met. Once again, remember one cannot give what one does not have. Building community means every member needs to decide, over time, each member will do everything they can to assure everyone gets their goals met. Realistically, not everyone may get their goals met, it, of course, depends on what the goals are, especially if the goal is immoral, illegal, greedy, or cruel. An individual's desire may not be realistic or achievable for some reason, so negotiating what is really desired is necessary for the existing "need" to be met. It is essential to find out what the goal was behind the desire and see if that goal can be achieved.

It is rare to find a person who is without desires. Usually, at some time everyone, has some type of desire, regardless of how momentary and fleeting. Thus when two or more people meet and authentically actively listen to each other, just about anything is possible. Typically, during the first meeting, individuals obviously or covertly determine social acceptability, "pecking order," areas of similarity, and what type of sexual or plutonic attraction, if any, is occurring. Each person makes a critical determination of the other person, often solidifying if there will be any further interactions during the first impression.

This first impression of each other will be a difficult impression to reverse.

For each action or inaction, there are always consequences, some intended and anticipated, some not. For instance, in structured situations or some other highly monitored setting, most often, we feel compelled to "go along to get along," regardless of one's immediate, authentic thoughts. In these situations, the authentic behaviors of "trapped" individuals are supplanted by backstabbing, lies, lack of necessary communication, and other diabolical actions or inactions. When two or more individuals engage as competitors, each contender's focus is twofold: first to impede other individuals' use of their power and disrupt their performance achievements; and second to use influential contacts, money, or whatever is necessary to become the victor. For this type of community, Truth is presented as trickery, and teamwork is built on pragmatic fabrications to substantiate one's position. In this situation, those whose core values are self-centered and economically driven quite often are called dynamic—or cold-blooded. Today's diverse workforce most often stretches the veil of political correctness to a translucent transactional exchange of "this for that:" with only the naïve falling for the illusion of mutual satisfaction.

Now, sustaining an illusion is possible, especially if the illusion works for our own personal benefit. However, all illusions break down sooner-or-later when emotional, financial, and social pressures challenge the conjured harmonious and healthy commune's environment perception. What more and more of us are figuring out is that repetitive stories, cellular memories, primal instincts, and our needs for personal security have turned into kindling, which has rapidly degraded and carelessly discarded into a tender box, presoaked with flammable accelerants. Individuals who lived tottering on the edge of fissure-infused communities must contribute to the community restoration, or face deprivation and alienation: or leave. A major community fissure is political correctness, which only works as a façade. The arrival of COVID-19 overnight took nationwide unparalleled draconian steps, under the disguise as political correctness to include but not limited to:

- allowed sanctuary cities and civic riots
- enforced business and school closures,
- enforced involuntary devastating economic repercussions,
- homeless population increased no or inadequate Federal/ state aid,
- insufficient medical facilities,
- insufficient medical staff,
- insufficient medications,
- insufficient mental health care,
- lack of food and dry goods
- required home quarantine,
- restrictions to assembling if allowed businesses churches open,
- restrictions to travel,
- social distancing indoors and out,
- surveillance of all forms of communications, and
- wearing face masks.

The year 2020 reset the social order creating a new lower caste system. An assault on one's health and emotional welfare, the previously unknown isolation and sensory deprivation from and between loved ones and friends shattered mental wellness and deprived physical expressions of compassion and endearment. Mask wearing not only obstructs emotional clues often clarity of verbal conversations is diminished. Either one could not hear what was being said, or the words were "garbled" by the mask's interference. The attempt to refashion and destroy every giving and receiving emotional interconnectedness was too well orchestrated to have been accidental or unforeseen. The vast majority of Americans demand the reinstatement of our Constitutional governance contract along with our Bill of Rights. Using the COVID-19 pandemic as the catalyst for the diabolical restructuring of America is like watching a degraded film of a mediocre novice magician. It sucks, and we want recompense for the abuse of our time and the intentional infliction of our emotional distress and false imprisonment.

BUILDING COMMUNITY: LEADERSHIP, AWARENESS, AND QUANTUM PHYSICS.

"It was the best of times; it was the worst of times." Charles Dicken's famous opening statement in his "A Tale of Two Cities" (1859) not only captured "France's state of the union,"—it seems to also describe quite appropriately our "state of the union?" His opening line covers the duality of France's friction of revolution, resurrection, and of course, the hope for a better life for its citizens. Discussing multiple governance theories, change plans, and leadership competencies when "mastered" will produce "good grades." But, in real life, what does it do for us? Well, "now that the rubber has met the road, less talk; do something!

Without belaboring the obvious, there is significant concurrence that the U.S. today, in the beginning months of 2021, nationally we are frozen with fear (of just about everything), emotionally imbalanced, exhibiting wavering" behaviors, hallucinations, withdrawal from reality, self-centered and often operating lawlessly without remorse. And this is on a good day. Often the only interrelatedness and/or entanglement exercised by a large portion of our population occurs as each individual pursues their own advantage to "win."

So how do our local, state-wide, and federal elected and appointed officials meet their personal needs and wants, consider the good of their constituents, and preserve our Nation before it explodes under the heaviness of greed, more greed, and ultimate overreaching unlimited power? *The transformation of a collection of individuals into a group, and then into a community of individuals, and then God preserve us, an integrated and diverse Nation?* First, community member, at each communal level, has to relinquish some personal prerogative.[50] Each community, at every level, must be a group of leaders whose delegated authority combines for the enrichment of the whole, not a group led by individuals or cliques[51]. As Americans, we believe in competition, but with this confusion, scarcity (actual or perceived) of basic necessities, all competition will do is fuel civil unrest and wars.

Each community has to ensure that basic survival needs are met before more altruistic governance goals will gain priority. *We, each of us, must reconnect with our own spirit and then establish common goals at the homestead level.* Initially, each community needs to identify its geographical boundaries and make "alliances with "others," existing in intersecting boundaries. Once people get the hang of this, individual communities enlarge, "wealth," technical expertise, and individual needs will be met more often. Basic survival needs must be provided, to include reliable food and shelter, medical attention, self-worth assurances, companionship, and work paying a living wage.

Individuals within a community take pride in achieving through collective efforts, realizing that achievement through collaboration creates something greater than the "whole." At this stage, the prevailing spirit is one of peace.[52] The spirit of community is not unique to "Christian tenets." For those who have a Christian orientation, community is the beginning of preparing for our Holy ascent: community is the manifestation of the Holy Spirit.[53] For others who are not Christian, the community needs to identify and list the core values of other religions/spiritual beliefs.

At this beginning juncture, we are not trying to allocate goods, services, or "special individual needs." *The goal is to get an accurate understanding of what the core values of the amalgamated collection of individuals contain. Once this list has been approved by all participants—with all the apparent contradictions listed, then it needs to be printed and displayed prominently in print and electronically available to everyone. Yes, here is the first opportunity for individuals to be delegated tasks with authority to accomplish this "mission." At this stage, diabolical contradicting religions have to agree that basic civility is mandatory within the group, or there needs to be another group formed.* A common understanding inclusive of all established core values, establishes what basic civility is with children also being required to follow these standards.

Fine, enough talk. Now do something.

Virtually any group of people can accomplish building community if the members know what they are doing and why. They may even have a review scheduled to see if basic community interactive core values are actually representing all conflicting core values. The vast majority of people are capable of learning and complying with the rules of community.[54] It is not unusual for at least one individual to fold her arms and say, "I ain't playing this mess." Well, usually, she will start joining in little by little because the skeptic in her realizes this "mess" is actually transformational. And for, perhaps for the first time, she wants to be a part of her community and be a part of the friendships and joyfulness. So, do not be surprised when she slowly integrates herself into the community. Do not make a "big deal" over the fact she has joined the spirit within the community. Just welcome her by warmly accepting her presence and learn to enjoy this individual. For some individuals, this may be the first time they have ever been acknowledged by others in a positive way, acknowledging she has value. Forming a community by design entails:

- a lawful process,
- attentiveness to youthful needs within the community,
- awareness of the communities diversities,
- clearly stated principles,
- continuous dialogue amongst members,
- practiced agreed upon core values and laws equally administered.
- purposeful attention to shifting situations, and
- witnessing and being responsive to chaos.

At any age of a community, obstacles threatening the continuation of the commune's mutual harmony can occur. A healthy community typically goes through cycles, all communities do, not just newly formed ones. Psychologist Bruce Tuckman came up with a phrase that contains all the elements in this circular procession of developing communal governance and interaction as: "forming, storming, norming, and performing. For those who are interested in learning more about Tuckman's change plan, go to: Forming, Storming, norming, and performing—From MindTols.com[55].

Leaders who purposefully initiate a change plan (sometimes called an action plan) have a better than average chance of achieving the changes need to meet situations and maintain cohesive, inclusive core values with ethically and inclusively attentive care. As the community matures, it "gains a collective life of its own, the community becomes "greater" than any individual member. Over time it is normal that community members will come and go, some reenter, and sometimes leadership changes. The one thing that will doom a community is if it attempts to remain static.

When the leader and/or the members insist on resisting all changes, the communities' life dies. If this happens, then you have to try again, something different. Sometimes it is an accomplishment just to get more than two or three people to come to the first couple of meetings. Communities at each progressive development need to take the group's pulse to see if restructuring is needed. When needed, acknowledgment of the specific apparent need for changes should be accurately and simply stated. Those communities that have open, authentic, and transparent leadership typically adjust and survive. Over time, each member's unique knowledge, skills, and abilities should have an opportunity to lead some project that should be successful. Encouraging every individual to take some leadership responsibility for supporting some aspect of the communities essential functions is important. Especially if each individual volunteers, what it is, they are going to do to enhance the community. Finally, leaders and members must make allowances for members to witness and contribute to the communities 'stories,"

Realism within the context of community is necessary. The existence of realism supports individuals who think and "buck" the trends.[56] Individuals with distinct personalities and opinions, particularly if presented in a favorable way to support the community, prevent "group think" or "mob psychology." A lot of the time, it may not necessarily be what is being presented, but the manner in which the idea/concern is presented. However, "community" is also a group that is developing a way to work on an issue together until all basic interests are reflected in the discussion(s) outcome. This type of dialogue can be quite time-consuming, but if approached with everyone's intent to actually hear and understand the concerns of all, it can be amazing how a new approach to governance and toleration can be achieved. Each meeting should have at least one topic of discussion that has already assured consensus. Be sure and end on this issue, so people leave with a sense of unity and accomplishment.

To build a community requires time, patience, and commitment. Cliques, factions, and "sides" must be given up replaced with sometimes more than one option of governance. If one is remaking the energy at the particle level, entirely new creations are possible. The members must know how to listen to each other and how to reject each other's proposals "saving face," if at all possible. On the other hand, a "community," within the context of being a group of all leaders, is a group that has achieved decentralized authority, which might work, perhaps a trial run is best to test this new approach.

Applying quantum physics and voice creates
form that builds community.

Sometimes the need for restructuring community is the result of a catastrophe, which typically means death, destruction, and scarcity intensifies the fear and disorganization. Scarcity moves us to explore more diversified ways of interacting so that we can continue to live together. Disasters also imply that outside help (hopefully), will intervene so outside constraints and conditions to receiving aid may lead to a more authoritarian approach which is needed in the physical rebuilding of one's community. This is the process of specialization when professional rescue services and basic survival commodities are disbursed according to "well tested" response protocols. In the past, we have looked at "competition" as an explanation of our behaviors. Wolinsky (1993), on the other hand, presents an entirely different approach to building and maintain community. He contends that the properties of nature at the scale of sub-atomic atoms are all made of the same particles. At this level, nothing exists unless and until someone is aware of a thing's existence (remember Schroeder's cat). *Thus the contention when striving to be inclusive to all community members, it is paramount to remember that Awareness Precedes Appearance and, voice is energy, energy creates form.* God's spoken Word creates form:

> "And the Word was made flesh, and dwelt among us (and we beheld his glory, the glory as of the only begotten of the Father,) full of grace and truth." (John 1:14).

Operationally, quantum consciousness asks each individual to practice the philosophy that "everything is made of emptiness, with form being condensed emptiness."[57] Quantum consciousness is essentially an entirely different way of perceiving "reality." This approach provides a way to recognize that the dialogue within the community is not about removing, diminishing, replacing, or giving up core values and needs. *The discussion is about us having the ability to rebuild anything we can conceive and agree on. So, what does this new construction look like if we combine our wants, needs, and desires so that we all can benefit and develop within our community.* Undoubtedly someone will say, "This is the craziest thing I've ever heard of." The response then is, "Yes, you are absolutely right. We already know what we had, now we are trying something new. You can bet it will look/be strange because we have never built anything together before." Once people get the hang of "thinking without opening the box (Schrodinger's cat)," the community is able to take its first "deep breath" as they start sharing their consciousness and unleash their full individual potentials.

What more does Wolinsky have to offer us with regard to practicably applying quantum consciousness to help us deliberately consider our religious/spiritual tenets and core values when making decisions or starting something completely new? Well, Wolinsky actually has seven different levels of conscious awareness that develop as we and become comfortable with accessing an enlightened awareness of Christ's Consciousness.

Level 1. Survival consciousness.
Level 2. Relationship consciousness.
Level 3. Self-esteem consciousness.
Level 4. Transformation consciousness.
Level 5. Internal cohesion consciousness.
Level 6. Making a different consciousness.
Level 7. Service consciousness.

Earlier, we briefly discussed Schrodinger's cat theory. *The "bottom line" to Schrodinger's experiment is that eventually, somewhere in the midst of all the calculations, one has to admit: "And the miracle occurs;" then energy creates form. (Of course, we know the miracle is God.)* In summation, quantum physicists agree that energy creates form. Their experiments have shown the occurrence, but precisely where in the "wave" and exactly how a form is created has remained elusive. Quantum physicists also concur that the quantum leap from energy to form is the occurrence of the "miracle." Herbert (1985) stated that there is no reality in the absence of observation and that observation creates reality.

Then Werner Heisenberg, a German physicist and philosopher went on to discover (1925) a way to formulate quantum mechanics in terms of matrices, "The Uncertainty Principle." For this discovery, he was awarded the Nobel Prize for Physics in 1932.[58] Basically, Heisenberg's principles state that there is a fuzziness in nature. Thus there is a fundamental limit to what we can know about the behavior of quantum particles. The most we can hope to calculate are "probabilities" for where things are and how they will behave. If you are interested in learning, the following is a great introductory link, found in the Guardian link, for more in debt consideration.[59]

Practically, the importance of this level to leaders, managers, and followers is that they are empowered to take the "quantum leap," take the dare and move beyond being a passive witness: to becoming actively involved in creating something new. Now we can better understand the importance of the self-fulfilling prophecy[60] phenomena. The self-fulfilling prophecies not only reassure or distress our personal conception of reality, one is creating reality differently (Watzlawick, 1984). All boundaries are observer-created rather than inherent. It is the quantum jump that takes consciousness beyond "simply" judgments and evaluations," it introduces us to the experience of underlying unity.

Now we can revisit the statement, "Everything is made of emptiness, and form is condensed emptiness" the statement attributed to Einstein. Everything in the physical universe has form; form creates what Bohm called the explicit order of sizes, shapes, mass, and density. In order for there to be separate forms, there has to be consensual boundaries that create the distinction between you and me. The consensual boundaries constitute how we normally perceive the world. When we comprehend that what we perceive as dense and physical objects are composed of the same particles and waves, then the limited, isolating experience of you-ness and me-ness dissolves.[61] Quantum theory, in a certain sense, regards the world as made out of waves (like waves in one's bathtub) rather than out of things. Quantum entities and their attributes combine according to the rules of wave addition rather than according to the rules of ordinary arithmetic. When waves meet, their amplitudes add, as stated in the rule called the "superposition principal." The superposition principle is as important in the quantum world as arithmetic is for everyday life. Quantum waves are oscillations of possibility; they carry no energy at all; for this reason sometimes they are called "empty waves." A quantum wave's intensity (amplitude squared) is a measure of probability. Because the quantum wave carries no energy, it is not directly detectable—we never see any quantum waves, only quantum particles. Quantum theory predicts the results of measurement with unsurpassed accuracy, so physicists use quantum theory to measure the world itself, because former "particles" now show their wave aspects, and former "waves" behave like particles.

Quantum theory reflects the fundamental unity of being, by describing all "quon's" the same way: Herbert's statement,[62] "One description fits all," is a bit misleading because quantum theory does not "describe" entities at all, it "represents" them. Quantum theory applies to all physical entities without exception. Numerous authors' discussions of leadership and management actually are describing the experience of the "end-point" of quantum consciousness, the "fundamental freedom" At this point the separated, individual self-hood transcends, through conscious awareness and entanglement, comprehends the necessity for community consciousness.[63] This is the true underpinning of "building a community," underscoring the critical, long term affects that purposeful discernment in selecting both leaders and the followers require when building a community. Every single member of the community contributes a direct cause and effect, intended or not, whether they participate or not, in the building of the community.

Consciousness, cohesiveness, "power over," and community.

The "art" of skillfully using power and influence to secure, maintain, and elevate one's social status, while effectively making as many contenders as possible for the same prized social recognition and power in politics. In the building of community, we have already witnessed that the ability to tell and hear stories is multi-purposed. Stories transmit facts, fables, morals, intergenerational kinships, and of course, the camaraderie between the storyteller and the listeners. If non-local real-time "knowing" is the hub, then non-local real-time "behavior manipulation" is the "spoke: connecting individual perceptions of time (linear, sequential, or circular) within community consciousness.

In times of uncertainty, strategic good decision-making is imminently related to survival. Split-second survival decision-making not only determines any specific individual's survival but ultimately culls humanity, determining the fittest and resourceful. With each progressive advancement of civilization (from hunter-gathers to an agrarian society, the industrial society, and now the technology era), humanity's electro-sympathetic consciousness in 2020 is being seriously studied by many aggressive and powerful individuals. Just consider as more of us become aware of God's Consciousness, there are individuals that presume an increased need to shackle our minds, movements, and dreams. For these individuals, there is no recognition that what they are accessing is God's Consciousness, to them, it is an integrated field of consciousness that is being scientifically investigated.

Today there are many countries other than the U.S. whose citizens are also awakening to the presence of a unified and integrated consciousness. Perhaps this is one reason that the New World Order and global domination seem to be ever encroaching on our individual lives. Further consideration of this theory is beyond the scope of this book. Other countries that have been working on non-local forms of information gathering, and manipulating non-locally, include but not necessarily limited to China, Germany, Great Britain, and Russia. An example of the practical application of non-local access would be to consider The World Bank's EDTECH team, based in Washington, D.C. This team used non-local protocols to monitor the effect of school closings due to the COVID-10 pandemic. Their website states that they will not be updating their currently posted web page (dated March 2020 to June 2020). The following information was extracted from The World Bank organization page: How countries are using EDTECH (including online learning, radio, television, texting) to support access to remote learning during the COVID-19 pandemic. For those interested in following up on their research on "managing continuity" and "improving and accelerating," visit their site: Lessons for Education during the COVID-19 crisis. Their web site indicates that they are actively working with ministries of education in dozens of countries, to include but not necessarily limit to the following:

1. Afghanistan
2. Argentina
3. Austria
4. Bangladesh
5. Belize

6. Bermuda
7. Bhutan
8. Bolivia
9. Brazil
10. Bulgaria
11. Cambodia
12. Chile
13. China
14. Columbia
15. Costa Rica
16. Cote D'Ivoire
17. Croatia
18. Czech Republic
19. Dominican Republic
20. Ecuador
21. Egypt
22. El Salvador
23. Ethiopia
24. Fiji
25. Finland
26. France
27. Georgia
28. Guyana
29. India
30. Indonesia
31. Italy
32. Jamaica
33. Japan
34. Jordan
35. Kenya
36. Korea
37. Kuwait
38. Kyrgyz Republic
39. Liberia
40. Libya
41. Madagascar

42. Malaysia
43. Maldives
44. Mauritius
45. Mexico
46. Moldova
47. Mongolia
48. Morocco
49. Nigeria
50. North Macedonia
51. Paraguay
52. Peru
53. Poland
54. Russia
55. Rwanda
56. Saudi Arabia
57. Serbia
58. Sierra Leone
59. Somalia
60. South Africa
61. South Sudan
62. Spain
63. Tanzania
64. Tunisia
65. Turkey
66. Uganda
67. Ukraine
68. United Arab Emirates
69. Uruguay
70. West Bank and Gaza
71. Zimbabwe

For more information, contact their website directly at: https://www.worldbank.org/en/topic/edutech/brief/how-countries-are-using-edtech-to-support-remote-learning-during-the-covid-19-pandemic

Other studies regarding non-local communications are concentrating on electronic emissions of individuals and other life forms. The research seems to show that depending on the strength and focus of electronic emissions, predicting the uniting of previously segregated associations may be possible. These united and/or intermingled links can now be shown to predict the achievement of a critical mass, create form, and influence systems and processes.

Allow yourself to imagine the advantage you would have in all kinds of situations if you knew in real-time, during an interaction with someone, or even before the interaction occurred, everything you needed to know? Reverend Robert H. Sculler's simplistic but profound statement covers this situation, "What would you do if you knew you could not fail?" How solid and secure would your self-esteem be if you knew that your facts about another person, place, or object were accurate before your interaction even started? How would social, work, and international political interactions be different; if every single person knew, that every other person had equal nonlocal real-time "knowing," about you and your intentions toward them? How would interpersonal boundaries change? Would security systems for documents become obsolete? Would business and political negotiations be different when any negotiator could, at will, have non-local access to any information, at any time, and distance regarding your negotiations strategies, financial data, deal-breaker(s), and final and best offer? Of course, negotiations would have an entirely different approach and perhaps even goals: would there be more "win-win" outcomes for both parties?

The importance of retold stories that entrain cellular memories[64] becomes extremely important in retaining and maintaining an individual's mental health and sense of security. Any individual with this reliable ability to gather, analyze and synthesize tangible and intangible information, regardless of constructed security barriers or restrictions on distance or time, would indeed be formidable. The only natural restraint on such an individual would be anyone equally or more adept, with the same or similar abilities. Talk about transparency! So, in such a world, how do you navigate social interactions, raise children, exist in a work environment, negotiate business deals, lead people? What would leadership look like when followers have the ability to know what the leader knows as soon as, if not before, the leader comes to her conclusions or decisions? How is any individual's social "game-playing," business relationship with employees and customers, nation's political propaganda needs to be altered? Does the engagement of war fundamentally change when "knowledge is no longer power," but "knowing" is power. (Yes, but there will always be "power," the source and the use of it may change, but there will always be "power." The only variable is whether or not an individual's "knowing" is always 100 percent correct 100 percent of the time. Then of course, reliance on Jesus, if directed, the answer us always 100 percent depending on what you ask. *One must ask God, first of all, the right question(s), then test to make sure God provided the answer (by testing). If these stipulations have been met, then you know you can rely on God because His truth and guidance are 100 percent correct, 100 percent of the time.*

CHAPTER 5

. . . .

What Normalized Occult Practices?

> The God of Abraham, and of Isaac, and of Jacob, the God of our fathers, hath glorified his Son Jesus: whom ye delivered up and denied him in the presence of Pilate, when he was determined to let hm go. But you denied the Holy One and the Just, and desired a murderer to be granted unto you; And killed the Prince of life, whom God hath raised from the dead; whereof we are witnesses.
>
> Acts: 3:13–15

> And there shall in no wise enter into it anything that defileth, neither whatsoever worketh abomination, or maketh a lie; but they which are written the Lamb's book of life.
>
> Revelation 21:27

There are many reasons that change happens, anticipated or not. When change is happening or suddenly "just shows up," we internalized "the change" personally. Typically our first assessment deals with the nuisance factor and the overall disruption to our life? How a person reacts or fails to react, is a result of the individual's mental maturity, problem-solving skills, adaptability to continuous learning, and finally: does the person have the will to take definite action. These concerns are particularly essential if the change is something you must comply with or suffer severe negative repercussions. The less control you have regarding the change's mandated behavior or project completion, the greater your agitation and desire to sabotage the change outcome. The greater choices you have in implementing the change, the more you become vested in the change outcome and success. If you perceive that you have a reasonable time to comply with completing the change plan and have some built-in "dry runs," the change process helps you get used to the change and realize that you have transferrable skills that give you some mastery in this new change.

The change we will consider here is when, what, why, and how did the U.S. culture make the drastic switch from having our national norm be Christian based? An overview of the exponential escalation of a wide variety of occult practices will be considered. The acceptance and normalization of the occult community within the U.S. are still spreading. We will take a look at many components that have simultaneously occurred and intertwined, resulting in the changes of our laws, growing social intolerance of traditional Christian values and morals, and the fractured cohesiveness of the family unit's interactions and guidance of their youth. We will consider a limited range of religious/spiritual norms that may exist within our average American communities. God's Word and Jesus Christ warned people that there are many thoughts, actions, and inactions that are categorized as an abomination.

By the late 1950s and into the 1960s and beyond, we have seen what in the past has been the unprecedented acceptance of "opening all the closets" and making public one's personal business, especially on social media. Of course, fashion follows freedom, so social influencers establish attitudes, clothing attire, and personalized looks. Social status, real or constructed, especially on social media, maintain: consistent behaviors and attitudes, always presenting tangible trinkets, the latest technology, travel, and consumption of excellent food cuisine. Additionally, networking and affiliating with appropriate politically correct causes and politicians "see and be seen" at "in vogue religious/spiritual meetings" and fund-raising functions that incorporate in some way occult rituals and practices. These are just a few examples that, knowingly or not, were lured by anti-Christ believers into severing a Christian's loyalty and connection with God. Any participation, by a Christian, with the occult in the past would have been scandalous: the individual would have been said to have "fallen away" from the church. What used to be a counterculture's predominant rite of passage for young adults is now the entrenched behavior of flaunting Jezebel's defiant spirit. There is a prevailing attitude in a huge segment of our nation of individual presumption of priority, an aggressive lust for notoriety, power, and immunity from accountability. Oddly enough, today's predominant Jezebel spirit permeates all social classes, every gender identification, economic status, and religious and spiritual affiliation. This laissez-faire attitude syndrome is not as tolerant as proclaimed. The pervasive, glaringly obvious lack of civility is either painstakingly denied because of naivety, stupidity or defiance among and between all age groups; is staggering. *People are seemingly turning a blind eye to the fact that personal core values determine one's behaviors and expectations.* One's behaviors may be suppressed and changed for a brief time, but one always returns to her authentic belief and core values. Following are some of the increasing acting out behaviors occurring in our nation, which has publicly increased over the last sixty years:

- Intolerance, traditional religions are demeaned, sometimes persecuted.
- An increasing number of traditional Christian and Non-denominational services are now motivational pep rallies and actually preaching spiritualism.[65]
- Witchcraft and magic, as well as other various occult activities, may commonly be witnessed in commercials, movie and TV programs, half-time entertainments, and a host of other general public venues.
- Historical pagan idols are displayed, making worldwide appearances in major cities.

- Self-centeredness, most occult practices reject/ignore rules and laws, indifferent to other's emotional or religious sensitivities.
- Alister Crowley's[66] quote: "Do what thou wilt shall be the whole of the law," succinctly: is the mantra of this age and solidifies the normalization of today's occult practices here in the USA.

WHY OCCULT BELIEFS AND PRACTICES HAVE PROLIFERATED AMERICA?

Today, there are numerous ways various individuals and/or groups develop their core values regarding religious/spiritual: work ethics, interpersonal relationships, and civic sense of community. Over time Americans have become aware that our collective culture has dramatically and fundamentally rewired our concept of interpersonal connections. We expect the ability to connect with each other 24/7 through an array of electronic communication tools. COVID-19 has trained employers, employees, customers, and constituents that it is normal to go through a maze of electronic filters (either by phone or online) to get an electronic pre-coded response. Talking to a "real person" is now an exception for most business transactions and often personal correspondence.

The 1960s was a decade that held many significant emotional events that collectively propelled our populace into futuristic frenzies grounded in structured history. The 1960's decade hosted the following "game-changing" social realignments, ignited primarily based on (real-time) technology (TV) and the Baby Boomer generation activism. These two factors witnessed in particular by Baby Boomers (in the 60s), the following selected significant decade events:

- Age of Aquarius/Psychedelic Sixties,
- Apollo 11 Moon landing, first steps.
- Assassination of Martin Luther King,
- Assassination of President Kennedy,

- Civil Rights Movement (Dr. King, Malcolm X, Little Rock Nine),
- Cuban Missile Crisis,
- Timothy Leary: psychedelic LSD, Moto "Turn on, tune in, drop out."
- Vietnam War,
- Women's equal rights movement also called Woman's Liberation. States pass laws against spousal abuse.
- Woodstock Festival, 400,00 in attendance

American core traditional values took pride that immigrants blended seamlessly into the "melting pot," with Christian values the primary "ingredient" in the pot. The problem with this opinion is that it was not held by all minorities, immigrants, and a substantial number of U.S. citizens that did not follow the Christian faith. Along with other changes occurring within the U.S., non-Christians started to "push back" against the "Founding Fathers" of the U.S., who based our laws, morals, and civic models on Christian tenets and core values. These often-antagonistic core values include but are not necessarily limited to the following:

- age cohorts,
- conscious awareness,
- education: accredited or not.
- entanglement theories,
- love/belonging dependencies.
- nationality/race,
- one-world government,
- power/abilities to influence others,
- psychological balance,
- religious/spiritual practices,
- respect from others,
- safety fears,
- self-actualization achievements, and
- social/economic status.

Admittedly each of the above categories had more or less prominence in certain states within the U.S. However, collectively each of the above elements morphed into accelerants, which facilitated and sustained the expansion of occult practices. There is still no single conclusive factor propelling occult, metaphysical saturation because the inundation is still occurring.

This book is not intended to rehash all the previous discussions regarding "what is happening to the U.S. morality and civility. *In this book, we are taking a different approach by looking at the array of predominant occult practices available to suit any desire. Additionally, we will be looking at the simultaneous support from the judicial and "traditional Christian" sectors that have supported the spread and normalization of occult practices.* Yes, there has an upswelling acceptance of assorted occult practices. However, without the support of our nation, collectively changing and/or adding laws to facilitate the protection of behaviors that previously were either illegal or socially ostracized practitioners.

Simultaneously, the various Christian denominations increasingly accepted many "good works and affirmation" as equal justification showing "love thy neighbor" and "thou shall not judge" mentality. With these twin changes over time of both moral and acceptable behavior, psychological imprinting of "strange flesh;" enabled dynamic support from:

1) U.S. courts,
2) Christian Churches toleration, and the
3) economic clout from anti-Christian reformists.

How have these three primary catalysts transformed the core values of the U.S.? How has the skewed acceptance of other gods provided a "helping hand" to today's power-driven, narcissistic, self-gratifying social dynamics? *Perhaps the biggest question for Christians should be, when did so many of us have such dark, unfulfilled holes in our souls that occult practices seem to satisfy us; and Christian tenets do not?*

Americans, at least in the past, most desired and fought for the freedom of choice and the right to free speech. So, how did so many misinterpret the concept of a "one world overseer" get mistaken for a laissez-faire government (one that does not interfere in the marketplace or basically anywhere else? A laissez-faire attitude is "cool, man, it's okay," one does not get involved in anyone else's behaviors or activities. *Unfortunately, history has shown when a populace finally revolts against a laissez-faire leader, typically, the new leader tends to be either autocratic or totalitarian (both are despotic, just different flavors).* What is the difference? Typically heading an Autocratic "government" is one individual having unlimited power. In a Totalitarianism government, the "government's control and regulation extends to every aspect of public and private life. So now, the question is: why would anyone think either of these two choices is appealing? Why is it that so many individuals strive for a One World Government?

Do people not understand that a philosophy that assumes the right to (total) self-gratification also shoulders the responsibility of total self-reliance to take care of one's self? For an individual to live totally self-reliant, the individual either has a short life, or at some time must get assistance from others. Additionally, a philosophy of self-reliance presents an unsurmountable fractured family interdependency, mentoring, and relations. The deal-breaker, insubordination, being displayed within family generations, employers, friendships, and business ethics internalizes (sometimes displayed) acrimony, distrust, isolation, and violence. The following Table 2 presents a selected (but not necessarily limited to) overall representative range of occult practices available within the US.

Table 3. The selected array of occult practices which have been normalized in the U.S.

Birth Date	Deceased	Generation	Name	Spiritual Tenet Significant Contributions
1503	1566	Transition from the Julian Calendar to the Gregorian calendar.	Nostradamus	French astrologer, physician, seer, and author.

1831	1891	Age of Enlightenment. Also, American, French, and Haitian revolutions.	Helena Petrovna Blavatsky	Russian occultist, philosopher, and Co-founded the Theosophical Society in 1875.
1869	1916	USA, Populist Movement: oriented coalition of agrarian reformers. Internationally beginning of globalism.	Grigori Yefimovich Rasputin	Russian mystic and self-proclaimed holy man to Tsar Nicholas Alexander II
1875	1947	USA, Populist Movement: oriented coalition of agrarian reformers. Internationally beginning of globalism	Alister Crowley	English occultist, ceremonial magician, poet painter, and novelist. Founded the religion of Thelema was their prophet. Called himself the Beast. Favorite quoted statement: "Do what thou wilt shall be the whole of the law."
1877	1945	USA, Populist Movement: oriented coalition of agrarian reformers. Internationally beginning of globalism	Edward Casey	Clairvoyant, and consultant
1880	1949	USA, Populist Movement: oriented coalition of agrarian reformers. Internationally beginning of globalism	Alice Bailey	Prolific writer of theosophical subjects. First writer to use the term New Age.
1904	1997	Interbellum Generation	Jean Dickson	White house psychic and astrologer. President Nixon's administration

1920	1996	Greatest Generation	Timothy Francis Leary	Psychologist advocated psychedelic drugs.
1921	1999	Greatest Generation	Malachi Martin	A Roman Catholic Jesuit priest. Popular author and speaker on various topics to include exorcisms, Satanism, Liberation Theology
1930	1997	Silent Generation	Anton LaVey	Founder of Church of Satan and the religion of LaVeyan Satanism. Author, musician, priest.
1933	2013	Silent Generation	Ingo Swann	A self-proclaimed psychic who focused on "consciousness research." Experienced altered states of Consciousness.
1933	1999	Silent Generation	Ron Wyatt	Discovered Noah's Ark in Turkey, the Arch of the Covenant and other sacred relics.
1936	1973	Silent Generation	Sylvia Brown	TV Psychic and profit, personal readings.
1945	NA	Silent Generation	Whitley Strieber	Author of horror novels and his alleged experiences with nonhuman entities. Affiliated with The Day After Tomorrow blockbuster.
1945	2018	Silent Generation	Art Bell	Original Coast to Coast AM broadcaster, internationally syndicated paranormal radio show. Also an author.
1949	2012	Baby Boomers	Tom Horn	Was Executive Officer of Sky watch TV and ancient mythology and paranormal Christian phenomena. Author and one of first to launch new internet coverage of the supernatural.

1950	NA	Baby Boomers	George Noory	Host on Coast to Coast talk paranormal radio show. Personal interest in paranormal and ufology. Original member of Pentagon's Stargate program (a code name for psychic investigation of military and domestic intelligence
1950	NA	Baby Boomers	L. A. Marzulli	Author, lecturer, filmmaker, and supernatural researcher (for example, Nephilim, created The Watcher series and UFO Physical Evidence film. Legally extracted material for DNA testing from the enigmatic elongated skulls found in Peru.
1950	NA	Baby Boomer	Retired Major Edward Dames	Remote Viewer is a consultant to managers so they can "access all their energy. One of the original teams Pentagon used ESP called "R.V." for more than two decades.
1962	2016	Baby Boomers	Ms. Cleo	TV Hotline, Tarot Card readings
1969	NA	Generation X	John Edwards	Psychic, medium, TV Series Crossing Over, and author.

The one observation that appears to be clear, without a more detailed analysis, is that starting with the year 1960, there seemed to be an increased interest in a wide range of occult practices and philosophies. As the US made technical communication advances, the demand by the population at large wanted psychic guidance, support, and advice. *Individuals apparently wanted to have the "edge;" on life, and unanticipated occurrences at work and home. People wanted power "over" something. They wanted to be able to snoop into the business of others surreptitiously and win: win at something.* There was also an increased interest in speaking with the dead: seances, channeling,

R.V., and of course out-of-body experiences. Some people want to be both unique and powerful, so they went for the "real magic." Today more than ever, we can clearly witness some "magicians" who are actually using paranormal assistance to perform some of their "acts."

Some individuals are mesmerized by old idols, spells, and charms. Last but not least, many are performing rituals to ancient gods with all the idols and accessories necessary to perform their rituals. On August 17, 2019, the satanic idol Baphomet[67] arrived in Arkansas and was displayed on the Capitol grounds. This exhibit is a winged goat creature with some human features and was displayed at a rally for the First Amendment. The First Constitutional Amendment prohibits the government from making laws that regulate an establishment of religion or that would prohibit the free exercise of religion or stifle freedom of speech. From Arkansas, it went to New York and serval other major cities in the U.S. In New York City, the exhibit was to be displayed near the destroyed trade centers. Because the public at large was outraged, the idol went elsewhere but returned after a couple of months. This time the Baphomet idol was placed in a less conspicuous and sensitive spot in the financial district.

What is acutely displayed in this particular story is the intolerance of individuals who wanted to exercise their rights to Baphomet being displayed: and the complete intolerance, for say, Christmas tree decorations to be displayed. Intolerance is being more and more confused with a right: to bully, persecute, file legal suites, demand interlopers be fired, and anyone else who is not in your peer group. The U.S. is systematically being fractured and restructured to something that stands a good chance that the change in the U.S. will resemble an autocratic, oppressive society similar to Stanley Milgram's study of obedience to authority way of life. What we are currently experiencing is not an experiment, it is life trying to recreate Milgram's study. (See Endnote Sixteen for expanded discussion of Milgram's breakthrough study.) Now here is the "thing": most occultists as well as defiant citizens "want to do their own thing." Yet, they increasingly support the "new norm" of the One World Government, which is 100 percent oppressive. So, how is this supposed to work for "them?" Interesting.

BASIC SOCIAL NORMS AND THE RETURN TO "NORMAL."

Some sociologists contend that every eighty to ninety years, there is a crucial event, a crisis that has destroyed the social order and creates a "new one." The new social order may redistribute the preference(s) of race, socio-economic class, the value of education, or other markers. Increasingly, technology and social networking, educational institutions, and businesses reward certain behaviors, alliances, and political affiliations: all of which may be diametrically opposite to the "way things were." These shifts tended to encompass a broad scope of behaviors, attitudes, social interactions, and ethics of work.

In today's job market, we see multi-generational, international, and local job applicants all competing for the same position. The obvious possibility for employment bias occurs when the job applicant and the employer come from significantly different age groups backgrounds, have language difficulties, and different employer/ employee relations expectations. All of these changes have occurred in the midst of the mechanization of jobs increase, internet business transactions for all kinds of goods and services are available 24/7. COVID-19 is still a source of sustained depression within our nation. For the first time since our Declaration of Independence, we, as a nation, are divided over whether or not the U.S. republic has been overthrown for socialistic governance. Especially if any one or more of these assertions are true, how could we (the U.S.) ever go "back to normal?" What the heck was "normal?" Obviously, it was not an acceptable norm for all of us, or we would not be in this house divided. Did we just witness a coup in our last presidential election? *So, the new situation is not "a new norm" because we have not fully constructed it yet. And, the "Old Normal" was never sufficient for all of our citizens, and we sure as heck do not want to go back to that.* **This is the definition, in action, of chaos.**

As decades pass, the U.S., as well as other parts of our world, over time, have all experienced all types of natural and human-caused catastrophes (examples: economy, famine, plagues, wars, and weather). These significant emotional distress situations seemed to occur more frequently now, have a greater strident impact, and are ostensibly emotionally and economically harder to recover one's equilibrium. It seemed as if people were either in a drug-induced "time out," too narcissistic to notice, or just simply living in a fantasy world to not know these events happen all the time, somewhere on earth. Only now, with better technology, we get to hear and see these events, often in real-time, where before it may have taken months if we heard about the event at all. The term "normalcy" was first used by Republican candidate Warren G Harding (1865–1920) during the presidential campaign to describe the condition of the U.S. prior to its entry into World War I (1914–1918). It was also the condition to which the nation would supposedly return, according to Harding's promise, if elected President. Voters liked the idea of returning to normalcy. Harding the biggest plurality victory ever. After Harding's election, his primary problem, of course, was to implement his promise to return to "normalization." The problem of accurately defining "normalcy,' is still problematic. To Harding, his definition was a foreign policy of isolationism and a domestic policy of increased economic freedom. Since then, the term "normalcy" became an American lexicon during 1857, as a slang word for "normality."

Recently the following statement was found during an internet search regarding the normalcy bias. However, there has been no definite proof so far regarding who stated the following quotation. This quote can be found many times without verifiable citation to the author of this statement. I am presenting it because it is a good summation, in my opinion, of the theory of normalcy.

> "The normalcy bias" refers to a mental state people enter when facing a disaster. It causes people to underestimate both the possibility of a disaster occurring and its possible effects. This often results in situations where people fail to adequately prepare for a disaster, and on a larger scale, the failure of the government to include the populace in its disaster preparations. The assumption that is made in the case of the

normalcy bias is that since a disaster never has occurred that it never will occur. It also results in the inability of people to cope with a disaster once it occurs. People with a normalcy bias have difficulties reacting to something they have not experienced before. People also tend to interpret warnings in the most optimistic way possible, seizing on any ambiguities to infer a less serious situation."

(Author unknown)

While anecdotal, it is worth considering that just perhaps, this might be one reason some Christians, and many people in general, display rebellious disbelief and behaviors regarding God's steadfast Word.

HOW DID WE BECOME ENTHRALLED IN OCCULT PRACTICES?

A large majority of the U.S. population, at some time, has dabbled in one or more of the various types of occult practices. Growing up, I used to watch the women at baby showers "play this game." The "mother" would use a pendulum to determine the baby's gender. Now we have ultrasound, so mostly the pendulum swings to see if "so-and-so loves me"? Perhaps a loved one has died, and a dear friend or friendly acquaintance asks if you would like to go to a seance or attend a presentation where a medium will connect you with your dearly departed. Or perhaps there is a local psychic fair, and we all decide to go together because it sounds like fun. "We might even have a Tarot card reading. I do not believe in it any more than I did my Magic 8 Ball, but sometimes the results are more personal than I thought…unnerving."

Or, perhaps a nationally known magician is in town performing his magic/illusionist show for a night. As you can see, a large number of us are introduced or nudged by family or friends to attend one of these (or an assortment of other practices) as entertainment. Once exposed, the curious among us want to see how "it" works. And the more that is learned the more the fascination. So, many feel driven to know more. The "need to know" can turn into a compulsion, especially if you have "proof" of whatever you choose to do, is accurate or mostly accurate. Over time, you and thousands of others have dabbled in the occult "harmlessly," so within a short time, occult practices have become mainstream.[68] The internet has made "visiting" a psychic so much easier, and by connecting by internet, email, or video conferencing, the client can remain anonymous if so desired. (But, if one is going to a psychic, and they can "expose the unknown," why doesn't the client realize if the reader is really a "psychic," then he knows all about you. The clients never seem to think about that.)

Most probably, only if you have had an unbelievably bad experience at one of these entertainment events, you will never go back. Otherwise, you enjoy the experience and are fascinated about how this stranger knew so much about you and your desires, family, and other personal information. The more you visit one or more psychics, the more curious you become. If so-and-so can access this information, why not me? Surely this cannot be what God is calling an abomination. Yes, this is exactly what God is calling an abomination: this and any other occult practices.

You pick your rationale, to continue to seek "forbidden knowledge," start enjoying status points as you show your newly learned skills to friends, families, and participate as one of the "readers" in your first psychic fair. You might even begin rationalizing that, "I am not doing anything wrong. "I am just listening, reading, learning, trying it out to see if it works. It is the professional psychic/magician/ illusionist that is the spirit practicing individual and the one who is defined as an abomination." Just because you have convinced yourself that you are a neutral spectator, God's view is different. Yes, in God's opinion, you are an abomination too. "Regard not them that have familiar spirits, neither seek after wizards, to be defiled by them. I [am] the LORD your God" (Leviticus 19:31).

New Age practices intrigue and captivate a phenomenal number of individuals to take lessons to learn: non-local viewing (Remote viewing, R.V.). The mesmerizing power to the unlimited access to information regardless of distance, time, living or inert targets, on-demand, is and seduction on steroids. This is especially alluring because all RV practitioners will vehemently contend that RV is not a psychic practice of any kind. This is a skill that, with proper training, anyone can achieve when specific protocols are used. The allure of such power to intrude on whoever, whenever, for whatever reason is irresistible to most. Especially individuals driven by greed, need, "power over, blackmail; and/or searching for secret religious/spiritual knowledge. Non-local viewing lessons or viewers who gather information for you about someone or something are abominations.

- A man also or woman that hath a familiar spirit, or that is a wizard, shall surely be put to death: they shall stone them with stones: their blood shall be upon them.

  Leviticus 20:27

- The graven images of their gods shall ye burn with fire: thou shalt not desire the silver or gold that is on them, nor take it unto thee, *lest thou be snared therein: for it is an abomination to the LORD thy God. Neither shalt thou bring an abomination into thine house,* lest thou be a cursed thing like it: but thou shalt utterly detest it, and thou shalt utterly abhor it; for it is a cursed thing.

  Deuteronomy 7:25–26

- To keep the commandments of the LORD, and his statutes, which I command thee this day for thy good? *Behold, the heaven and the heaven of heavens is the LORD'S thy God,* the earth also, with all that therein is.

  Deuteronomy 10: 13–14

- For *rebellion is as the sin of witchcraft, and stubbornness is as iniquity and idolatry.* Because thou hast rejected the word of the LORD, he hath also rejected thee from being king.

  1 Samuel 15:23

Dr. Wayne Grudem and Dr. John MacArthur[69] are this Chapter's primary scriptural authorities used as a teaching reference for us. First, an introduction to Dr. Grudem, and his source of scholastic expertise in Christian Doctrine, relied upon in this section. Dr. Grudem is our esteemed theologian, seminary Professor of Theology and Biblical Studies, an author who has published twenty-two books. His book used as our reference is "Systematic Theology."[70] His theological view is that Christianity, Judaism, and Islam have different but complementary roles and responsibilities in marriage, family life, and religious leadership. Hopefully, this disclosure regarding his Religious tenets and core values will assist you, as it has me, in coming to my own conclusions while reviewing his statements regarding; First, What is the Christian's (doctrinal) significance ascribed to the Beatitudes with regard to our daily interaction with God and our actual behaviors? And second, what is the meaning of "The Church in 2021?" Is it a "person, place, or spiritual meeting place of like souls? Grudem's discussions are fascinating, considering all the various Christian denominations apparently have been considered in his discussions. One thing that is beginning to be glaringly apparent is that some who proclaim to be Christians are shopping for "self-improvement and empowerment. These "Christians," seek to obtain prestige, superhuman powers and abilities while being rewarded with tangible economic gratification and god like status. The fact that individuals with this intent may not have obtained these desires may leave them feeling:

- confused with an invisible deity, therefore, God is alien,
- deprived—others have powers/spells,
- dissatisfaction no carnal enjoyments,
- feeling set-up persecution is allowed,
- God is prejudice,
- God is punitive,
- justice dispensed haphazardly,
- no free will,
- performing wonders but not smarter,
- shafted faith, not work is rewarded,

- some prayers denied, not fulfilled.

In general, Christianity appears to many to be a drag because "our rewards" only come after death, and supposedly, nothing earthly is enticing. Let us face facts, the bright lights, glitz, fortune, fame, with all the creature comforts one wants is most often obtainable through one or more occult practices. Most if not all occult practices promise to give the participants;

- ability to have own spirit guide,
- ability to communicate with spirits, therefore, becoming essentially "all-knowing."
- command of the natural elements, time, and effectiveness of spells cast,
- earthly rewards not necessary to die to achieve,
- keys to long a life (sometimes promising immortality),
- mastery of physics (matter and energy),
- respect and recognition with requisite economic gains,
- worship Aleister Crowley's infamous precept, "Do what thou wilt shall be the whole of the law."

Finally, the recruitment of individuals into various occult practices is typically friendly, caring, fun, compelling; and you are indoctrinated that you are extraordinary. In some instances, you are told you can achieve god status. In addition to the prevalence of "occult recruiters," laws within the U.S. at every level have significantly relaxed regarding morality, family values, civil disobedience, civility, civic pride, and personal accountability. Christian metamorphosis, since the late 1950s has supported the variety of "bibles" now marketed. Americans have become lazy, stating that the standard King James Version is too hard to understand. Therefore numerous various versions of the "Bible" have been "dumbed down," some of which have completely omitted some scriptures and/or changed the meaning of some scriptures. Some churches will use a "Bible" but then say the scriptures must be considered allegorical, often suggesting something opposite of the scriptures. Church services range all the way from "traditional sermons" with scriptures presented as the spine of the minister's message. Music during services, or sometimes the service is the ministry of music, with the music ranging but not necessarily limited to:

- "updated traditional hymns"
- alternative
- avant-garde,
- bluegrass,
- electro,
- electronic,
- folk,
- hip hop,
- hip hop,
- Laughter—discordant
- new age,
- rap,
- Simultaneous individual utterances, and
- tribal (from any nation).

If these forms of music have gospel lyrics that praise God, in many instances, the lyrics are indistinguishable, and even if the lyrics are coherent, God being praised is rarely, if ever, specified. Often strobe lights or other visual distractions accompany some of the performances; thus, sober contemplation during a "musical ministry" may put one in a trance or epileptic fit, but a praise of God is unlikely.

In conclusion, the short answer to how we, as a nation, became so mesmerized and enthralled in the occult is the following:

1. A degrading and/or omission of the Bible, God's inspired Word.
2. Family values changed, reflecting narcissistic gratifications coupled with pervasively liberal abortion laws, gender transitioning at will, and religious laws designed to "attempt"

to make God and His church into an organization for eunuchs.

3. The popularization of assorted occult practices is so common they are not now even seen as occultic but as one's spiritual path.

4. The rise in the pursuit of the perceived benefits, status, power, and prosperity: arrogantly displayed by psychopaths, narcissists, and other "negatively indwelled individuals, has set a new standard of success and achievements.

"WHAT IS THE CHURCH"?

The "Church" today, almost universally, is a generic noun, suggesting a morphing collection of individuals that form congregations (with or without a designated building for worship). Originally, "The Church" clearly denoted Christians were followers of Jesus Christ, the Son of God. "The Church" typically elicited some type of emotional reaction and clearly set apart believers in the God of Abraham, Isaac, and Jacob from all others. Here, our definition and purpose of "The Church," is explained by Dr. Grudem based on his extensive study and analysis, provides his thoughts regarding what the Church is.[71] There tends to be two prevailing thoughts, different but not necessarily contradictory. The New Testament authors see Jewish and gentile believers alike, are now united in the Church. Together they have been made:

- For he is our peace, *who hath made both one*, and hath broken down the middle wall of partition between us; Having abolished in his flesh the enmity, even the law of commandments contained in ordinances; for *to make in himself of twain one new man*, so making peace;

    Ephesians 2:14–15

- "Now therefore ye are no more strangers and foreigners, but *fellow citizens with the saints, and of the household of God* (Ephesians 2:19).

On the other hand, there are strong arguments that view the church as not beginning until Pentecost. This argument maintains that beginning with Matthew 16:18 and 18:17and then continuing in Acts, and the Epistles[72] people did not have to be assembled in public worship, any place is acceptable. Paul calls Christ the "cornerstone" of the Church (Ephesians 2:29) and suggests the Church did not begin until Christ Himself laid the foundations of life, death, and resurrection.[73]

- Luther and Calvin's view on the marks of a true church are still held true today. The Word of God is too often not being preached. Increasingly false doctrines or doctrines of men have been substituted for scriptures.
- The results produce anything but a true church.
- A true church will hold to:
  - Christian doctrines concerning salvation,
  - the person of God,
  - the person or work of Jesus Christ.
  - Salvation is by faith, not works,
  - The correct administration of the sacraments (example: baptism and the Lord's Supper),
  - There must be a personal relationship with Christ in prayer and Bible study.
- The three purposes of the Church's ministry to God, ministry to believers, and ministry to the world: and keeping these purposes in balance.
  - Ministry to God: Worship. The Church's purpose is to worship God, not just preparation for something else. This is a self-fulfilling major purpose of the church. *The church is to be filled with the Spirit* and then to be "singing and making melody to the Lord with your heart. (Ephesians 5:16–19)

○ Ministry to Believers: Nurture. *The church has an obligation to nurture those who are already believers and build them up to maturity in the faith—which is to mature in Christ.* (Colossians 1:28). Until we all attain the unity of faith and the knowledge of the Son of God to mature manhood, to the measure and stature of Christ (Ephesians 4:12–13).

○ Ministry to the World: Evangelism and Mercy. Jesus told his disciples to make "disciples of all nations." (Matthew 28:19). Evangelism and Mercy are the prime goals of ministry to the world. It is noted the New Testament's focus is on giving material help to those who are part of the church (Acts 11:29; Cor. 8:41; 1 John 3:17).

We entered into this discussion because we wanted to know, precisely if possible, what theologically speaking, is meant when one uses the phrase "The Church." With Grudem's extensive knowledge of God's Word, competencies in Biblical and theological research, and finally his ability to teach us in terms we can understand pointed out that:

1) The church is now a blinded fellowship of Old Testament, Jewish believers, and Gentile believers.

2) There are those who have an equally persuasive contention that The Church did not exist until after Pentecost.

3) There is significant concern that the Word of God is not being preached, instead, there are false doctrines (deliberately preached or by ineptitude). Some doctrines devised by dubious, purposefully rebellious, and driven money and power have preached as if recounting God's Word, while they have personally inserted enhancements to God's Word. Finally, *Grudem emphasizes that there are three purposes of the church's ministry (1) worship, (2) nurture, and (3) evangelism and mercy.* Having said this, Grudem strongly contends that it is imperative that The Church diligently

strive to keep a balance of The Churches, "feeding" both new and seasoned Christians to mature into God: and support all three ministry purposes of the church equally.

THE BEATITUDES.

Many of us have either heard of or read from Matthew 5: 3–12, Matthew's account of Jesus' Sermon on the Mount, what has become known as "The Beatitudes, provided below:

> And seeing the multitudes, he went up into a mountain: and when he was set, his disciples came unto him: And he opened his mouth, and taught them, saying, Blessed are the poor in spirit: for theirs is the kingdom of heaven. Blessed are they that mourn: for they shall be comforted. Blessed are the meek: for they shall inherit the earth. Blessed are they which do hunger and thirst after righteousness: for they shall be filled. Blessed are the merciful: for they shall obtain mercy. Blessed are the pure in heart: for they shall see God. Blessed are the peacemakers: for they shall be called the children of God. Blessed are they which are persecuted for righteousness' sake: for theirs is the kingdom of heaven. Blessed are ye, when men shall revile you, and persecute you, and shall say all manner of evil against you falsely, for my sake. Rejoice, and be exceeding glad: for great is your reward in heaven: for so persecuted they the prophets which were before you.
> Matthew 5: 1–12

A personal disclosure.

Have you ever wondered why this particular sermon, The Sermon on the Mount, is held in such high esteem, I sure have. I am concerned because after hearing and reading the Beatitudes many times, I cannot explain the foreshadowing groundbreaking importance of Jesus' prophetic sermon? I know I should be able to, but for some reason, I cannot, or my attempts always seem "off." Therefore, I am turning to two long-standing, respected, and academically esteemed Christian religious scholars to help me understand the Beatitudes.

Prevailing on both Dr. Wayne Grudem[74] and Dr. John MacArthur to guide us through the following discussion regarding the Beatitudes. In my opinion, Dr. Grudem's analysis differs from Dr. MacArthur in that Dr. Grudem answered more contractual and other legal relationships between us (myself and you); Jesus Christ, God, and the Holy Spirit. On the other hand, for me, Dr. MacArthur specifically explained each individual scripture within the Beatitudes. Together, their analysis is profoundly helpful, enlightening, and amazing. Wow, no wonder this particular sermon is held in such high spiritual esteem.

I have selected several scriptures from the Beatitudes that either resonated with me or had completely confounded me. I did not have a clue, and, fortunately, I have always searched for a better, deeper understanding. I understand that I may not have picked the scripture(s) you might. I therefore strongly encourage you to read for yourself all twelve of the Beatitudes, with a comprehensive explanation provided by Dr. MacArthur for each of the twelve pronouncements by Jesus.[75]

These two superb theologians supported each other's presentations and, for me, gave a full, rich, and new appreciation of the scriptures. I hope the following presentations provide the same or similar enlightenment, appreciation for the fullness of Jesus' words in this particular sermon. *The Mercy of God, Jesus Christ, and the Holy Spirit and my/our relationship to the Holy Trinity are unique, protective, loving, merciful, and everlasting.* I hope you have had a similar experience to mine, learning something new and absorbing how inextricably those of us who are the "children of God" are everlastingly bound to him, awaiting our eternal reunion.

Dr. Wayne Grudem's analysis regarding the Beatitudes.

The Beatitudes are a covenant, a contract, regarding man." A covenant is an unchangeable, divinely imposed legal agreement between God and man that stipulates the conditions of their relationship."[76] While a covenant is unchangeable, it may be superseded or replaced. *When man enters into an agreement with God, the provisions of the relationship are "divinely imposed," man can never negotiate with God or change the terms of the covenant*[77]. At the heart of God's contracts with man is that God will be man's God, and those accepting the contract shall be his people (Jeremiah 31:33; 2 Corinthians 6:16 et al.).

What is unique in this particular contract is it is first made between God, and Jesus, while other covenants are between God and man. The second significant difference is that *when a contract occurred between God and man, God's contract was dictated by him, man had no input into the contract: man's only option was to accept the contract (on an individual basis) or not.* The articles of the Beatitudes *covenant between God and Jesus is that Jesus had equal standing, and the negotiation was mutual.* This justifies one of many reasons we consider Jesus to (rightfully) be our intercessor. Contractually, Jesus had the right to die in atonement for man's sins, so that man could, through Jesus, achieve salvation. This new covenant, between God and Jesus, made the old covenant, between God and man obsolete. The new covenant superseded the old one. "This new covenant is the "eternal covenant" (Hebrews 13:20) in Christ, through which we shall forever have fellowship with God, and he shall be our God, and we shall be his people."[78] Dr. Grudem goes on to say that this contract is representative of covenant theology, which emphasizes the continuity between the Old Testament and the New Testament.

Dr. Grudem goes further, saying: "…the condition of continuing in the covenant is said to be obedience to God's commands."[79] In both the Old or New Testaments, obedience alone is insufficient and does not "earn" any additional merit. *However, obedience to Christ in the New Testament is seen as necessary evidence that an individual is truly a believer and a member of the new covenant (1 John 2:4–6).* The promise of grace in the new covenant is the promise of eternal life with God. Thus, the reason this contract is called the "covenant of grace" is that God's grace is extended to us entirely unmerited and is extended to those whom He has redeemed. "This new contract is the "eternal covenant" (Hebrews 13:20) in Christ, through which we shall forever have fellowship with God, and He shall be our God, and we shall be his people."[80]

Dr. John MacAruthur's analysis regarding the Beatitudes.

Dr. John MacArthur[81] is a fifth-generation pastor and the senior pastor of Grace Community Church in Sun Valley, California, since 1969. His pulpit ministry," Grace to You," reaches worldwide, with satellite offices in Australia, Canada, Europe, India, New Zealand, Singapore, and South Africa. For our purpose, we are relying on Dr. MacArthur's Study Bible[82], which painstakingly goes through each and every Bible scripture in Matthew to analyze the Beatitudes scriptures in detail. The following selected scriptures for discussion addresses scriptures that grasp the essence of the sermon. Following are the selected scriptures from what is commonly known as the Beatitudes, Matthew 5:1–2, 3–6, 8:

- "And seeing the multitudes, "he went up on a mountain, and when He was seated His disciples came to Him. Then he opened His mouth and "taught them, saying:"
  - "…This sermon is a masterful exposition of the law and a potent assault on Pharisaic legalism, closing with a call to true faith and salvation. Christ expounded the full meaning of the law, showing that its demands were humanly impossible. *This is the proper use of the law with respect to salvation: it closes off every possible avenue of human merit and leaves sinners dependent on*

162

nothing but divine grace for salvation. Christ plumbed the dept of the law, showing that its true demands went far beyond the surface meaning of the words and set a standard that is higher than the most diligent students of the law had heretofore realized."

- "Blessed are the poor in spirit, for theirs is the kingdom of heaven."
  - o Blessed, the word literally means "happy, fortunate, blissful." Here it speaks of more than a surface emotion. Jesus was describing the divinely bestowed well-being that demonstrate that the way to heavenly blessedness is antithetical to the worldly path normally followed in pursuit of happiness. The worldly idea is that happiness is found in riches, merriment, abundance, leisure, and such things. The real truth is the very opposite. The Beatitudes give Jesus' description of the character of true faith, poor in spirit. The opposite of self-sufficiency. This speaks to the deep humility of recognizing one's utter spiritual bankruptcy apart from God.

Note: Dr. MacArthur uses the New King James Version.

- "Blessed are those who mourn, for they shall be comforted."
  - o "This speaks of mourning over sin, the godly sorrow that produces repentance leading to salvation without regret."
- "Blessed are the meek, For they shall inherit the earth.
  - o Meekness is the opposite of being out of control. It is not weakness, but supreme self-control empowered by the Spirit. The fact that "the meek shall inherit the earth" is quoted from Psalm 37:11.
- "Blessed are those who hunger and thirst for righteousness.
  - o This is the opposite of the self-righteousness of the Pharisees. It speaks of those who seek God's righteousness rather than attempting to establish a righteousness of their own. (Romans 10:3, Philippians 3:9).

What they seek will fill them, i.e., it will satisfy their hunger and thirst for a right relationship with God.

- "Blessed are the pure in heart, For they shall see God.
  - Not only with the perception of faith, but in the glory of heaven. (Hebrews 12:14, Revelation 22:3, 4)

WHAT DID JESUS SAY IS THE UNPARDONABLE SIN?

I remember when I was a little kid, attending Nana's church, we would often hear the sermon on "The Unpardonable Sin." Quite frankly, all I can remember is the word "blasphemy." So, naturally, I took this occasion to do some research using both Dr. Grudem and Dr. MacArthur's spiritual guidance and expertise on the Unpardonable Sin. While working on another chapter in this book, an impression led to a YouTube Bible lesson on the Unpardonable Sin taught by Dr. John Barnett, Pastor/Teacher at DTBM Online Video Training, The Master's Seminary, Kalamazoo, Michigan.[83] I strongly suggest that you listen and watch this video for a clear and overarching combination of Dr. Grudem's and Dr. MacAruthur's concurrence on these scriptures. Dr. John Barnett's class on what Jesus says is the Unpardonable sin can be viewed on the following link: https://youtu.be/REdr6ibRGd0

This video will be particularly helpful for those with a learning style enhanced by audible and visual aids along with written information. For convenience, the 11 scriptures concerning the Unpardonable Sin: Mark 3:20–30 KJV, naturally including the specific scriptures: 3:28 specifically stating that *all* sins will be forgiven; and 3:29 saying except for the unpardonable sin…blasphemy against the Holy Spirit. If you are wondering how in scripture (28) Jesus says *all* sins will be forgiven: and then in the next verse **(29) Jesus turns around and says the only unpardonable sin is blasphemy.** Frankly, this is where Dr. Barnett's class online filled in the missing lesson I needed to understand. Hope you find his video helpful too.

And the multitude cometh together again, so that they could not so much as eat bread. And when his friends heard of it, they went out to lay hold on him: for they said, He is beside himself. And the scribes which came down from Jerusalem said, He hath Beelzebub, and by the prince of the devils casteth he out devils. And he called them unto him, and said unto them in parables, How can Satan cast out Satan? And if a kingdom be divided against itself, that kingdom cannot stand. And if a house be divided against itself, that house cannot stand. And if Satan rise up against himself, and be divided, he cannot stand, but hath an end. No man can enter into a strong man's house, and spoil his goods, except he will first bind the strong man; and then he will spoil his house. ***Verily I say unto you, All sins shall be forgiven unto the sons of men,*** **and blasphemies wherewith soever they shall blaspheme:** ***But he that shall blaspheme against the Holy Ghost hath never forgiveness,*** **but is in danger of eternal damnation: Because they said, He hath an unclean spirit.**

Mark 3:20–30

Dr. Wayne Grudem's analysis regarding the Unpardonable Sin.

Dr. Grudem discusses several different interpretations within the Christian denominations regarding the *Unpardonable Sin, Mark 3:20–30 KJV.* This work will focus on Grudem's fourth analysis,[84] from this point forward, he points out:

- *that sin consists of unusually malicious, willful rejection and slander against the Holy Spirit's work attesting to Christ and attributing the works of Satan.*

- A closer look at the context of Jesus' statement in Matthew and Mark shows that Jesus was speaking in response to the accusation of the Pharisees that "it is only by Beelzebub, the prince of demons, that this man casts out demons" (Matthew 12:24). The Pharisees had seen Jesus' works repeatedly. He had just healed a blind and dumb demonic so that he could see and speak (Matthew 12:22). But the Pharisees, in spite of clear demonstrations of the work of the Holy Spirit in front of their eyes, willfully rejected Jesus' authority and his teaching and attributed it to the devil. So it was irrational and foolish for the Pharisees to attribute Jesus' exorcisms to the power of Satan—it was a classic, willful, malicious lie.

- Jesus explains, "if it is by the Spirit of God that I cast out demons, then the kingdom of God has come upon you" (Matthew 12:28). Jesus declares this warning: "Whoever is not with me is against me, and whoever does not gather with me scatters" (Matthew 12:30). *There is no neutrality*, and certainly, those who, like the Pharisees, oppose his message are against him. Jesus then says, "*Therefore I tell you, every sin and blasphemy will be forgiven people, but the blasphemy against the Spirit will not be forgiven*" *(Matthew 12:31)*. The willful, malicious slander of the work of the Holy Spirit through Jesus, which the Pharisees attributed to Satan, *will not be forgiven.*

- The context indicates that Jesus is speaking about a sin that is not simply unbelief or rejection of Christ, but a sin that includes:
  - A clear knowledge of who Christ is and of the power of the Holy Spirit working through Him.
  - A willful rejection of the facts about Christ that His opponents knew to be true, and
  - Slanderously attributing the work of the Holy Spirit in Christ to be the power of Satan.
  - In the case of the hardness of heart would be so great that any ordinary means of bringing a sinner to repen-

tance would already have been rejected. Persuasion of the truth will not work, for these people have already known the truth and have willfully rejected it. In this case, it is not that the sin itself is so horrible that I could not be covered by Christ's redemptive work, but rather that the sinner's hardened heart puts him or her beyond the reach of God's ordinary means of bringing forgiveness through repentance and trusting Christ for salvation. *The sin is unpardonable because it cuts off the sinner from repentance and saving faith through belief in the truth.*

- o The fact that the unpardonable sin involves such extreme hardness of heart and lack of repentance indicates that *those who fear they have committed it yet still have sorrow for the sin in their heart and desire to seek after God do not fall in the category of those who are guilty of it.*

Dr. John MacAruthur's analysis regarding the Unpardonable Sin

Note: Dr. MacArthur uses the New King James Version, *Mark 3:20–30 KJV*:

- *...is coming to an end.* An expression only used in Mark which refers to Satan's ultimate doom as head of the demonic world system.
- ...enter a strong man's house and plunder his goods. One must be stronger than Satan to enter his domain, bind him, and free people from his control. Only Jesus has such power over the devil.
- *Assuredly I say unto you (in the King James Version it is, Verily I say unto you).* "Mark's first use of the expression, which occurs through the Gospels, was employed as a formula that always introduced truthful and authoritative words from Jesus.

- Whenever someone deliberately and disrespectfully slanders the person and ministry of the Holy Spirit in pointing to the lordship and redemption of Jesus Christ, he completely negates and forfeits an possibility of present or future forgiveness of sins, because he has wholly rejected the only basis of God's salvation.[85]

What is meant by saying a Christian is "back-sliding or has fallen away?"

Jean Piaget[86] is credited for the statement: "Through association there is assimilation." More likely than not, your first introduction to the occult may have been watching a relative or friends discuss an expected baby's gender. Perhaps you noticed someone reading the paper's daily Horoscope. Did you ever play around with a pendulum to get a "yes or no" answer? At some time, have you had a psychic read Tarot cards: often an introduction to the realm of magic, power, and domination of the elements. Do you watch, read, or listen to radio programs that focus on the spirit world, discuss aliens, interview physics, or other "spiritual" our unique unexplained phenomena?

There are innumerable ways people are innocuously introduced to some form of the occult. In addition, focusing on which ones of the occult options lure you, the people in the occult community are so intriguing, friendly, and helpful in teaching you the craft. The forbidden knowledge identifies you as special. The positive results and validity of whatever practice you are drawn to give you knowledge beyond your imagination. You have developed a range of psychic friends and associates and become involved in this community, workshops, lessons, and the urge to "spy" on others comes as second nature. You now relish the charade of being ordinary to family, friends, workmates, and so forth.

If you are a Christian, you figure that God gave you this power, calling, anointment, after all, there are Angel Tarot cards, and you know your guardian angel by name. After all, God made you in His image, and you talk with him all the time, often in a special spirit language. At first, there is a twinge of guilt (not sinning) that Deuteronomy 18:10 just might be addressing what you are doing.

> There shall not be found among you any that maketh his son or his daughter to pass through the fire, that useth divination, an observer of times, or an enchanter, or a witch.
>
> Deuteronomy 18:10

The point here is that most Christians that "backslide" typically do not do so out of willfulness. *They often unknowingly "ease" their way in, incrementally, into acrimonious and anti-Christ behaviors and/or activities.* After a while, your time is spent more and more with individuals teaching you your new "calling" and less time with your Christian prayer partners. Your vocabulary starts to change, deleting frequently words of praise and gratitude for God and Jesus, and more discussions about challenging, acknowledging your guardian angel, and the healing powers of crystals, candles, hypnotism, and so forth. While Deuteronomy 18:10 seems to be the most universally known scripture addressing the sinfulness of participating in the occult, the following scriptures address and support the prohibition of witchcraft and other occult practices to include but not necessarily limited to:

The Old Testament KJV: The occult is forbidden.

- 2 Chronicles 33:6 (causes his children to pass through the fire, observed times, enchantments, witchcraft, familiar spirit, wizards)
- Isaiah 47:8,9,10,13, (8) given to pleasures, dwellest carelessly, sayest in thine heart, I and none else beside me (9) sorceries, enchantments (10) thou hast said in thine heart, I and none else beside me (13) astrologers, stargazers, monthly prognosticators
- Isaiah 8:19 (familiar spirits, wizards, the dead)
- 1 Chronicles 10:13 (familiar spirit)

- 1 Samuel 15:23 (rebellion, witchcraft, stubbornness, iniquity, idolatry, rejected the word of the Lord)
- Leviticus 19:31 (familiar spirits)
- Leviticus 20:6 (familiar spirits, wizards, whoring)
- Leviticus 20:27 (familiar spirit, wizard)
- 2 Kings 21:6 (pass through the fire, observed times, enchantments, familiar spirits, wizards)
- Exodus 22: 18 (witch)

The New Testament KJV: Occult Forbidden

- Galatians 5:19–21 adultery, fornication, uncleanness, lasciviousness, idolatry, witchcraft, hatred, variance, emulations, wrath, strife seditions, heresies, envying, murders, drunkenness, and reveling)
- Galatians 5:20–21 idolatry, witchcraft, hatred, variance, emulations, wrath, strife, seditions, heresies, envying, murders, drunkenness, reveling)
- Acts 19:19 curious arts
- Revelation 21:8 fearful, unbelieving, abominable, murderers, whoremongers, sorcerers, idolaters, liars)
- Revelation 22:15 sorcerers, whoremongers, murders, idolaters, whosoever loveth and maketh a lie.

Of course, there are other ways, addictions, crime, and so forth, for an individual to "backslide." But this work is concentrating the occult, thus the previous discussion. God's Word, as dictated to Moses in the 10 Commandments, is steadfast and unchanging. His admonishment to man clearly states that He is a jealous God not allowing any graven images, any likeness (of Him), and man shall not bow down or serve any other god. Clearly, this admonishment carries into the new administration established by Jesus Christ's sacrifice and shedding of His blood on Calvary's cross. If nothing else, these scriptures state as a steadfast fact; that sin is the one thing that will keep us away from salvation.

Old Testament KJV: Sin separates man from God.

- "But your iniquities have separated between you and your God, and your sins have hid his face from you, that he will not hear" (Isaiah 59:2).

New Testament KJV: Sin separates man from God.

- "If we confess our sins, he is faithful and just to forgive us [our] sins, and to cleanse us from all unrighteousness" (John 1:9).
- "Whosoever committeth sin transgresseth for sin is the transgression of the law. also, the law" (1 John 3:4).
- Even as Sodom and Gomorrah, and the cities about them in like manner, giving themselves over to fornication, and going after strange flesh, are set forth as an example, suffering the vengeance of eternal fire.

1 John 3:4

Benevolently, God does allow us to repent for our sins, because everyone is under the condemnation of sin, our nature is sin-filled and carnal: Our redemption:

- "For by grace are ye saved through faith; and not of yourselves: {it is} the gift of God: Not of works, lest any man should boast" (Ephesians 2:8–9).
- But without faith it is impossible to please him: for he that cometh to God must believe that he is, and that he is a rewarder of them that diligently seek him. By faith Noah, being warned of God of things not seen as yet, moved with fear, prepared an ark to the saving of his house; by the which he condemned the world, and became heir of the righteousness which is by faith.

Hebrews 11:6–7

- For all have sinned, and come short of the glory of God; Being justified freely by his grace through the redemption that is in Christ Jesus: Whom God hath set forth to be a propitiation through faith in his blood, to declare his righteousness for the remission of sins that are past, through the forbearance of God; To declare, I say, at this time his righteousness: that he might be just, and the justifier of him which believeth in Jesus. Where is boasting then? It is excluded. By what law? of works? Nay: but by the law of faith. Therefore we conclude that a man is justified by faith without the deeds of the law.

  Romans 3:23–28

THE UNITED STATES SUPREME COURT: TRADITION VERSUS CHANGE.

To paraphrase David Horowitz,[87] the U.S. Supreme Court is the highest tribunal in the nation to hear controversies related to the Constitution or laws of the United States. This court is the final arbiter of the law and, as such, is expected to dispense equal justice under the law and be the interpreter of the U.S. Constitution. The Court's power to reinterpret the Constitution can be very broad, and its authority, of course, is absolute. Therefore, in the last couple of decades, we have seen that radical and/or minority groups ("minority" as in percentages of the American population, as well as racial minority groups), if they win their case, have been able to impose their will on all Americans. The Court has given radicals a powerful lever they could never have achieved through the democratic process. With an insurmountable lever, they moved the nation and advanced their dream of a liberal liberated future in a way they could not have previously imagined.

The establishment and scope of the U.S. Supreme Court

The following description of the U.S. Supreme Court's background, description of duties, and pertinence of each decision are taken from The Court's official web page <u>About the Supreme Court | United States Courts (uscourts.gov)</u>.

Article III of the Constitution both establishes the Supreme Court's federal judiciary. Article III, Section I states that "The judicial power of the United States, shall be vested in one Supreme Court, and in such inferior Courts as the Congress may from time to time ordain and establish." Although the Constitution establishes the Supreme Court, it permits Congress to decide how to organize it. Congress first exercised this power in the Judiciary Act of 1789. This Act created a Supreme Court with six justices. It also established the lower federal court system. Today there is one Chief Justice and eight Associate Justices of the United States Supreme Court. The Justices are appointed by the President and are confirmed by the Senate. Typically the Justices hold the office for a lifetime. The salaries of the justices cannot be decreased during the term of office. These restrictions are meant to protect the independence of the judiciary from the political branches of government.

Article III, Section II of the Constitution establishes the jurisdiction (legal ability to hear a case) over certain cases, for example, suits between two or more states and/or cases involving ambassadors and other public ministers. The Court can hear a case on appeal or almost any other case that involves a point of constitutional and/or federal law. Some examples include cases that involve the United States as a party, cases involving Treaties, and cases involving ships on the high seas and navigable waterways (admiralty cases).

When exercising appellate jurisdiction, the Court, with few exceptions, does not have to hear a case. The Certiorari Act of 1925 gives the Court the discretion to decide whether or not to hear a case. Typically the Court agrees to hear about 100 to 150 of the more than 7,000 that ask to be reviewed each year (if you figure they hear 150 cases a year out of the 7,000 cases asking to be heard) is less than

1% of the submitted cases for any specific term. Once a decision is handed down, there are no further appeal rights.

Supreme Court's establishment of the power of their decisions started a change within the US that heretofore had been unprecedented. Many Christians youth and liberal theorist are seduced by the egalitarian appeal of the Court's decision declared victory to a previously felt dream for non-discrimination. At the time, conservative individuals were irritated. Apparently, they did not understand the full scope and the full force of the law behind the Court's ruling. Defeated opponents of the victorious appellant were either consciously blind or blatantly aware this new progressive approach "flew in the face" of Christian tenets. Many religious/spiritual/ and other liberally minded individuals were either beguiled into supporting what "felt right and was socially progressive, thus acceptable. It did not take Christians long to realize that this decision relegated Christ to being either unknown or dismissed, as Christian's Lord and Shepherd, while simultaneously made conservatives civilly tolerate "apostasy Christians:" the tragedy, many did not have a clue about the reach and depth of following 1803, landmark decision.

As the Court's official website states, "The Supreme Court plays a very important role in our constitutional system of government. First, as the highest court in the land, it is the court of last resort for those looking for justice. Second, due to its power of judicial review, it plays an essential role in ensuring that each branch of government recognizes the limits of its own power. Third, it protects civil rights and liberties by striking down laws that violate the Constitution. And finally fourth, it sets appropriate limits on democratic government by ensuring that popular majorities cannot pass laws that harm and/or take undue advantage of unpopular minorities. In essence, it serves to ensure that the changing views of a majority do not undermine the fundamental values common to all Americans, i.e., freedom of speech, freedom of religion, and due process of law."

This overview of the United States Supreme Court has been provided by the Supreme Court's official web page. It has been incorporated into this book as a self-described (by the Supreme Court) enabling act, authority be a final appeal court for those selected to be heard and to impress and underscore, for us, the important, lasting, sometimes, culture-changing decisions that the Federal and State governments must comply with the court's decision. Having reviewed why the following selected Court decisions are considered "landmark cases," it is because these decisions, among others, and have definitely changed the U.S. culture, laws and reshaped our collective futures to some degree.

SELECTED SUPREME COURT DECISIONS IMPACTING THE 19TH AND 20TH CENTURY.

In 1803, the Marbury v. Madison decision.

The Court's best-known decision, for exercising extreme power in their judicial review, and/or the ability of the Court to declare a Legislative or Executive act in violation of the Constitution. The enabling jurisdiction is not found within the text of the Constitution. See the first discussed in the following Selected Supreme Court decisions, in the Marbury v. Madison decision where it established their power within federal and state governance, by hearing the case of Marbury v. Madison.

In this case, the Court had to decide whether an Act of Congress or the Constitution was the supreme law of the land. The Judiciary Act of 1789 gave the Supreme Court original jurisdiction to issue writs of mandamus (legal orders compelling government officials to act in accordance with the law). A suit was brought under this Act, but the Supreme Court noted that the Constitution did not permit the Court to have original jurisdiction in this matter. Since Article VI of the Constitution establishes the Constitution as the Supreme Law of the Land, the Court held that an Act of Congress that is contrary to the Constitution could not stand. In subsequent cases, the Court also established its authority to strike down state laws found to be in violation of the Constitution. Therefore, the Court has the final say over when a right is protected by the Constitution or when a Constitutional right is violated.

In 1875, the Dred Scott decision.

The Supreme Court held that since Scott's ancestors were imported into the U.S. and sold as slaves, he could not be an American citizen. Since he was not a citizen, he had no jurisdiction to sue, which meant that Blacks who were living free in the North were barred from federal courts. Additionally, the court held that under the Fifth Amendment, slaves were property and any law that deprived a slave-owner of their property was unconstitutional. Many believed this decision was one factor leading to the Civil War.

In 1962, the Engel v. Vitale decision.

New York schools adopted a daily prayer after it was required by state law. Five families disagreed, and Steven Engel sued on the basis that it violated the religion clause of the First Amendment. The Supreme court held that reading an official prayer at school violated the constitution because it was an "establishment of religion. Justice Black wrote the majority ruling stating that the very practice of establishing governmentally composed prayers for religious services was a breach of religious freedom in America. This meant that any state-enforced prayer or reading of the Bible in a public school would be suspect. This case also established the enforcement of separation between church and state. As these three decisions laid the path to wanton being normalized. At the same time, occult practices were going mainstream on TV, radio talk shows, various classes, and occult individuals demonstrated their magic powers and a range of titillating "powers, mental knowing, and the ability to talk to spirits who always knew the answer to the question(s) you really asked.

In 1963 Murray v. Curlett combined with
Abington School District v. Schempp.

One year after striking down school prayer in Engle v. Vitale, the Court voted in Madalyn Murray's favor and Schempp's favor: Pennsylvania's prayer statute legally sanctioned or officially sanctioned

Bible reading and prayer in public schools is unconstitutional. The court concluded that no matter the religious nature of the citizenry, the government at all levels, as required by the Constitution, must remain neutral in matters of religion, "while protecting all preferring none, and disparaging none." The court thus rejected the contention that the Establishment Clause forbade only governmental preference of one faith over another.

In 1973, the Roe v. Wade decision

The U.S. Supreme Court ruled that the Constitution of the U.S. protects a pregnant woman's liberty to choose to have an abortion without excessive government restriction. The majority of Americans contended that the United States Declaration of Independence, the Bill of Rights and the seventeen amendments, the common law practices, developing judicial system, and the educational foundation; all acknowledged Christian tenets were the foundation of our nation. Thus, began the crafty, slow replacement of Christian family values and acknowledging that from conception, a baby in the womb is a human being and has a right to life.

In 2015, the Obergefell v. Hodges decision

The 2015 decision *Obergefell v. Hodges*, which declared that same-sex couples have a constitutional right to marry under the 14ᵗʰ Amendment guarantee to equal protection of the law.

THE GENERATIONS MEETS THE NEW AGE SPIRITUALITY

In 1967, the recording group, The 5ᵗʰ Dimension, recorded the blending of two songs originally written for the musical stage play Hair; by James Redo, Gerome Ragni and Galt McDermot. The two melodies, "Aquarius" and "Let the Sunshine In," were released in the spring of 1969 and spent six weeks at number one on the

U.S. Billboard Hot 100 pop singles. This song morphed into a New Age National Anthem here in the U.S. We were flooded with TV, radio, written advertisements that all types of psychic experiences were available. We were encouraged to explore self-realization, spiritual oneness, and we were most certainly mesmerized by the power and knowledge to be found "only" by occult studies.

An overview of the decade 1960–1970 cannot be discussed without including the Hippy movement: a countercultural movement that rejected the mainstream American mores, values, and tangible markers of "success:" the acquisition of personal and real property. Timothy Francis Leary, a psychedelic drug advocate, was in his heyday. Born October 22, 1920-died May 31, 1996, at age 75, his anthem was; "Turn On, Tune In, Drop Out." In 1967 nearly 100,000 youth invaded Haight-Ashbury in San Francisco, California; for what became known as the Summer of Love. This summer's notoriety was developed by the news media's focus on the hippy movement, the underground alternative youth culture's communal living in cooperative collectives, and sometimes "off the grid." The goal, besides getting stoned, was to interact harmoniously with the world, make peace, not war. Traditional Christian family values, to include marriage between one man and one woman, often gave way to "living free and having an open relationship, with anyone one, the village raises the children, and mother earth can and will supply all our needs if we are just in tune with her.

Those were the days, and as the haze of smoke wafted away over the years, many former hippies; cleaned up, became managers and CEOs and…politicians.

CHAPTER 6

. . . .

Leadership, There Is Always A Leader

I therefore, the prisoner of the Lord, beseech you that ye walk worthy of the vocation wherewith ye are called, With all lowliness and meekness, with longsuffering, forbearing one another in love; Endeavoring to keep the unity of the Spirit in the bond of peace. There is one body, and one Spirit, even as ye are called in one hope of your calling; One Lord, one faith, one baptism, One God and Father of all, who is above all, and through all, and in you all. But unto every one of us is given grace according to the measure of the gift of Christ.

Ephesians 4:1–7

A leader must have at least one follower. The leader may be formal or informal, elected or self-appointed, serving for a specific task or for an extended and undetermined length of time. Some leaders are more of a manager than a leader, or depending on the situation they may perform both as the leader and as a manager. A leader always has an impact on her followers, good or bad, however if indifferent, there is a serious problem. Indifference causes the most damage to the relationship between the "leader" and followers, equally problematic is that productivity and achievement of goals and future planning often fails. When a leader fails to discern "who" and "what" her voice creates or sustains, often undesirable outcomes occur to include false assessment of facts and/or situations, financial miscalculations, fractured interpersonal relations, and treacherous partnerships and work outcomes. *Fortunately, when she is conscious that her core values provide the foundation for her spiritual-energetic constitution, her degree of confidence, productivity, and interpersonal relationships radiate authenticity, trust and facilitates achievable goals, productivity, and profits.*

The definition of leadership in this work contends that leadership is grounded in the conscious choice among real alternatives. The assumption is that competition and conflict may be elements faced at some time during the leader's duration. Leadership includes the art of encouraging followers to act for certain goals that represent the values and motivations, the wants and needs, the aspirations and expectations of both the leader and is inclusive of all followers. In other words, Warren G. Bennis' 1959 metaphor in his work, "On becoming a Leader," stated: "Defining leadership is like defining "good" art, it's difficult to describe, but you know it when you see it."

Every leader has at least one leadership style. Great leaders have a range of "styles" that increase as his leadership matures. His knowledge of different leadership styles to meet unique situations is critical, especially if there is diversity in the workforce, constituents, and or customers. As the leader matures, the greater the chance, he becomes a Transformational Leader, displaying the following characteristics. Does the leader:

- present a clear declaration of his core values, which include compassion, service, social justice, inclusiveness, integrity, and the building of community?
- practice a value of inclusion so that her contributions incorporate the common good above self-interest?
- demonstrate he able to examine situations from many perspectives, propose alternative courses of action, seek feedback, and is open to ambiguity and paradox?

- have a holistic approach in her leading? Does she strive to balance a personal and professional life, displaying authenticity and a commitment to life-long learning?
- does he establish and prioritize specific goal achievements, receive input from others, and facilitate inclusiveness from all followers?
- regularly display that she has the required knowledge, skills, and abilities to delegate tasks to achieve goals and timetables?
- authentically behaves in a manner that shows *he like his followers* and treats each person with dignity and as an individual?
- *have a sense of creativity and a vision that her followers believe they collectively co-created?*
- behaviors that reassure his followers that his executive management's core values are consistent with his core values,
- interact with, form alliances, and network globally when necessary, and finally
- do her family, friends, and acquaintances model ease in culturally diverse interactions both formally and informally?

There are dozens of identified leadership styles example: Authoritarian, Charismatic, Dictatorial, Servant, and Situational, among a host of others. A full discussion of the various leadership styles is outside the scope of this work. Many of the best leaders have a range of different leadership styles that may be alternated dependent on the situation. Leadership flexibility is best when: dealing with diverse groups, international communications, labor organizations, and many other situations. Continuously relating to a homogenized selection of family, friends, associates, and groups; leads to limited future planning/ideas, increased failures in problem-solving, and recycled enthusiasm, and faulty self-auditing.

THE BASICS, WHAT IS LEADERSHIP?

Leadership at best begins as the reoccurring, unquenchable pursuit of knowledge and shaping reality—anchored securely within your trust for a better future. As we all know, the birth of a dream is a whole lot easier than bringing that dream to fruition. Far too many dreams get stifled along the way, often sabotaged by self-doubt, duplicitous family and friends, naysaying work associates, or perhaps just the zillion other life encumbrances. For some reason, regardless of the inherent frailties incumbent with leadership, we recognize, respect, and follow inspirational leaders. So, perhaps now is as good a time as any to take a moment to consider why and how leadership wields power, affects character, and modulates change.

The power and influence of the leader, authority figure, to influence followers to follow orders was researched in this most recognized and respected series of studies conducted by Stanley Milgram's 1961, Obedience to Authority[88] experiment. Followers showed they were willing to "take orders" from the leader even when they knew the consequences of following orders would inflict significant pain on others.

With actual or implied leadership comes formal and informal power. Leaders and those to whom they delegate administrative powers continuously direct and change lives. Leaders: some morally altruistic, some diabolical, have been quite charismatic and thus inspired others to reach formally considered unachievable and miraculous feats—or led individuals into the depths of depravity and inhuman acts. From the office bully to the full-blown tyrannical national leader: some leaders cause catastrophic change while others just profoundly mismanage. *Milgram's experiment, scrutinized the power over others, leaders wield, was later reenacted and filmed by artist Rod Dickinson Exhibition,[89] have verified that both the leader's core values and leadership style define the leader's character and behaviors, but the power inherent in being the leader is what commands the followers.*

Some individuals are initially drawn to leadership because of the power, money, and prestige of being the leader. Some individuals are drawn to leadership because of the ability to marshal dreams and turn the intangible into reality. Some individuals are placed in leadership roles by their followers because the leader is inspirational, which meets some common need to actually get something done for the common good. And, some individuals, intimidated by the demands of meeting other's needs, making decisions, and sacrificing personal goals and relationships, shun even the most intermittent informal leadership roles. Leaders may face accepting the leadership role because circumstances and opportunity present the opportunity, *but no one becomes an accidental leader.* Leadership is knowingly taken on (even if not outwardly admitted).

What makes an exceptional (here the implication is a good) leader is that with each acquisition of a leadership role, he realizes he has to be a continuous learner. Leadership is time-sensitive, and as such, the leader has to comprehend the difference between knowing what the goal is, and comprehending the multifaceted, multileveled materials, human capital, political entanglements, and unanticipated changes must be successfully juggled. All successful leaders exhibit the ability to delegate responsibilities (okay, some have delegation issues and strictly scrutinize the delegation, this is poor leadership). Leaders who are compelled to do everything themselves retain the leadership position briefly. *Inept managers typically last a lot longer than controlling leaders because inept managers make sure they have a host of others to blame for malfeasance.* Novice controlling leaders, on the other hand, are both highly visible and ultimately responsible, therefore subject to being expendable scapegoats.

Simply put: Leadership is a verb, an action (even if the "action" is indecisiveness). The position of leadership is a powerful position, and with power comes wealth or access to wealth. Thus by occupancy, the leader (voluntary, involuntary, formal, or informal) is viewed by followers as a powerful person to whom they defer both respect and the authority/responsibility of leadership. The study of leadership (whether formal or informal), the stewardship of leadership, the responsibilities of leadership, and the outcome of leadership (on individuals and groups) is real, operationally significant, and impacts us, in hundreds of ways, every day.

The implications of both Milgram's original 1960, Obedience to Authority research and the 2002 Obedience to Authority Reenactment have resounding implications. The responsibilities of today's business leaders, administrators, managers, and first-line supervisors as they set the tone and maintain the work environment. *Executive management and those to whom they delegate administrative authority are culpable for resulting hostile work environments even if they "only allow" bullies and predators to reign unobstructed.* When leaders either overtly or tacitly condone despicable employees, turn a blind eye toward bullies, and sanction predators within their administrative authority, the leader is culpable along with subordinate staff; and stringent disciplinary action, up to and including termination, should be enforced.

If followers see that leaders are "authorized" to behave in a dysfunctional, hurtful, hateful way, they will "allow" the activity to occur. While men and women have some differences in leadership styles, the power of a leadership position remains unaltered. The lure of power, prestige, often wealth, and "access" to assorted privileges: is the same across class or gender lines. Milgram's studies tell us, in harsh and disturbing terms, what we already knew: human beings are capable, even under less than extreme conditions, of doing bad things, particularly when placed in a context where they are carrying out orders or doing what is "expected." So, you see, both the leader and the position of leadership are phenomenally important.

God says a leader is a shepherd.

Reviewing what man has said about what leadership is, God has the final word about what a leader actually is. This statement is not said to be dismissive of the preceding profound statements regarding leadership. However, very few came even close to the precise, steadfast, all-encompassing simplicity of God's Word. The following selection of God's pronouncements regarding leadership are being presented both from the Old Testament and the New Testament KJV. *This discussion of leadership has a two-fold purpose. First, to once again show that there is no contradiction in God's Word over time. Secondly, to show that in both administrations (Old and New Testaments) that according to God, leadership is shepherding.* There are many scriptures discussing and describing leadership. Following are selected scriptures from each administration, which is by no means to be mistaken for the only scriptures on this topic.

The Old Testament: God the Shephard.

- Which may go out before them, and which may go in before them, and which may lead them out, and which may bring them in; that the congregation of the LORD be not as sheep which have no shepherd.

  Numbers 27:17

- The Lord is my shepherd; I shall not want" (Psalms 23:1).
- "He shall feed his flock like a shepherd: he shall gather the lambs with his arm, and carry them in his bosom, and shall gently lead those that are with young" (Isaiah 40:11).
- Hear the word of the Lord, O ye nations, and declare it in the isles afar off, and say, He that scattered Israel will gather him, and keep him, as a shepherd doth his flock.

  Jeremiah 31:10

- As a shepherd seeketh out his flock in the day that he is among his sheep that are scattered; so will I seek out my sheep, and will deliver them out of all places where they have been scattered in the cloudy and dark day.

  Ezekiel 34:12

- For the idols have spoken vanity, and the diviners have seen a lie, and have told false dreams; they comfort in vain: therefore they went their way as a flock, they were troubled, because there was no shepherd.

  Zechariah 10:2

- Woe to the idol shepherd that leaveth the flock! the sword shall be upon his arm, and upon his right eye: his arm shall be clean dried up, and his right eye shall be utterly darkened.

  Zechariah 11:17

The New Testament: Jesus the Shephard.

- But when he saw the multitudes, he was moved with compassion on them, because they fainted, and were scattered abroad, as sheep having no shepherd"

  Matthew 9:36

- And before him shall be gathered all nations: and he shall separate them one from another, as a shepherd divideth his sheep from the goats.

  Matthew 25:32

- Verily, verily, I say unto you, He that entereth not by the door into the sheepfold, but climbeth up some other way, the same is a thief and a robber. But he that entereth in by the door is the shepherd of the sheep. To him the porter openeth; and the sheep hear his voice: and he calleth his own sheep by name, and leadeth them out. And when he putteth forth his own sheep, he goeth before them, and the sheep follow him: for they know his voice. And a stranger will they not follow, but will flee from him: for they know not the voice of strangers.

  John 10:1–5

- *I am the good shepherd, and know my sheep, and am known of mine.*

  John 10:14

- *And other sheep I have, which are not of this fold: them also I must bring, and they shall hear my voice; and there shall be one fold, and one shepherd.*

  John 10:16

- Now the God of peace, that brought again from the dead our Lord Jesus, that great shepherd of the sheep, through the blood of the everlasting covenant.

  Hebrews 13:20

- And when the chief Shepherd shall appear, ye shall receive a crown of glory that fadeth not away.

  1 Peter 5:4

IMPORTANCE OF LEADERSHIP IN CHANGING AND CHAOTIC TIMES

Leadership in times of change must focus on identifying the common voices among core values when dealing with unanticipated, catastrophic change. Why? Because an individual's ability to adapt is directly linked to their ability to synchronize their leadership skills, their core values, and of course, their mastery of contemporary transferrable (street common sense, academic, and continuous learning) problem-solving competencies. Today's multifaceted socially and economically adept individuals (this is you and me, by the way) must be able to "step back from the future, clearly state dreams and goals, and merge both with a plan and purpose. Your ability to survive and thrive is handicapped by the following if you are unable to adjust:

- a dreary soul,
- addicted to something,
- depressed,
- fearful,
- obsolete,
- out of work,

- remorseful,
- strident, and
- *unable to hear God's still small voice and obey.*

Those of us who can adapt, who can keep refurbishing our work skills and competencies by continuously learning, will prosper. The continuous learner who is able to civilly tolerate working in a diverse workforce will successfully navigate the several dozen different job changes required during his working career. Those of us able to be flexible enough to assimilate into both shared work environments and the more isolated home-based work locations will prosper in our post Coronavirus pandemic's "New Norm." Today's body of Christ must be inclusive, incorporating core values in social interactions, business policies and procedures, and community affiliations. Yes, it is possible to have a core value-based business that is productive and profitable. "New" and fluid reliance on technology and networking must not obliterate the human spirit; but it can help find like-minded individuals with the same or essentially the same core values. There will always be a need for some jobs that will require humans, not entirely reliant on robotics. But, even these jobs will be highly mechanized, demanding basic computer operational skills as well as repair skills, if nothing else. So, the term "Leadership Voices™" includes the common elements identified when Transformational Leadership principles are consciously used to manage, motivate, and affirmatively manipulate our apprehensions, appreciation, and adaptability facing life changes.

CORE VALUES INTEGRATED WITH LEADERS' PROFICIENCIES ARE ENHANCED.

As already stated, it is crucial that leaders comprehend that those individuals to whom they delegate authority are authorized representatives to staff, labor organizations, customers, and the community. The Good will of both the leader and followers precede both performance, product, and service efficiencies and durability to clients and the community in general. Even if the leadership has a monopoly or autocratic grip on procedures and processes, subversive retaliation smolders against the leader. Effective leadership and "good" management:" work values/ethics, productive workforces, and healthy work and living environments require authentic and effective communications. Some types of verbal communication, rather than just simply being "bad communication skills," are harmful dismissive, and abusive.[90] The recognition of verbal abuse, although increasing, tends to focus on personal relationships. The preponderance of the literature to date recognizes verbal abuse as a legitimate, distinguishable form of psychological exploitation and brutality. Effective leaders and "good" managers envision, form, and sustain productive and healthy work environments, with communication skills being an essential component of accomplishing their objectives. An overview of the literature that specifically relates to leadership, organizational development, and management reveals that, while communication is much discussed, the closest acknowledgment of psychological abuse is limited to the areas of fear, discrimination, self-esteem/morale, self-fulfilling prophecy, or "looking-glass" assessments.

Charles Cooley's "Looking Glass" study[91] concluded that our ideas of "self" come from how we appear to others, how we think they judge our appearances, and how we feel about all this. https://lesley.edu/article/perception-is-reality-the-looking-glass-self

Over the last nineteen years, most people have learned about the characteristics of verbal abuse and the extensive range of pain, suffering, and sometimes mental distress resulting from sustained verbal abuse. Affirmative Action discrimination laws, corporate policies and procedures, and political correctness have all placed individuals in a position" to know, or should have known," that verbal abuse may have serious consequences. *There are still, unfortunately, some holdouts that still hold that in the "game," of the goal acquisition, retention, and expansion of power; the end justifies the means."*

These powerful holdouts have both connections and power to allow them to "reason," that good and evil are reduced from absolute to relative categories; the determination of whether an act is good or evil depends (according to them) entirely on the basic assumption of one's system of values. If the basic or core value is assuming and maintaining power, then assuming power, regardless of the means used, is good. Thus the ways of acquiring, consolidating, and expanding power are good as long as they accomplish their task, as long as they are efficient. Therefore, utilizing efficient means is "good," and the use of any inefficient means is "bad." Machiavelli's book "The Prince" (1513) saw no problem with using insults or harm to coworkers, subordinates, or others with whom one comes in contact through his position of power.

There is agreement that power, in the sense of domination over others, is an excessive assertion.[92] In the "traditional" hierarchical organization, many men and women equate or integrate their position in the organizational hierarchy with their identity. If a leader or manager has associated their personal identity with their position within the hierarchy, then any shift to a different system of values provokes fear. All suggest that there is another kind of power, one that influences others, which sustains its potency and authority from networks, not hierarchical composition.[93]

A person's expectations or beliefs determine his behavior and performance, thus achievement and productivity coincide with a manager's rising expectation for individuals performing job tasks, so; high supervisory expectancy produces better leadership, which leads employees to develop higher self-expectations, which motivate workers to exert more effort. Frankly, this domino's approach to ultimately increase performance and supervisory expectancies might indeed work: but it is sloppy and time-consuming. It is given that the expectations of the leaders and managers can powerfully influence the employee's behavior and performance. However, the employees have to respect the supervisors and can trust their authentic assessments of employees, being non-partial, fair, and correct. Employees also need to know that if improvement is needed, the supervisor will assist them to achieve the acceptable performance standard, with or without a reasonable accommodation. One of the fundamental principles of leadership and management is that constructive comments or communications are necessary to realize positive performance expectations, and not every communication is attached to some sort of "corrective action plan." In conclusion:

- we tend to accept impressions that reinforce our basic identity,
- we tend to resist circumstances that do not clearly indicate our demise if we do not change,
- unless there is a significant emotional event that alters our basic self-concept, we will ferociously continue with our current self-assessments,
- we will change ourselves *if we believe that the change is the only way* to preserve ourselves,
- we are unable to change if we cannot find our recreated selves in a new version of the world, and finally
- we must be able to see we will absolutely fail in this new situation; then and only then will we make *the sustained effort* to change.

We will always move in the direction of our number one value and away from what threatens that value[94].

WHAT IS TRANSFORMATIONAL LEADERSHIP VS. PROACTIVE MANAGEMENT?

Transforming leadership occurs when individuals engage with each other so that both leader and follower raise one another to higher levels of motivation and morality. Power bases are linked for mutual support and common purposes.

Proactive Management Principles, on the other hand, are the collection of the leader's (or those to whom administrative authority has been delegated) typically attend to the day-to-day operational job tasks, methods, means, and kinds of work to produce the product, service, or consultation that brings in revenue and profits. First-line supervisors through mid-management have the distinguishing responsibility of meeting production/service goals and internal supervisory responsibilities, which may include but not be limited to:

- conducting employee performance evaluations,
- designated fiscal management of necessary office supplies and other durables,
- meeting with Labor or administration at first level grievances,
- other production accountability as delegated, and
- training employees.

Thus, first-line and mid-level managers have a significant role in the overall organization good will, employee morale, and productivity, and representing on a daily basis the business' stated goals, objectives, and community relations. Transformational Leaders must train, nurture, and ensure proactive managers establish and maintain a work environment honoring diversity, stimulating productivity, encouraging excellence, and aggressively supporting a work environment free from harassment and discrimination. Competent, purposeful blending and balancing one's personal core values, actively mediating conflicting interpersonal communications, and facilitating productive work systems earmark proactive management principles. *Yes, these mid-level managers have a tremendous responsibility, one could say they are the stabilizers of the organization.*

What if anything is so different about leadership in chaotic times? Anytime someone leads, if they lead for any period of time, they will encounter change: in goals and process, procedures and staffing concerns, fiscal highs and lows, and definitely various types of leadership skills required. *Perhaps a better question would be, specifically, what leadership characteristics distinguish an otherwise "ordinary individual "from those leaders who are visionaries and also proactive in their management.* Each level of leadership must comprehend that who they are (up to the Chief Executive Officer) will be defined by subordinate leadership staff; based on core values and leadership styles of those to whom the leader has delegated authority. First-line supervisors are the leaders of their staff, and thus they hold leadership responsibilities that define the entire command of leadership.

A common by-product occurring with change is fear. Leaders and those to whom they have delegated authority must effectively and deliberately present a clearly cohesive adherence to company values and purpose statement. There must also be a working 360-degree feedback process through tumultuous times. Succinctly put, leaders must provide:

- clearly stated definite production/service and standards,
- state clear timelines and processes, sign off of all employees stating they have been made aware of these previously stated stipulations,
- practical fine-tuning and change plans occur if needed, with clear procedures to request and approve all change plans,
- each job classification understands the mandatory duties, and if there is a "family within this classification," there must be clearly stated the distinguishing characteristics between each level within the job classification.
- employees need to know where their stipulated work fits in the total change plan and what specific job classifications, if any, will be laid off, retired, reclassified, absorbed into another classification…or other plans, and
- each section of satisfactorily (or better) goals completed on or before date accomplished change component: celebration by all contributing staff of each goal achieved.

Business owners and "ordinary workers" share the same concerns regarding profitability and stability: they want all they can get with the expectations that the business' profitability will be fairly shared; not necessarily equal, but definitely fairly. Being an effective leader provides the best chance to strategize, obtain, and maintain power (reduce the necessity for labor unions) and stewardship. Being a transformational leader provides the best chance to envision the optimum outcome for all concerned, be aware of the nuances of change, and consistently envision unconventional possibilities. All leaders that are flexible, visionaries, and proactive managers have the best chance of effectively leading through stressful, fearful, and chaotic events. The entire organization would really love to be proud of their leader!

Everyone leads sometimes. Everyone is a follower sometimes. Some leaders are elected, some appointed, and some because they are "natural" leaders within the group and emerge as the leader. Some people follow because they are unwilling, unable, or disinterested and "go along to get along." *Some individuals who are "incidental leaders," disenfranchised followers, or apathetic group members facilitate chameleon and/or despotic leaders.* All leaders have some degree of power. The degree of power and the money, that always annexes power significantly determine a leader's ability to influence others. It is always important to distinguish between a leader's power and a leader's ability to manage. Some leaders have no clue about civil behavior or about proactive management competencies. It is therefore essential to recognize that all leaders, over time, face changes; only a few leaders create, nurture, and practice an ethic of care and proactive leadership during changes.

During chaotic global pandemic times, some individuals kept their jobs, retained their small businesses, or started to rebuild independent work opportunities from scratch. During the year 2020 through the first half of 2021, elected officials pandemic leadership-imposed: virus draconian business lockdowns, civilian isolation/quarantines from families and religious/spiritual services, and social distancing. These actions were supposed to suppress and thus end the pandemic communicability. The enforced mandatory closures and/or impossible restrictive operational guidelines to "remain open" failed miserably, especially for small businesses. There was no inclusion of citizens in monitoring the success of these excessive and strident population lockdowns. Neither did citizens feel that elected officials showed any ethic of care: toward them, their staff, or their community. The repercussions incurred by business, ordinary citizens, as well as the mental and financial impact associated with the tragic virus-related loss of life, will probably show an extended unanticipated significant emotional scarring. Those individuals lucky enough to be able to work from home on their jobs also sustained isolation from co-workers, a hodgepodge of juggling family care, achieving internet work productivity, unanticipated expenses setting up "home work stations, attending to non-resident family emergencies, and harnessing energetic minor children restricted to quarantine living restrictions. This is an example of real-life chaos.

Thousands of employees who worked from home in quarantine isolation; did so without training to consider production control or customer services. These harsh, immediate changes in work method, means and kinds added the fear added the overlooked "work depression," resulting from the lack of informal job-related information exchanges and general co-worker camaraderie. Labor contracts, depending on the employee's work classifications, caused as much fear as the thought of staying at work and catching "the virus." To make matters worse, these work closures or work from home requirements vacillated. Sometimes a business could open with restrictions and then were told to close again. Many businesses closed permanently, unable to exist due to the expensive modifications with no customers to actually do business with to make the required facilities changes worthwhile. Small businesses took a particularly strong hit. Depending on their business financial health, if businesses need to take a short-term loan to pay employees, banks knowing that these businesses were ordered to close may not have extended loans. Yes, much later, Congress came up with stimulus checks to assist businesses, individuals on worker's compensation, private citizens that met various stipulations, and moratoriums on evictions from homes and apartments during the virus pandemic. But, when these short-term subsidies end, the chaos from the taxes necessary to cover the "stimulation hand-outs" will be catastrophic. As Margo Channing (Betty Davis) said in the 1950 20th Century Fox Production, "All About Eve:" *"Fasten your seat belts boys, it's going to be a bumpy night."*

As a result of inconsistent closing mandates, the COVID-19 virus pandemic economic scourge is responsible for accelerating post-traumatic stress, disrupted community internal caring and sharing, and established a new, desolate poor class of formally employed individuals. Obviously, the vast majority of our elected officials, at every level, have miserably failed as leaders. Most elected officials have also failed at being proactive managers. This colossal failure did not happen accidentally, this collective mass failure had to be planned: one must work aggressively to be a total failure.

Not to end on a tragic or hopeless note, be reminded that these inept leaders are not immortal, they can and eventually will be replaced. Most importantly, always remember that everybody leads sometimes, so start leading where you are. There is no such thing as "too little leadership, all leadership matters, especially Transformational Leadership. We, the people, developed this country, still live here, and we as leaders and community sages can and will revive our spirits, core values and turn on our lights. Light the path for our upcoming generation, who will soon become elected and appointed officials, business owners, and international corporation heads. It is imperative that they learn from this generation that experienced this travesty what never to do again. It all starts with:

- knowing whether or not you serve God, god, or not sure what, if anything,
- from knowing your religious/spiritual foundation tenets, you can now declare your core values, therefore
- your behaviors naturally are driven by your core values,
- the "looking glass effect" supports your self-ideal because you will see no need to "change."

Humans will continue to face unexpected sickness pandemics, devastating natural destruction, and for some, even wars. There will be times, of course, where a dictatorial leader is required in an emergency situation. But even a dictatorial leader that is astute will keep an eye and ear open, giving the population some input regarding resources needed, leadership appearances and words of encouragement, and seeing some actual improvement in living conditions. Yes, even an intelligent dictatorial leader can transition, okay, just a little bit, to a situational leader, and through continuous learning—over time—become one of the best transformational leaders.

CHRISTIAN TENETS AND AMERICAN WORK ETHICS.

This segment discusses American work ethics, management styles, and the toleration of verbal abuse in the work environment. Undoubtedly the more verbal abuse of any kind is tolerated, encouraged, and even established a predator/prey work environment, the more individuals can rely on the fact that this environment is planned, not accidental. Only the CEO and Executive Board of Directors will know the actual benefit(s) achieved from such a "business plan." Interestingly a specific conversation most often will never occur, there is just an implied agreement to support management's productivity and profitability achievements. Obviously, there is a significant power, money, and political protection that is enabling this climate (with or without lawsuits and other attempts to extract recompense) to continue to exist. In that case, short of an exorcism, if you cannot stand the environment, get out at any cost and move far away. Yes, Jesus said to "turn the other cheek" (Matthew 5:39), but nowhere did I see Him say that you had to stay there if you had an opportunity to leave before being "slapped" on the cheek. But if you are "stuck" in this situation, then the following is instructed by Jesus.

> But I say unto you, That ye resist not evil: but whosoever shall smite thee on thy right cheek, turn to him the other also. And if any man will sue thee at the law, and take away thy coat, let him have thy cloke also. And whosoever shall compel thee to go a mile, go with him twain. Give to him that asketh thee, and from him that would borrow of thee turn not thou away.
>
> Matthew 5:39–42

197

John Calvin and the American Work Ethic

John Calvin (1509–1564) was a French reformer and theologian. The overall impact of Calvinism resulted in the following core values relating to the American Work Ethic, as we know it. [95]

- The improvement of society and government depends on the improvement of human beings. Therefore, a critical arena for reformation was the church, for in his opinion, only through the grace of the Holy Spirit could the human heart reform.

- Utilitarianism, another essential value for which Calvin regularly evaluated human society for its utility. This same principle, however, gave Calvin's social ethic a degree of flexibility. For example, he contended that one should act "rightly" for one's-self but not put pressure on others to follow their example as if it were a rule.

- Calvin also thought private property was fundamental to social order. Calvin believed that each person should possess what is his own: that acquisition of property might vary, but each person should increase her means by ingenuity, physical strength, or any other means. In short, Calvin equated political order with each individual "holding "her own."

Take a moment to reflect. Does this "work ethic" resemble any management philosophy where you work? This particular work ethic, while having much merit, also has the necessary ingredients required to cultivate and sustain bullies, determinedly difficult people, and predators. Ever wonder why senior executives and administrators know the bullies and predators (many of them are managers and supervisors) behaviors toward individuals in the workforce, yet nothing is ever done to change or stop the offensive practices. *Well, senior executives and administrators subscribe to the Calvinist's conflicting ideas of expecting that individuals should act right but not pressure others to follow their example; while simultaneously holding that the individual is totally responsible for her failures, then the burden of "getting along" is transferred to you.* Meanwhile, you and the bully are expected to "hold your own" and advance by ingenuity, physical strength, or any other means. *Thus you, the prey, not the disruptive, abusive, predator are responsible for your own circumstances.*

Max Weber and the American Work Ethic

Max Weber (1504–1558) was a social and theological researcher and analyzer. His analysis of Christian (and particularly Protestant) tenets is given significant recognition for forming the core of the "Protestant Ethic," or work ethic in the sixteenth century. *This work ethic enabled the emerging merchant class to accumulate wealth, keep profits, claim extensive personal freedom and is the primary basis for capitalism.* The core values established are:

- Work is a calling. Unlike other societies that traditionally regard work as a means of survival, the equation of work to a calling provided significant motivation for producing or more than is necessary for survival.
- Success as a sign of grace. Success in one's occupation was a clear sign of divine favor, therefore provided motivation for "hard work."
- Individuals as monitors of their own state of grace. The individual alone is responsible for his own fate. As with Calvin, this philosophy diminished or released employers from obligations to employees.
- Capitalistic enterprise was separated from the pursuit of gain. The desire for wealth has historically existed in many places throughout time thus had nothing to do with capitalistic action.
- True leadership means receiving power from God, and its use is to serve people in God's way. God rules, not leaders. People matter most, not techniques.

- Weber maintained Puritanism had a direct and immediate impact in forming the moral outlook affecting the lower and middle "working classes" by establishing the "virtues" of the "faithful" employee.
- Note: late in life, Weber modified his contention that Protestantism was a *contributing factor to capitalism, not the ultimate reason* supporting capitalism.

Everett Hagen and the American Work Ethic.

Dr. Everett E. Hagen (1907–1993), While definitely more contemporary, Hagen's contribution had a profound impact on our now "traditional" work ethics. His contribution was what he called the "innovative personalities." Some personality traits are attitudes about reality. This shift in attitude about reality occurs when established, predetermined, ascriptive norms are undermined by social mobility, resulting in stratification of hierarchies which determines the following norms:

- When an individual, group, or occupational category loses its status, a gap appears between the prior status and the later status.
- Individuals within this "fallen" category do lose face thus, they do not retain the regard they believe they deserve. Thus the gap between the self-defined deserved past status and the current lower status.
- This discrepancy has real-world consequences such as lower levels of income, power or both. This results in a diminished social circle and, therefore, "powerful" connections.

Does this "work ethic" resemble any management philosophy where you work? This particular work ethic, while having much merit, also has the necessary ingredients required to cultivate and sustain bullies, determinedly difficult people, and predators. Low self-esteem, loss of self-esteem, and fear for one's self-preservation are intrinsically interwoven when there is "structural inconsistency," and the individual perceives they have no status or their status is in jeopardy. This could turn volatile if there are underpinning mental issues. We witnessed on TV the first mass tower shooting by Charles Joseph Whitman, the Texas Tower Sniper on August 1, 1966, and the escalation of shootings, bombings, and other terrorist activities have accelerated from 1966 forward.

THE RELATIONSHIP BETWEEN CONSCIOUSNESS AND GOD'S STEADFAST WORD?

Consciousness and/or awareness is a process of self-reflective information absorption. Consciousness occurs as intellectual enlightenment or illumination, which adds a state of moral exaltation, a quickening of one's moral senses, and the appreciation that one is in possession of eternal life. It is in this state that one typically perceives the world as a mystery, and in this state, visionaries abound.

Consciousness is necessary to distinguish an individual from every other living creature and other natural elements. Consciousness is a connective link between one's body, instincts, and images. All consciousness recognizes "other" entities and interprets what is perceived. Consciousness, in this sense, acts as one's personal filter of facts, situations, new occurrences, titillating dreams and desires. Yes, there is also a feeling of belonging and shared emotional connection.

There are three forms or grades of consciousness: (1) the Simple Consciousness, (2) the Self-consciousness, and (3) the Cosmic Consciousness. Generally, conversational exchanges tend to discuss Cosmic Consciousness. Why, because this is the highest form of consciousness, both subjective and objective, which reaches for ultimate enlightenment, is the resting place of world peace and goodwill, and for many is the fertile and ethereal horizon of God.

Along with cosmic consciousness, intellectual enlightenment or illumination occurs, extending to a state of moral exaltation, producing an indescribable feeling of elation, joyousness, and a quickening moral sense. Depending on one's specific religion, spiritual, creed, or cult identification: there is a sense of boundless freedom, a connection to eternal life, and the awareness that one is complete and accepted. Consciousness has no limitations, is a part of the "whole," and for religious/spiritual individuals, this is where there is connection, infusion with God.

Consciousness involves bringing visions to the threshold of decision and action so that one can coexist in the "real world," to achieve and enjoy relationships, tangible achievement, and be a steward within one's community. The acquisition of various powers and global interconnectedness is not the goal, it is the bi-product of submission and obedience to God and the acceptance of Jesus Christ as our contracted intercessor to God. This need to link, to unify, necessarily implies a distinction of self from another, not the absorption of "others."

LEADERSHIP AND CONSCIOUS AWARENESS.

So, how do we as individuals and leaders retain our conscious awareness, discernment and manifest our wishes, hopes, and dreams through change, catastrophic change, and berserk chaos? The "problem" occurs primarily because, typically, we resist admitting change constantly occurs. Most leaders defy things have "changed" enough to require a "new" consideration, approach, action, and/or future plans. No leader wants to become obsolete; however, all but transformational leaders will admit that consistency is an illusion. The seductive and illusionary appeasement found in the familiarity of tradition, stability, safety, and profitability routinely appeals to:

- the cynic because there is always a reason and to the mystic there never is,
- the historians because the past is constant, to visionaries it depends on the history if it supports the current visionaries goals,
- the infiltration of the change; for instance watching a sunset you are cognizant of twilight and then the darkness of

the night, but you cannot specifically identify the precise instant night settled in, and

- one's intent and discipline: your individual intent and discipline may be minimal, but the actual change may be more far-reaching and encompassing than anticipated.

It would be so much easier if we could limit change to isolated, independent segments of our lives. Sometimes crisis, resulting from chaos, occurs because there are so many unrelenting changes occurring in every facet of our life simultaneously. And being human, sustaining intent and discipline continuously, in every facet of life concurrently, cannot be done. One can only stretch so much, and things start to break down, sometimes called panic attacks, nervous breakdown, acute depression, and other assortments of explanations why a person just "shuts down."

So, picking and choosing which strands of our lives to leave unraveled while we attend to selected occurrences in our lives create stress because there is no rest and recuperation time. Thus the traumatic acceleration incurred from both unrelenting pressure and sustaining our goals and achievement timelines does not pair well with reliance on God. The "how" and the "why" of how we pick the people we do, the ideas we value, and our physical geographical locations we pick; are dependent on what we value and how we prioritize our values. Community, economics, energy, environment, infrastructures, self, and survival; each independently and collectively comprise our core values as well as weave the fabric of our social norms. Individual adaptability is contingent on: whether or not we learn, how we learn, how we interpret and apply what we learn: and most importantly, what we pass on to our next generation. Conscious awareness absolutely creates the collective intent driving the changes that interconnect humanity, our behaviors, and lives.

For this reason, the fact that we are all interconnected, each of us is the sum of our inherited past, our environment, and our unique values, vision, and voice. One thing that all humans share is our need to survive. Regardless of our community and the advancement of our nation, state, community and neighborhood we all have to work—do something to eat. True, some societies have a "safety net" for those unable or unwilling to work, but many societies do not. People, in general, are expected to "work" do something of value that contributes to sustaining their lives, or they die. This is one reason our "work" is so important to us, and we spend so much time plotting, achieving, being tormented by, or being defined by what we do, and our power typically dependent on the amount of money we make. As individuals, our ability to detect the subtle shifts that precede our need to do something differently from what we have previously done is unique. For many of us, that first "warning," the "change forerunner," is usually ignored, camouflaged, or disabled. Many of us miss the subtle creeping facts that we must adjust. Some, but not necessarily all of the hits that should prove to be the warning that shifts are already occurring, will include the following but not necessarily limited to:

- changes of volume and array of editable and/or durable necessities (groceries, toilet paper, mechanical replacement parts, increased self-service purchasing),
- smaller permanent work forces,
- continuous expansion of independently contracted employment,
- continuous quality improvement more reliant on technology,
- continuous development of niche services and customers,
- changes in the neighborhood (neighbors moving, loss of jobs, property values diminish, and so forth),
- sophisticated incorporation of dialogue and consensus building to support negotiated contracts, which were previously not committed to paper, and
- balancing the interdependencies of personal lives and extended unpredictable work schedules, serious and/or sustained long-term family illness.

Working conditions necessitate changes more frequently than ever anticipated. Our adaptability requires us to use every part of our being to marshal both the internal fortitude (discipline) and strength (intent) just to "keep up" as we vacillate from fear to impudence includes the following, but is not limited to:

- approaching our personal "employment" as a small business enterprise:
- clearly self-articulating our vision and values,
- coherently expressing our transferable work skills and competencies,
- engaging in continuous education—both academic and vocational,
- using technology optimally in achieving work excellence and productivity,
- exhibiting savvy regarding work rights, responsibilities, and coping with diverse personalities while engaging in competition for shrinking jobs and benefits,
- learning and applying the "art" of humility, strength, speaking clearly and mindfully, and the value of silence.

But just how far and how often can we bend and sway with the hundreds of changes we face each day? How do we know when that last "insignificant" change we made over time turn out to be an indication of the chaos to follow? When is that instant we "snap" like Michael Douglas' character William in the movie *Falling Down*? [96] This 1993 Warner Brother's release is about William Foster, "the average white-collar working stiff," who just wants to get home to see his daughter on her birthday. Unfortunately for William, this day has had one too many changes required of him to adapt to the journey home. The film at first implies that it is the traffic jam that is his breaking point. However, as the movie progresses, we see that when William got up that morning, he had already passed his capacity to make "just one more adaptation. After this point, just about everyone William encounters "loses."

What is implied but not explored in the film is whether William's termination from his job as a defense worker was his "breaking point/final change," or, was it something that happened prior to his being fired? Like most of us we never know when the final change, exceeding our endurance, will occur. We just know that we can no longer adapt to one more thing. When we lose our ability to cope, what does that look like? This film shows the violent aftermath resulting from the failure to adapt to the morning rush hour traffic. There is significant reason to be concerned that after the year (2020) many of us faced: dramatic, unwanted, restrictive, embarrassing, and demoralizing changes simultaneously in many life functions; for many of us, change intolerance is on a short-lit fuse.

How each of us morns or snaps, our intolerance of the next change in many ways resembles how we process grief, so faultlessly researched[97] by Dr. Elisabeth Kubler-Ross' acclaimed findings regarding how we deal with death and dying:

1. Denial and isolation. Initially, we tend to deny that anything has taken place, we may even withdraw from our usual activities and associates.
2. Anger. We tend to vent our anger toward the person or situation that inflicted the change or brought the message that change is needed: even if realistically nothing could have stopped the change.
3. Bargaining. We attempt to bargain (beg, threaten) with anyone we perceive as having power over the situation, and/or we bargain with our spiritual source if we recognize one.
4. Depression. A feeling of paralysis, fear, disorientation, hate, apathy, or any mixture starts to fill the void of helplessness. We may or may not have any physical behaviors that accompany depression.
5. Acceptance. Acceptance means the inevitability of the change is comprehended, but it does not necessarily mean that it is understood, agreed to, or incorporated.

Does change always have to push us to the brink of our breaking point? If not, how then do we skirt some of the inherent traumas' of change—big or small? We have repeatedly heard that we need leaders, and if we have one, a good one, this leader can go in front of us, and guide us, through change. How and where we find the necessary leader(s) is a search that is almost as old as people living in communities. Some of the questions associated with our need for leadership is, other than how we find our leader include:

- Once we have found our leader, how long do we keep her?
- Is the same leader good for all things, or do we need to change our leaders depending on the situation or time?
- Does the leader have to "know everything," or is his ability to just motivate me enough?
- When does the leader's vision become obsolete?
- When do I need to take over as the leader?
- If I do take over as the leader, who are my followers, and do I want them following me?

Whether or not leaders are born with innate "leadership" characteristics or they are "made" is a debate that may never be settled. Effective leadership does not just happen, it can be developed to include the following essential components:

- Competence in technical area(s) most beneficial to changes occurring.
- Exhibits basic communication skills in human relations and "grief" counseling.
- Development and use of interpersonal skills.
- More use of active listening skills than giving directions.

Daily many of us are feeling the increased pressure from isolation, the lack of physical contact with loved ones and friends, that have separate living dwellings. After a sustained period, especially when complicated with the realistic fear of disease, prolonged serious illness, and fear of personal death and dying family and friends during a global pandemic virus. We collectively become easily irritated, restless, mean, and/or fearful, replacing our previous enjoyment of camaraderie and self-fulfillment with realistic, pragmatic fear.

We need strong, transformational leaders grounded in wisdom and our collective voices and values. Disappointment when our leaders fall significantly short of being transformational, they are in fact, are: autocratic, compromised, greedy, and transactional (this for that). Each of us needs to understand our tolerance: to and with changes because the only thing constant is change. Are you prepared to step in and lead? If not you, who…if not now, when?

Just remember that as Christians, you are always responsible for your actions and interactions, which means that God and His Word should always be our gyroscope and compass:

- "I am the LORD: that is my name: and my glory will I not give to another, neither my praise to graven images"

  Isaiah 42:8

- Thou shalt not bow down thyself unto them, nor serve them: for I the LORD thy God am a jealous God, visiting the iniquity of the fathers upon the children unto the third and fourth generation of them that hate me.

  Deuteronomy 5:9

Civility does not mean agreement, nor does one have to accept another's values, ethics, or religious/spiritual tenets. A directive imposed by law and subject to prescribed punishment will have both compliance and elusive defiance. Forcing someone to "accept" another's religion/spirituality core values only results in superficial compliance or outright revolt. Within the U.S., individuals use to be required to follow the laws or work to change them. Now citizens are told that this is the law, regardless of their personal religious tenets. You are compelled to:

- All Torts and Criminal law offenses,
- Assaults (specifically),
- Backstabbing,
- Battery (specifically),
- Bullying,

- Cyber-attacks of any kind,
- Defamation,
- Gaslighting,
- Gossip,
- Intimidation,
- Lying
- Predatory activity, and
- Verbal abuse

It is important to remember that one's intentions are unknown until there is some type of behavior and/or action. However, it is extremely difficult for an individual to have a sustained intention and not have that intent over time "bleed" over into some type of action and/or behavior. It is your action/behavior which you will be held accountable for, and some activities, behaviors cannot be undone, nor can the damage done to another be taken back. *Once again I emphasize that acceptance of different core values is not required. Toleration is required when and if interaction does not void your core values.* Remember, your core value is something you are willing to die for, it is the essence of who and what you are.

If your primary tenets will be violated, then this is an entirely difficult and different situation that historically has led to war. So, unless both parties are ready for war, perhaps the best outcome is to stop any and all associations. This is problematic, you say…well, so is war. Of course, force and immediate threat of bodily harm require disengagement immediately and probable intervention of the law.

This book recognizes that not every gathering of individuals wants to, or needs to, work toward building community/teamwork. However, this book supports the premise that those work environments, community affiliations, and social relations that purposefully encourage, and support community building, are engaging in the spirit of continuous learning, compassion, and toleration. When individuals work to construct a safe, productive, transforming environment; *following the Servant and Transformational Leadership modeled by Jesus Christ,* it is amazing how a diverse community has each other's backs and accomplishes communal dreams.

CHAPTER 7

· ·

Transformation Takes Time: My Journey

> For I know nothing by myself; yet am I not hereby justified: but he that judgeth me is the Lord. Therefore judge nothing before the time, until the Lord come, who both will bring to light the hidden things of darkness, and will make manifest the counsels of the hearts: and then shall every man have praise of God.
>
> 1 Corinthians 4:5

Now that we have gone through the stress factors many of us face, what do we do besides lament our woes and fears? We do something restorative, creative, and invigorating. Then we rejoice. Christians celebrate joy within the promises of God's love and Jesus' intersessions while marshaling the battle in the spiritual realm.

> And the sons of strangers shall build up thy walls, and their kings shall minister unto thee: for in my wrath I smote thee, but in my favour have I had mercy on thee. Therefore thy gates shall be open continually; they shall not be shut day nor night;

that men may bring unto thee the forces of the
Gentiles, and that their kings may be brought.

Isaiah 60:10–11

In other words, hold on, redemption is possible, and so is peace
and joy in Jesus' name. *This chapter is about your doing something different, something positive and empowering, and allowing yourself some dedicated protective time to do something to express yourself in a positive way.* If, due to circumstances, you can only carve out "perhaps," five
minutes, then do it at least twice a day. If your dwelling has way too
many people for the size of your dwelling, there is always the old "I'm
in the bathroom or laundry room" sanctuary. The actual location and
time of day/night are not important. In your cocoon of healing, once
entered, you will spend not less than five minutes, of course, you can
spend as much time as you please. The purpose is to start truthfully
recognizing how you feel. If you have children, consider whether
you want them to join you to learn how to give themselves quiet,
protective time. This may be difficult at first, most of your time may
be trying to remember what relaxation felt like. Ask yourself how
do you feel, then express the feeling in at least one of the following
examples 9or something else):

- affirmations,
- breathe deeply,
- build, carve
- crafts,
- dance,
- doodle, color,
- exercise,
- look in a mirror
- paint,
- play music,
- play with toys,
- pray, meditate,
- sew,
- sing,

- some type of movement!
- wood working,
- write.

The goal is to work up to the point that you have eventually carved out at least an hour of self-fulfillment time each day. This may take time, but how long this takes to reach an hour a day worth of protective time is a goal, and not long this takes to reach this goal. The point is that over time you will continue to realize you are important, valuable and you deserve some quiet, rejuvenating time. You are to make this contract with yourself and do at least ten minutes (if you are only doing five minutes at a time) and keep this fulfillment time every day for twenty consecutive days. Why twenty days, because "tradition states" it takes at least twenty consecutive days to establish a habit. Once you start recognizing your feelings and tending to them, you are taking your first steps toward being consciously aware and spiritually joyful. How can you hear God's still, quiet voice if you do not even recognize your authentic feelings and you are never still, quiet, or mentally emotionally capable of hearing anything "still and quiet?"

MY BIOGRAPHICAL SCRAPBOOK

Most biographies are written in prose, sometimes presented as a diary, collection of letters, or in manuscript format. The medium used to express yourself, relax and enjoy life is endless. Personally, I like expressing myself as a writer. So, as an example of what I am asking you to consider doing, I am presenting my condensed bibliography in selected poetry. My expression is written. When I started, I had no idea that I would be adding to my poetry throughout the years. Now, I am so pleased I did. I get to watch myself retrospectively every time I pick up "My Scrapbook" and praise God I have lived long enough to know God has never given up on me, not even now. I have shared this book with very few, but trusted family and friends until now. Now, I'm willing to share one way, the way I chose, to express and enjoy my creativities whims.

A bit of personal disclosure here.

Once I got started remembering how to recognize my feelings, my horizons opened to me. My physical fulfillment time alternated primarily between exercise (light weights, swimming, and dancing) and, of course writing, at that time affirmations and poetry. I like the writing because that gives me something to date, and at times I go back and read what I had written. The affirmations and poetry in this section were written over a span of years. Now, looking back, I can see my growth and development. I knew I had feelings, I just never wanted anyone to know what they were. It has been extremely hard for me to include my poems in this work, but sometimes an example is better than an explanation. You will notice that I went through several stages ranging from rage to fancifulness. I also did paintings that go with each of these poems, I have not included them because I reserve this expressive art as "my eyes only."

This chapter demonstrates the actual transitions I had to undergo. The following biographical scrapbook is divided into the following five healing "transitions."

1. In the beginning.
2. Awareness Precedes.
3. Discipline Precedes Dominion: Consciousness opens.
4. Chaos is Transformational.
5. Balance the "I" within me.

I am not perfect today, but at least I am a consciously aware person. I have to admit that I do so appreciate being able to share my full self with God (yes, it took me a while to figure out he knew me better than I knew myself). Because I allowed myself to appreciate me, I was, I can appreciate me as I am now. And yes, I still have growth to become even better. My self-work is far from over. By raising my levels of conscious awareness, I have established a much better personal relationship with God and, of course, shepherded by my intercessor, Jesus Christ. I hear God's still small voice, and after testing to verify it is His voice (yes, I am still learning), I obey. For me pouring my soul out on paper for you to see me through your eyes strikes me as a perverted version of Salvador Dali's Surrealistic Art. Dali is my favorite artist! It is a major struggle for me to include this chapter. I am an introvert, and according to Myers-Briggs, I am an INFJ, which means I am quite private, and analytical. Prior to this publication, only three people have ever seen any of my poetry with my art for each poem. I think the stand-alone poetry is sufficient and appropriate in this book.

> *My poetry does not rhyme. Some poems are long, some are short. The heading for each section of the poetry gives you the overview of where my spirit swirled during this period. Then look at the titles of the poetry within that section. Even if you do not read one word of any poem, most will be able to follow my transition.*

Each of us is unique, so where I wrote poetry, you may build things, spin yarn, scuba dive. There is no limit to how you can access your inner joy, regardless of how weak or lost your joy may seem to be. Just keep in mind this is not supposed to be a solo adventure or a quest resembling William Shakespeare's "The Taming of the Shrew." So, consider who your confidantes will be, typically it usually consists of five or fewer people who may or may not be related to you. As you all start on your journeys together, yes, your will all learn from each other because you have some common characteristics or purpose: diverse backgrounds, decision-making strengths, and you all have a common goal: getting your sanity and joy back. Pick carefully: do they know what confidentiality means and adhere to keeping silent with any others outside your emotional sanctuary. You do not want anyone amongst you who are fickle, whiny, narcissist, mean, rude, backstabbers, blabbermouths, or the like. There should be some common ground regarding your religious/ spiritual belief if any.

Over time you will find that as your conscious awareness increases, you may be drawn to the spirit world. *The one caution I have to give you is that there are only two types of conscious awareness, one is God's, the God of Abraham, Isaac, and Jacob. Any other consciousness, regardless of how similar it may appear to be, is not the Christian's God. And drifting off and acknowledging any other consciousness than God, in His eyes, is an abomination.* Besides, you deserve the best, and God's accuracy and information, is 100% truthful, correct, and prophetically accurate 100 percent of the time. There are many spiritual pitfalls when one travels in the spirit world, hold tight to the hand of Jesus, read God's Word, and Jesus Christ is your protection. *God is a real, sentient being, and so is His son Jesus Christ, both having the perfected capability to perceive, reason, think, create, and both ARE power.*

I am a Christian, so the examples I use are based on Christianity. Whatever your religious or spiritual affiliation or lack thereof…you will need to search the doctrines and sacred writings of your religion/spirituality if any. Sometime during this developing increasing conscious awareness, many individuals become inquisitive about other religions/spiritual practices. Many other religious, spiritual practices imply they have an abundance of secret knowledge, powers, and or familiar spirits as guides. If you are a Christian, your primary goal is to be welcomed by God (the God of Abraham, Isaac, and Jacob) into His awaiting heaven.

Learning how to accurately discern people, places, and trinkets is one of the distinguishing characteristics of hearing and obeying the Word of God. Pack your "bug out bag," your Bible (for me, big letters), companion research tools, two good pairs of walking shoes, and an internal map to find God. There is none more powerful, accurate, compassionate, and loving than God. However, He does not play. Impostures will never be acceptable, no matter how much they mimic God.

As this book is written, we are still in the midst, in 2021 of the COVID-19 global pandemic, the end result remains to be seen. I have asked you to search your beliefs and the congruency, if any, between the two. Are your actions and behaviors guided by your identified core values? If you are unsure, follow your budget for the past year.

How you spend your money will promptly identify what your core values support. I have been the first to take my own "advice," and it has proved to be helpful in keeping my focus on God's Word and not fear death.

IN THE BEGINNING:

Kaleidoscope

Lonely, apprehensive uncharted course stalked by a fighting phantom. Deluged with transitional options, obsolete half-lives.

Belying the Dream of limitless trust and affection for exhaling self-containment. Disentangling definitions of success and shifting dimensions of vacuous fulfillment.

Senseless, timely, self-destructive competition with joyful feelings. Accelerating the change of Love and Dreams for disciplined celibacy.

Confronting feelings as an unthinkable acceptance of death. Flawed, senseless heroics submitted for Desires and muted self-esteem.

Sex roles and social changes suspended in traditional tears, perhaps incurably diseased. Aggressive retreat exaggerated by repressed needs to be held.

Increased sensual absenteeism and physical impressionistic narcissism. Self-fulfilling isolation and strangulation embrace nostalgia.

Obsession with time and space except when watching the sunset. Liberation necessitates dependence on Dreams, Love, and Time.

Trial and error work out the practicalities and responsibilities of love. Emerging reunion of man and woman building enduring, and evolving strengths.

Lonely, apprehensive, uncharted course stalked by a fighting phantom. Deluged with transitional options, and obsolete half-lives. LcshI © 1/82

Shadow Dancer

Void Black stage, a singular third eye watches a silhouette dancer.
Glowing red eye grained, amplified by a single candlelight.
Gracefully blacks move, lightly bouncing, carefree, supporting amateur dancer.
Hairless shapely figure, carrying an entire soul, portraying an entire life.
Shades of black and gray, bending, leaping, twirling, setting a three/four tempo.
Luminous white fingernails, touching two souls both the same; independently fused.
Gradient light blacks gracefully intertwined with light and air.
Tactile, introspective dancer communicates with space and time as shadows can.
Liquid, brilliant blacks, glide as if years were ice, scuff marks repairable.
Moisture not sweat spender in memories of forgotten potentialities.
Picturesque blacks, quiver dichotomies of life, immorality intricately curvaceous.
Mirrored darkness radiates sedentary tranquility flickers warmly with lights.
Angular grays, stratified, feeling raw, encased by four/eight time.
Learning new steps, changing shoes, souls…divining personalities.
Crescendo cracked Blacks, silhouette dancers merge to one.
Third eye shines identity of liquid outline choreographs capabilities.
Ultimate Black glows, passions and timing reconcile breathing: voluntary.
Soul's essence stratification, hollow lips smile and fade to void Black stage. LCHSI © 1982

The Awakening

Relinquished irregular vile façade: Wandering alone, wandering
   psychologically.
Icon's shattered, idealism challenged: only time, only movement.
It's time for me to stay: to remember, to restore.
Mine eyes see my image; clearly focused, clearly past.
Feelings first time in years; strangely erotic, strangely dead.
When someone goes away, someone has to stay to say Good-bye.
   LCSHI © 3/23/88

Drumming: Time Passes-1

So many things that matter, my face fades. Concentration on each
step, details, details.

> Image within my mind's eye, actually obscured.
> Attracting external presentation internally
> betrayed.

The dance within sets the theme, volume almost off. The bodily
frame minimally maintained awaiting the awakening.

> My thoughts molded by pressures, thoughts of
> love, wanting. Seeking companionship in all the
> wrong places, without.

Compromising until I could get to me, always tomorrow… Time
passes, time passes, time passes…time passed.

> The linking thread through time, the dance; in
> my mind. My body only half-able to perform,
> desires continue.

One day the drumming came, full volume, beautiful music. I responded, my body is dilapidated, my image shocked.

> Time passes and I'm dancing to the music, soul,
> mind and body. Dance slowly, dance with frenzy,
> dance to save my life.

I'm smiling as I dance, my life is being restored. Dance will sustain the battered ego, tattered image, and scared spirit.
Each breath, each pulses blood, fuses civility. Hear the drums: time passes, time passed.

LCSHI © 6/5/88

Drumming: Time Passes-2

So many things that matter, my face fades.
Concentration on each step, details, details.
　　Image within my mind's eye, actually obscured.
　　Attracting external presentations internally betrayed.
The dance within sets the theme, volume almost off.
The bodily frame minimally maintained awaiting the awakening.
　　My thoughts molded by pressures, thought of love, wanting.
　　Seeking companionship in all the wrong places, without.
The linking thread through time, the dance: in my mind.
My body only half-able to perform, desires continue.
　　One day the drumming came, full volume, beautiful music.
　　I responded, my body is dilapidated, my image shocked.
Time passes and I'm dancing to the music, soul, mind and body.
Dance Slowly, dance with frenzy, dance to save my life.
　　I'm smiling as I dance; my life is being restored.
　　Dance will sustain the battered ego, tattered image, and sacred spirit.
Each breath, each pulses blood, fuses civility.
Hear the hums; time passes, time passes, time passed. LCSHI © 6/5/88

Assimilation

Immortality came to me and spontaneously it left.
    Righteousness passed and paused and knowingly it left.
Indignation spent the night and seductively left.
    Time vagrantly ambled close and shamelessly it left.
Dependency applied for occupancy and necessarily it left.
    Foresight whimsically came to play and awkwardly it left.
Ordinariness forged synthetic truths and tentatively it left.
    Commonness etched my path and hauntingly it left.
Mortality came to me and iridescently it stayed. LCSHI © 4/5/82

Awareness Precedes: Enlightenment

Spiritual Awakening

Vision, like my colors are vivid.
The textures and patterns forming.
Grounded in beauty the chaos is comforting. LCSHI © 8/10/01

Touch

Communicates textures,
Radiates Assurance,
Transmits energy,
Confirms being alive. LCSHI © 08/99

Separation

You can exist in the dark, but you don't know it without touching
something or someone else.
    If you touch yourself in the dark, sometimes you startle your-
self. If you touch someone else in the dark, sometimes you find comfort. LCSHI © 2/98

Disentangling Definitions: Phase 1

There are times during a day when I sit and look, thinking about air.
I'd really like to focus on a topic, me: my essence of identification.
> Sometimes, I like cold sensations: tears, kisses,
> smiles, because they are fake. Introspective reality
> lubricates sensations. Sensations operate better
> anesthetized.

Infatuation truly felt, engaged fine linear lines across my face and
nails. Time, a real dimension, carves my heart and calluses my sub-
pitched inner affections.

> Quiet time absorbs…competitive enticements,
> unanswered longing; quiet despair. Seductively
> whispered almost promises, spin potentialities of
> potentials.

Suspended tranquilized passions are the result of touch. I am
untouched. Love is the projection of an image, an anticipated, projected narcissistic smile.

> There are times during a day when I sit and think
> about feelings…mine. I focus on an illusive dep-
> recatory, porous distant lover…and I squint.
> LCSHI © 2001

Disentangling definitions: Phase 2

Memories of textures, desires, impressions and needs merge into salty
sandy jewels. Threads of ambitions: blind, obscurant, mundane pleasures scrutinized into daydreams.

> Past actions, hurts, exuberant experiences abound
> in cotton like half-lives. Retrospection amplifies

reminiscent titillating awkwardness, stimulates memories.

Facades implicating reality in tender sparsely shared moments. Time moves. Self-conceited, seductively whispered almost promises, purposely endearing and illusionary.

Obsolete ecstasy tempered immediate physical responses, amnestic letters. Distant, lustful ramblings gravitate toward a specific point on a lopsided hedge.

There are times during a day when I sit and look, thinking about feelings...yours. I remember distant, porous flowers, given in narcissistic need...and...I sneeze. LCSHI © 7/4/83

Discipline Precedes Dominion: Consciousness opens every door

Distilled rage

True desolation is singular.
Immaculate isolation is a syncopated hum.
Time is one breath.
Despair is one too many deferred dreams.
    Rage is the frustration of yet another heartbeat.
    The dilemma: continue the breath or terminate the beat.
    Suggestion: keep the breath, the beat, and the dreams.
LCSHI © 8/93

Understanding Rage

If: I smile does that invite you to ravage my soul?
If: I share does that license premeditated emotional neglect?
If: I trust does that approve concession and verbal constipation?

If I laugh must my spirit be pillaged?
Does my friendship endorse prematurely ejaculated loyalty?
Must I live yet another year to achieve the anticipatory award?
Rage is the comprehension of social reality.
Comprehension is situational, time sensitive, strained through worn core values.
Rage requires time, effort, strength, and dedication: Laughter floats, is whimsical and sparkles.
Core value's resiliency: contingent on being anchored on The Rock not shifting sand.
LCSHI © 6/2006

Depression

Flattened lungs, impaired vision, mute quadriplegic bystander.
Peers sarcastically challenges bystander to pole vault.
Challenge accepted; trampoline used not pole.
Bystander wins: challenger is depressed. LCSHI © 3/93

Oscillating Heart

Quiet disturbed thoughts tediously accepted and distilled.
Icy fingers dripping mental fragmentations crystalize.
Surreptitious needs embrace elongated passions: indulged.
Shadowed morals adjust elaborate friendships, titillate.
Time ticks and slips, feelings exaggerated, pant.
Shame should be but isn't despair shouldn't but is.

Icy fingers touch: souls fantasize and pictograph.
Laughter whispers morphine, companionship taunts.
Subtle links seduce displaced magnetized slivers.
Evangelized elastic strand ebbs insidious delights.
Time ticks and slips, convenience erodes passions.
Discount would but didn't: independence wasn't but is.
Solitude invades aloneness, time displaces ticks.
Icy fingers probe, undulating fire responds.

Gestating image iconic, stimulating sensibility acclaimed.
Repentance mocks chastisement, serpent attracts serpent.
Fire scorched tongues: dehydrated climax stutters.
Love could be but can't: respect can't and isn't.

Quiet thoughts anesthetized; preferences suspended, devalued.
Romantic experimentation internalized; personal character etched.
Icy fingers fondle solitary chiseled tears.
Sobs internalized lightning: illumination distributes reciprocity.
Desperation isn't pulsating: Love isn't stolen.
Suspended convenience estopped, fidelity's a heartbeat. LCSHI ©
9/28/82

Repudiation

What I need and what I feel one day was set on a wheel.
And each hope, a golden spoke, gingerly melded my wheel.
My self-esteem, a platinum rim, affixed by Life on my wheel.
My dreams, a golden gyroscope undaunted turns my wheel.
    Destiny reappraised…is demanding another wheel.
    LCSHI © 7/7/82

Requiem: The chant

My soul's been twisted. Perverted guidance. Perverted doctrines.
    Original, imperfect translucent images. At home. At home.
Defective, misshapen sounds fail. Like rain. Like Shadows.
    Disturbed distinguished almost friends. Depraved genitals.
Depraved smiles.
Anguish exquisite penetrates chromosomes. Penetrating endow-
ments, Penetrating capacity.
    Belonging exclusively, peeling pervasiveness. Encroaching vital-
ity, Encroaching devastation.
Endosperm extinguished; osmosis killed. Embryo's sorrow. Embryo's
tears.
LCSHI © 3/23/88

Chaos is Transformational

Reflection or Mirage

If I could tell you what I wanted to, I would say:

Every rare once in a while, an interface sparks at, or, during an unanticipated moment. At this irretrievable moment mirrored recognition appears...fleeting.

The importance of the recognition is not in the improbability of the occurrence. The importance of the interface is that recognition is comprehended.

Centuries of explanation go unspoken as miles reflect probing eyes. Essence's isolationism is reprieved as souls, fleeting, touch. Time erodes the resistance of germinating intimacy and mischief.

Miscalculated probabilities are interwoven with intermittent needs. Tensions shared desired within unspoken deferred dreams.

Incomprehensibly, allocated time merges into daydreams and territorial lines. Sizzling recognition of reflected trust amplifies quiet synchronized heartbeats.

Ours is an unqualified refined glimmer of recognition. Space and time dictate propriety and restrained enthusiasm within limited meetings.

Approach the finely spun elasticity of longing gingerly. Anticipate duration but expect digressions. Promises appear transitory and mercurial. Fickle patience is volatile when longing for an occupied reservation.

Every rare once in a while an interface sparks at, or during an unanticipated moment. At this irretrievable moment...

I could tell you that I love you if you were here.
LCSHI © 2001

The File Clerk

Latest style.
    Lady's Night, Smoking!
        Pretty man, new ride, clean.
Slowly, seductively, an image; working, saunters in.
Lazily, religiously, with anticipation hips caress chair.
Deliberately, red shimmering lacquer is applied to fingertips.
Wet, glossy, stick fingers rhythmically type today's correspondence.
Rent's due.
    Child payments late.
        Eagle flew with syncopated despair.
Low, deep continuous back ache; low files.
Practiced pose, exaggerated walk during mail runs.
Lustful recollection of nights punctuates assembly line environment.
Stiletto heels, quinoa dress, office smock endures production.

No man.
    Shiftless lovers rotated.
        Periodic, accidental efforts toward promotions.
Wanton, youthful heart; tired limbs stroll in.
Leisurely exercised hips saturate confidential, familiar chair.
Pureed stamina endures discounted talents, hums tune.
Traditional shrewd subservient babble, plotting dignified progeny.
Exhumed cadence.
    Deferred dreams, astringent.
        New red polish, Ladies Night
        LCSHI © 11/10/92

Affirmation

Never question the irregularity of patterns, diversity of colors or obstacles that have been woven into the tapestry. There is strength and immortality in our collective hands.

All of the ordinary moments selflessly given transcend to extraordinary healing and protective energy. The interconnectedness of expressive touching and endearing moments that "just happened" provide the well-spring of unconditional love.

Love and strength surround, emerge, infuse life's gifts feeding the reservoir of love, trust, and consciousness. Hold the edges of your pain and bridge the trials of recovery, for as long as it takes. Never quit. Don't give up five minutes before the miracle.
LCSHI © 02/98

The Crystal

Pretend you are an object made of crystal and silver. Crystals (along with precious gems) reflect outer light as well as generate their own Inner Light. Silver is a precious metal that has lasting inner strength and outer beauty. Fill this object half with water, so that the remaining half is filled with air. You are now a vessel that contains all the necessary elements for life: that is lifeless.

Let this personification serve as a silent reminder for you to cherish your life and your Inner Light. Life is judiciously given and being quite fragile can be to easily taken. None but you radiate your elements and essence. You contain all the elements for life and have life. You are totally unique to the universe never to be duplicated or replaced.

As you journey on the dreams of your choices, remember that you are a crystal, and your heart has a silver core. You will always manifest your truth, do no harm, resonate in Consciousness.
LCSHI © 7/12/82

Balance the "I" Within Me

The Craving

Each morning as I awaken… I'm hungry:
    Confirmation of being alive.
During the day, as time passes… I'm hungry:
    Confirmation of being sensuous.
Denied recognition, reflections… I'm hungry.
    Confirmation of being hedonistic.
Deferred liquor, narcotics/hallucinogens, lusts… I'm hungry.
    Confirmation of being hedonistic.
Each night I anticipate morning… I'm hungry.
    Confirmation of being hedonistic.
Choices, decisions, definitions… I'm hungry:
    Confirmation of being aware.
Replenish cells, survive… I'm hungry.
    Confirmation of being
    LCSHI © 2/24/92

What If

Sometimes the most expressive, touching, and lasting "talks" just happen. You know not a conversation by appointment, but a "commune" by opportune moment. Like, in the course of baking bread, or reading together, or sewing, or dancing or working on the car—or—you know…some other extraordinarily "ordinary" occasion. Being is about the marvelous adventure in the never ending "what ifs."

Each tear is a treasure of your soul visiting your external senses. Never waste a tear. What if you ran out of water, would your perceptions, your consciousness dry up?

Each heartbeat, a rhythm to joy or sorrow, is a meter to the frailties and determinations of the human spirit. Never fail to listen to the beat of your heart! What if the rhythms went away, would your sentient nature dissipate?

Each moment is a testament to adventure, occupying space and consuming time. Never stop moving! What if explorations of your life, productivity, accountability, competency, accessibility and authenticity never progressed, would your stagnation render you sterile?

Each friend is a golden thread and is spun with endurance and appointment a position on the loom of your life. Never question the irregularity of patterns, diversity of colors or impregnability that you are inextricably interwoven into the tapestry of the lives of others. What if there were no "others," would you comprehend the meaning of your tears? LCSHI © 2/18/92

True Friends

> Are rare
> In Good times
> Through Bad Times
> Are guardian angels witnessing, manifesting Grace?
> LCSHI ©10/28/2000

Fanciful Working Classes

Sharp, transparent icicles frailly drip spontaneity and corporate laws. Quenching spirits, extinguishing fears, reflecting light.

Shimmering stainless steel spider webs, span time and bridge trends. Whispering consumption, taunting fanaticism, demanding fidelity.

Iridescent ants inhabit domestic hovels and sanction profits. Sharing goals, recording insight, storing idols.

Stained-glass dragonfly wings vibrate repetition and competition. Exposing morals, terminating characters, breeds professionals.

Retarded, incandescent amoebas fuse lives and absorb animation. Tapping barbarism, ambushing ambition, fondling corpses.

Bold black ink announces peace treaties and passe capitalization. Dying crops, evacuated careers, icicles form.
LCSHI © 10/18/82

Chromosomes: Transmitters of the Call

Bliss, the rapturous nucleus of each chromosome. Individually linked, energetically transmitting The Call, one's reason for life.

Image, the self-reflected paradigm, each physical nuance reflects the heart's answer to The Call. The separation of Grace from nature and fulfillment manifests ritualistic mores.

The triumph of libido, the impulse to life, opens the heart to one's Calling purely resonating harmonic echoes. The vitality of spirit moving according to the Call pulses rhythmically when unobstructed.

Nirvana, the "at oneness with the Call," evokes compassion for self, laughter, disregards timelines, and defines acceptance.

Image is self-definition, form the result of chromosome function. Each heartbeat anticipates Bliss, voice is energy, energy creates form.
LCSHI © 12/02/01

Girlfriends: Say Touchstone

Having history together, and still liking each other, now that's a girlfriend.
Cradling one another's dreams, when the dreamer is too exhausted to rock them, now that's a girlfriend.

Say girlfriend…yes, you touchstone, this anthem celebrates you. When I could not see…you were my eyes.

When I could not hear…you were my ears.
When I could not feel…you were my textures.
When I could not stand…you are my crutch.
When I could not think…you were my compass.
When I could not hope…you whispered, keep breathing.

Having long chats 'bout nothin', and loving the connection, now that's a girlfriend. Laughing together so hard your sides hurt, and you can't remember what started the laughter, now that's a girlfriend. LCSHI © 12/08/01

Chocolate and Parallel Universes

The lights are low, it's very, very quiet. Listening to the sounds of silence brings back memories I'd love to have:

There are times it occurs to me that each moment of every day we coexist with unlimited parallel universes. I'm here reaching out to you. You're there, only because I think you are, doing who knows what…as I reach out to you. All over this world people are eating, sleeping, living, and dying, in all types of conditions and economic strata. Sometimes this concept is almost too expansive to really "get," but it's important. Somehow it makes the phrase "*live in the moment*" the only phrase that really makes sense.

If each of us really have a hundred percent possibilities available to us one hundred percent of the time *until we decide*…then each decision is a turning point. And if there is no such thing as chance then each decision while made by free will only alters the circumstance and perhaps the timing we arrive at our destiny. If in fact destiny is preordained, then living in the moment must be the only important event in our lives since each decision counts, both limiting and expanding our life options.

I've been wondering about the importance of paranormal/psychic awareness. Silence is profound and very, very noisy. The stillness of one's breath, my breath is quite harsh in my ears. And then I become very aware that I'm observing myself watch my breath. Now this is kinda scary because it seems as though there are several ME's all of which have a common communication… otherwise how could I watch the watcher that's watching me? Some have called this our consciousness, as though this is the keeper of the moral "good" and "bad". Moral values are critical, perhaps that's why in these days cynics go to so much trouble trying to patronize the mundane and tout the nonjudgmental as being some sort of compassionate cesspool. I think the "paranormal" is in fact who we actually are, we've somehow… perhaps through centuries of education and socialization…lost contact with who we are.

How else do we explain how lovers just "know" who, where, and how their "other half" is? Time and distance ride the connection of love, and love is the bond, the electric current of consciousness. Now chocolate is a gift from God. It has all the essential elements necessary to provide comfort, sensuality, and release. It can be devoured in a gluttonous fashion; licked lazily and seductively with every tantalizing morsel savored; ignored out of fear that it's addictive and sinful or because the anticipated pleasure will produce passion so great the repercussions are animalistic.

So, the paranormal is chocolate, dripping with sensuality when hot, brittle when cold, wasted when ignored. The scent the warm, sweet, infusive earthy aroma of chocolate is the doorway to awareness. Taste and scent of chocolate are to our nerve endings what extraordinarily perception is to our comprehension of sights, sounds, and textures.

So, I'm sitting here, in the early morning silence, slowly licking a dark chocolate rum and cherry cordial. Savoring the melting chocolate as it runs down my fingers, rolling the thick milk chocolate on my tongue and deeply inhaling the velvet scent.

Wish you were here, and I'd feed you one.
LCSHI © 2/22/02

You've Got to Know How Much You're Worth

Am I worth the time of day, a desperate, gasping breath? Perhaps a lingering glance: exposed, appraised, flayed?

Pride and joy, stand up, dance. Mirrors, mirrors reflect and sparkle. Hiding the hinges, the whole, the value.

Is one breath more important than another? If so, which is most valuable, the constricted one of course. No promises each one a singular surprise.

Water will seek its own level, that's its nature. Inequality is a disservice, a minor key reverberating off each mirror.

If water knows its worth and naturally seeks its own level can I expect less from myself?
LCSHI © 2/23/02

CHAPTER 8

· ·

God: All Things Were Made By Him

> In the beginning was the Word, and the Word
> was with God, and the Word was God. The same
> was in the beginning with God. All things were
> made by him; and without him was not any thing
> made that was made. In him was life; and the life
> was the light of men. And the light shineth in
> darkness; and the darkness comprehended it not.
>
> John 1:1–5

Creating joy, happiness, peace, and having an optimistic outlook, especially in time of crisis, pain, deprivation, and despondency: may seem a ludicrous mockery. Depending on your level of energy, hopelessness, and apathy, please suppress your desire to destroy this book. It has taken me years to develop my conscious awareness, and I am still a work in process. I will always be a work in progress. When I was a little kid I once announced I was going to read every book in the world. Well we both know that cannot happen because daily, somewhere in the world there are several books being released most probably every hour. So believe me, I still have much to learn. *It is hard work to get over anger, betrayal, rejection, assortments of traumas, and many other circumstances of life. All of which we were attempting to cope with before the COVID-19 pandemic. The fact that any of us have mentally and physically survived is a testament to God's miraculous design of the human body and spirit.*

The traditional "rule of thumb" is that it takes twenty days for a habit to form. But with today's technology, I decided to see if I could find how long forming a habit will actually take. According to <u>How Long Does It Really Take to Form a Habit? 7 Things to Consider (healthline.com)</u>, "It can take anywhere from 18 to 254 days for a person to form a new habit and an average of 66 days for a new behavior to become automatic." And that is making the behavior modification every day during those 18 to 254 days. So, the pep talk for your developing conscious awareness is, cut yourself some slack if you find "this establishing a habit thing" a bit annoying. Just start over again (and again, and again…).

I strongly suggest you start with something simple. For instance, every morning, when you wake up, look at yourself in the mirror and say, I will take five deep breaths four times today. This you can do anywhere, you do not have to explain breathing, and by the fourth time, your nerves and apathetic attitude will be thankful you remembered to take deep breaths a couple of times. Many of us forget to breathe, which of course, over time does not do too much for your overall health. Another consideration, if you happen to like to watch and or listen to comedy shows, laughter is a great way to space out reality, get some deep breaths, and perhaps even share the fun with a family member or friend. These, of course, are just examples. We are all unique, so whatever small, no stress moment you choose to give yourself, find what works for you.

Affirmations, your own or one written by someone else can be tricky. Most of them actually state "I will," others imply "I will." Most affirmations state explicitly or implicitly "I want, or I need". At some point, it will occur to you that saying, "you want/will," may be assisting in your procrastination. *So ask yourself when will I move on?* There is no time limit for this, however growth is highly suggested. At some point hold yourself accountable for some evidence of your spiritual development. *Be sure and ask Jesus to assist you along this change plan.* The hardest part most probably will be trying to decide what you "will do," "want," and/or "need." Following is the progression I went through as my mental "selfie" clarified, got color, and had emotional support with picturesque natural backgrounds. For me, over time, I went through the following four progressive verbalized affirmations.

1. I will... I want... I need etc.
2. I am... I have... I appreciate etc.
3. I am thankful for... I have gratitude that... I share...
4. I am fortunate that... I am happy that... I am exceedingly blessed...

You can, of course, write as many affirmations on as many topics as you wish. Or, you can put more than one goal as your topic: your one goal "is" your affirmation. However, for your first affirmation, I suggest you start with one goal/want/ or need. The most important part of affirmations is that you separate out what is a "want" and what is a "need." For instance, if you decide you want to read the Bible, then I suggest you say something simple like: I will read one scripture four times today. Why just one scripture? Because some days, the last thing you will want to do is anything you have mentioned in your first affirmation. And saying you are going to read a chapter a day will be overwhelming. Say one verse...if you read more excellent. But your affirmation is your personal contract with yourself. Why write a contract that seems overwhelming to begin with? If you do, you are contracting for failure!

My first affirmation presented as an example.

My first affirmation took quite a bit of work for me to say exactly what I wanted. I discovered that the areas that I needed to do the most work were the hardest to write. I found out if you pay attention to your body as you write, you will learn quite a bit about yourself. I know I did. Dust off some of those dreams you once had and put some light on it. Then accomplish these long-overlooked dreams one by one. Here is a hint, when I went into the Peace Corps, my roommate during our introductory period was 75 years young. One of my paternal Great Aunts always wanted to go to college. So, at age 72 she enrolled at Youngstown University and graduated at age 76. When I last visited and spoke with her she was 105 years old. She was very proud she had her B.A. for 29 years. She died at 106, so she accomplished having her degree for 30 years.

Affirmation: The Healing

I deserve the best life has to offer.
I bend with adversity and survive.
I am shrewd and compassionate.
I emanate peace, love, and happiness.
I receive what I eminent.
I am entitled the luxurious survival of:
    My health,
    My spirit,
    My emotions,
    My finances.
I achieve success and affirm my right to excel.
I am loved, cherished, and respected by my mate.
I accept that my body is sacred, shapely, and sexy.
I respect myself and honestly love me unconditionally.
i go with God.
LCSHI © 3/3/1992

MY FINAL AFFIRMATION OF HEALING.

After several years I finally was able to write and achieve the following Affirmation. It may not take you several years to work with Jesus and develop your spirit to recognize that I (you) have been created in God's image. When you understand what it means to be covered by the blood of Jesus, and you have repented for your sins, the clarity, love, and blessings from God are phenomenal. I am far from perfect, but each day I learn more, love more, and praise God more.

As it turned out, my "affirmation" became a prayer. In retrospect, my prayer was way more "powerful" than an affirmation. At the time, I had no clue, but God knew.

> My Prayer: This Day:
> Today…may be my last, may it count.
> Today… God, please protect and guide me.
> Today… God, please protect my property; real and personal.
> Today… I appreciate:
>> Being alive…to laugh,
>> Being aware…to know,
>> Being hedonistic…to feel,
>> Being voluptuous…to love,
>> Being sensuous…to allure,
>> Being strong…to survive,
>> Being mortal…to be me,
> Today… I am shrewd and compassionate.
> Today… I radiate harmony.
> Today… I attract harmony.
> Today… I learn.
> Today… This day i go with God.
>> LCSHI© 4/9/92

WHAT SHOULD I LOOK FOR IN A NEW CHURCH HOME?

When looking for a church home, the task can be daunting, especially if you have no Christian denomination preference, it can be overwhelming. There is no "consumer guide" for finding a church. So you either rely on friends, family, our play hit and miss. If you are snagged by the various door-to-door missionaries in just about every city, you may be become affiliated because of the "love bombing" that occurs during the courtship. Pretend you are going to buy a car, and you, of course, know that the majority of car sales representatives work on commission. So you listen, take notes, but never commit to anything other than you will consider what they have had to say. You will contact them if and when you are interested in learning more.

However, in this day and age, the internet is a wonderful resource, use it as if your life depended on what you find out; because your life most certainly does. Dig for the religious denomination's "hidden tenets" that are not normally discussed in the recruitment phase. Look at the pros and cons you have accumulated. Then after that:

- Make sure you make an appointment to discuss these findings with the head/senior minister.
- *Ask the minister how he defines God.*
- *Ask if the minister believes in God.*
- *Ask if the minister believes that Jesus Christ is God's only begotten Son. And ask the minister if he believes that Jesus is both man and God. If he does not believe Jesus is both Son and God, then what exactly is Jesus?*
- What Bible is the Church's preference/suggestion if one were going to purchase a Bible to follow along during the sermons? Some of you may already have a Bible preference when searching for a new/different Church home. If your Bible's differ, then ask what is exactly the difference between these Bibles. There are many internet links that discuss the differences in the assortment of the Bibles. Here is a starter link for you to get a baseline and then compare and contrast other information to determine which bible you want. Pastor Mike Hoggard's (posted Dec. 27, 2020). The Difference: The King James Bible vs. Modern Translations. https://youtu.be/ZmFmzyPq3Lk
- Does the senior minister's ordained staff believe in God?.
- Does the senior minister and the Church's denomination believe in hell? If not, why not?
- Exactly how is one "saved/forgiven" from their sins?
- Who forgives us for our sins, and what "task/payment" do we contribute to be absolved?
- Are there any other books, teachings, video's and so forth that are used on a regular basis as a companion to the Bible?

If so, what are they? Which document has the final spiritual Word between these documents?

- What is the woman's role in the Church?
- What Church official offices can LGBTQIA+ hold? (FYI, see following)
  - The Q= identify as queer or questioning sexual identity.
  - The I = intersex individuals.
  - The A = asexual or "aromantic (used instead of not romantic)."
  - The + represents inclusion of spectrums of sexuality and gender.

Of course, you may have other questions of importance, be sure and ask them. For instance, some people believe in speaking in tongues. Other individuals want to know, how long or short, is the primary Service? Is Sunday recognized as the Sabbath day, if not Sunday, then what day do you recognize as the Sabbath?

If you interview more than one potential Christian Church home, you may be surprised at the different answers you may get. *Do not let them be vague, they need to be quite specific. Your eternal home will be compromised by an apostate minister. You want to find out now, not when you've "missed the rapture, and/or awaken from your sleep," and find your reservations have been confirmed in hell. (Hint, if your minister does not believe in "hell," this is a red flag.)* For Christians, our God is unique, the Alpha and Omega:

So shalt thou find favor and good understanding in the sight of God and man. Trust in the Lord with all thine heart; and lean not unto thine own understanding. In all thy ways acknowledge him and he shall direct thy paths. Be not wise in thine own eyes: fear the LORD and depart from evil. It shall be health to thy navel, and marrow to thy bones.

Proverbs 3:4–8

As Christians, we know that all glory is given to God in the name of Jesus Christ. Our existence is because of God, and we are saved by our faith, not our works. Jesus Christ is our intercessor, teacher, mentor, and shepherd. Our compassion and our love given open-handed has been modeled by Jesus, and we do so in the name of Jesus Christ.

> Through thy precepts I get understanding: therefore I have every false way. Thy word is a lamp unto my feet, and a light unto my path. I have sworn, and I will perform it, that I will keep thy righteous judgments. I am afflicted very much: quicken me, O LORD, according unto thy word. Accept, I beseech thee, the freewill offerings of my mouth, O LORD, and teach me thy judgments. My soul is continually in my hand: yet do I not forget thy law. The wicked have laid a snare for me: yet I erred not from thy precepts. Thy testimonies have I taken as an heritage for ever: for they are the rejoicing of my heart. I have inclined mine heart to perform thy statutes alway, even unto the end. (SAMECH).[98] I hate vain thoughts: but thy law do I love. Thou art my hiding place and my shield: I hope in thy word. Depart from me, ye evildoers: for I will keep the commandments of my God. Uphold me according unto thy word, that I may live: and let me not be ashamed of my hope. Hold thou me up, and I shall be safe: and I will have respect unto thy statutes continually.
>
> Psalms 119:104–117

This attribute of faith is important because during times of escalating chaos and excessive stress, depression and multiple outrageous simultaneous demands: there is often an overwhelming tendency for the darkness of depression to crush the life out of us, both literally and physically. Over time, several scriptures have been a comfort and source of strength for me during some of my darkest, chaotic, and spirit-numbing situations. I hope one or more of these scriptures may one day be of comfort to you if, in fact, you have not already relied on them, see the following Table 4: Selected scriptures that bring comfort and security.

Table 4: Selected scriptures that bring comfort and security.
Note: These selected scriptures are favorites of mine, bringing security, guidance, and joy. *These are presented purely as an example* to show how I typically and purposefully apply these scriptures to my personal attitude and behaviors.

Citation		KJV Content	Notes	Suggested Practical Application
Genesis	1:4	And God saw the light, that {it was} good; and God divided the light from the darkness.	God deliberately separated light from darkness. There is to be no confusion, no comingling.	There are many reasons a person refuses to or procrastinates deciding. Indecisiveness is a decision. One has to make a conscious decision to seek clarity and fairness. Relying on God's word means I will not evade or avoid God's stated expectations understanding my obedience is expected. Being human, unfortunately, I do not always immediately

				achieve this goal for a particular situation, but with practice over time, I do.
1 John	1:5	This then is the message which we have heard of him, and declare unto you, that God is light, and in him is no darkness at all.	Our behavior is a 24/7 witness to all others.	In my daily interactions, I strive to be authentic, without guile, compassionate, and attentive. I am aware that my actions speak louder than my words. I continue to strive for consistency.
John	1:5	And the light shineth in darkness; and the darkness comprehended it not.	Jesus Christ's light is our beacon (guidance), strength, protection.	Remember that an individual who has a core difference from you will not honor, appreciate, or understand you.
Psalm	119:105	Thy word is a lamp unto my feet, and a light unto my path.	"When we live in God's light, we have spiritual fellowship with him." Living in God's light is a VERB—we must act! Aggressively read the Bible and apply his word to our life.	Learning to walk in God's light, especially during tumultuous times, is often fraught with danger and/or distractions; and often a lonely path. Many temptations occur, depression and doubt can slip into lethargy and apathy. Staying on the path in God's light is the only path to salvation and truth. God's Word is my spiritual GPS.

Deuteronomy	27:16	Cursed {be} he that setteth light by his father or his mother. And all the people shall say, Amen.	God alone is our guidance, gyroscope, and salvation.	Our family and close friends are mortal. So, I have to be mindful to never confuse respecting a mortal's opinion or values…if the contradict God's Word. God provides the only path to salvation.
Ezekiel	28:17	Thine heart was lifted up because of thy beauty, thou hast corrupted they wisdom by reason of thy brightness: I will cast thee to the ground, I will lay thee before kings, that they may behold thee.	God admonishes there are repercussions for wrong choices. (All glory and adoration must be given to God.)	I often have to do a "reality check," to make sure pride, ambitions, wealth, and public acknowledgement do not entice me to make wrong choices. I have to remember that disregarding God's Word is the first step into backsliding. Continuous determined disregard of God's Word will cause my heart to harden, and thus, over time, redemption may be inaccessible.
1 John	1:7	But if we walk in the light, as he is in the light, we have fellowship one with another, and the blood of Jesus Christ his Son, cleanesth us from all sin.	If we choose God, his covenant to us is fulfilled.	Mortal man will never be perfect. God does not expect perfection. He expects consistent communication with Him and my active listening to His Word. and my obedience.

1 Thessalonians	5:9	For God hath not appointed us to wrath, but to obtain salvation by our Lord Jesus Christ.	God's promise of eternal life.	Jesus Christ shed His blood as a sacrifice for atonement for our sins. I need to keep reminding myself that as an individual I am loved; and through my faith not works, my salvation is assured.

CHAPTER 9

· ·

Personal Workbook

In that day shall this song be sung in the land of Judah; We have a strong city; salvation will God appoint for walls and bulwarks. Open ye the gates, that the righteous nation which keepeth the truth may enter in. Thou wilt keep him in perfect peace, whose mind is stayed on thee: because he trusteth in thee. Trust ye in the LORD for ever: for in the LORD JEHOVAH is everlasting strength.

Isaiah 26:1–4

Every change we make occurs, if and only if we relate to it and see some benefits. Our best motivation to change occurs when we see that what we want: invasion, strive for, will best be accomplished when we do something different than we have been doing.

This final chapter contains several questions that you are encouraged to consider and answer. There will be some space provided for you to answer in this book. However, you may choose to write your thoughts someplace other than in this book to preserve your privacy. Over time you may choose to add or change your initial thoughts. The following link http://www.Facebook.com/profile. php?id=100000603619065 is to my Facebook page, Leadership Voices™, for those who wish to discuss their thoughts with others regarding this book. The exercises encourage you to explore your personal thoughts, opinions, and behaviors regarding change, so dive in and consider the following two initial questions.

- Personally, what is your relationship between the inevitability of change and your level of fear and/or resistance to change? Remember, it has been said, "If you don't like something, it will change. If you do like something, it will change. Life and time always change."

  _____

  _____

  _____

  _____

- List your core values (you are encouraged to have no more than three). If you have more than three you want to list, go ahead, You will then, over time, combine, reduce, or find you have something else that really stands out as how you "prioritize" what you do and why you do it. If you do not have a clue, you have really never considered this before, do not worry, just write something, anything down. This chapter will help you define what your core values are.

  1) _____
  2) _____
  3) _____
  4) _____
  5) _____
  6) _____
  7) _____

- Do your core values allow or hinder you from recognizing that changes are constantly occurring? If you have had a hard time figuring out your core values, do you often have a hard time making up your mind about what to do? Do you often allow others to influence or decide for you what you want to do or resist? Explain.

_____

_____

_____

_____

- The degree to which we adapt to change depends on how flexible, innovative, and determined you are to adapting (regardless of your liking the circumstances). Do you find this to be a statement about you? Explain.

_____

_____

_____

_____

- When was the last time you had to adapt to changes that were out of your control? How did you do? What was it and how did you adjust? Explain.

_____

_____

_____

_____

The following exercises are intended to encourage you to explore your personal thoughts, opinions, and behaviors. How many core values did you identify, if any. Remember, as you may add to or delete what you have originally identified as a core value. Why, because you may determine that some of the items you identified were strong but secondary beliefs. *Remember, a core value is something you are willing to die for.* The Coronavirus Pandemic is a situation requiring behavior in response that has not been previously necessary. Situations change, but not necessarily your core values. Were you living during the COVID-19 global pandemic? If so, what was your experience? Were you personally impacted in some way during this pandemic? If not, have you heard stories from family and/or friends that were impacted? How do their stories affect you, if at all?

Remember a core value may be religious, spiritual, ethical, economical, and so forth. *Your core values are who and what you are.* Review your core values and determine which core values have been challenged, if any? Explain.

_____

_____

_____

_____

Has this pervasive, exhausting, isolating, viral pandemic altered in any way your beliefs as well as your behaviors?

_____

_____

_____

_____

Here is a hint, if you are still having difficulty determining what a core value might be, look at how and on what you prioritize spending your money. That is a good start, especially during limited funds, what you value becomes abundantly clear and determines your priorities and often your ability to stay alive?

How do you prioritize your skimpy funds?

- <u>FAMILY:</u> Self, immediate family, extended family, and so forth. What do you choose? Explain.

_____

_____

_____

_____

- DEVOTION CONVICTION: Self-reliant, religion, spirituality, occult practices, agnostic, atheist? What do you choose? Explain.

_____

_____

_____

_____

- FISCAL RESPONSIBILITY: Self-reliant, providence, indulgence, chance, do you gamble? What do you choose?

_____

_____

_____

_____

- SOMETHING ELSE: Please describe

_____

_____

_____

_____

THIS WORKBOOK IS PRESENTED FOR YOUR BENEFIT.

Each of the following questions are crafted to encourage you to think about yourself, your dreams, your achievements, and lessons learned from failures. *This means you do not have to answer any question or answer questions in order.* You can take as much time as you want. And you may change, add to, or delete any comments or thoughts. You can write your answers in any form you can understand and relate to. So, you can "explain" your answers as; a painting, drawing, compose music, build something, or in any other way that expresses who you are and how you comprehension change, feel about any required change, and reason through things, which determines your behavior. This time is for you. If you choose to share this information with anyone, it is entirely up to you. Once again, this questionnaire is strictly voluntary.

Personal Background Baseline

These questions establish your uniqueness based on your familial upbringing, community associations, and ethical and moral influences in your youth.

1. How do you choose to declare your gender:
    NOTE: It is understood that an individual's gender and body go beyond one's reproductive functions. This question is strictly asking about your declared gender, *not interested in your sexual proclivity*. This question is being asked exclusively to see if there is a trend developing amongst those who choose to answer some or all of this questionnaire. We in the U.S. have faced, since 2020, unprecedented changes, hardships, and disorientation in the U.S. resulting from the COVID-19 global pandemic. If you have any concerns, there will be a space that will state "none of your business," should you choose to select this option.

    At this time, of course, if you choose to answer these questions personally, then there is no need to concern for your privacy. You will have full control of whether or not you respond to these questions in the space provided in this book or in some other format.

    However, in close proximity to this book being published, there will be some individuals who will wish to share their answers, with others and a website will be available to accommodate those that choose to do so. Check the Leadership Voices™ Facebook web page for updates.

    Everyone who in the future chooses to answer the questionnaire online can be assured their privacy will be maintained. Each individual filling out the form online will format a unique ID code so that there will be no way to individualize any responder to any particular answered questionnaire. *If, after this web site is activated,* you have further questions or concerns, please contact me at lead-voices@aol.com

a. Female _____
b. Fluid _____
c. Hermaphroditism ___
d. Male _____
e. Non-binary transgender _____
f. Transgender Man _____
g. Transgender Woman _____
h. Currently undecided _____
i. Other designation _____
j. Not your business _____

2. In what country were you born? _____
   a. Did you live in the U.S. between the ages of 1–10 years old? Yes____ No____

3. Where were you living in January/February 2020? _____
   a. Did you travel (in the U.S. or internationally)? _____
   b. If you traveled internationally did you have problems getting back to the U.S? Please explain.

   _____

4. Were you in another country, were you able to get home easily, or was it a hassle? Explain.

   _____

5. In what state (province, region, etc.) did you live in January 2020?
   a. If in U.S. what is your zip code? _____

b. If home is a country other than the U.S., what country?

_____

6. Do you live in a:
    a. City_____
    b. Small town _____
    c. Rural area_____

7. What is your level of education:
    a. Completed some or all of primary school _____
    b. Completed 8th grade _____
    c. Completed 10th grade _____
    d. Completed 11th grade _____
    e. Completed 12th grade or GED _____
    f. Attended Vocational School or Community College

       ____

    g. Completed Vocational School or Community College

       ____

    h. Achieved Batchelor's Degree _____
    i. Achieved more than one Batchelor's Degree (How many) ____
    j. Achieved Master's Degree _____
    k. Achieved more than one Master's Degree (How many)

       ____

    l. Achieved Doctoral, MD, J.D. DDS, or other _____
    m. Achieved more than one Doctoral, MD, J.D. DDS or other ____
    n. Other type of accredited education not earned in U.S.?

       _____

Please explain:

_____

8. Do you own a business, contract out your work, or do free-lance work? Yes _____ No _____ Still looking, not sure what to do _____

   a. If Yes, do you work full or part-time? _____

   b. Do you work more than one job, if so how many? _____

   c. Has your business/employment been adversely impacted by the 2020–2021 COVID-19 pandemic in the U.S.? Please explain:

   _____

   d. Have you been able to obtain other work if business closed or you were laid off? If yes, in the same or similar job? Please explain:

   _____

   e. Have you been able to get another, totally different job? Please explain:

   _____

   f. Have you started your own business (one or more)? Please explain:

   _____

9. Do you feel your religious/spiritual tenets held at bay "serious fear and/or major depressions? Yes _____ No _____ "Please explain:

   _____

10. Do you feel your religious/spiritual place of worship/congregation was supportive of you during this time of distress and uncertainty?

    Yes _____ No _____ Please explain.

    _____

11. Do you have a child/children? (What ages, living at home?)

    Yes_____ No _____ How many?_____

12. If you have a child/children, did this place an additional burden, in any way, on how you coped with the required changes needed to educate, feed, and clothe your children. Explain.

    _____

13. Do parents or other relatives live with you? Yes _____ No _____

    a. Did they live with you prior to January 2020?

        Yes _____ No _____

    b. Are any individuals living with you physically in January 2020, if so were any of your household mentally and/or physically fragile?

        Yes _____ No _____

14. During the year 2020. have you had to provide Hospice care, and/or have a death of a significant family member or close friend due to the COVID-19 virus. If Yes _____ (Please accept our condolences.) No _____

15. Do you have to home school children? Yes _____ No
_____

   a.   If so do you also work from home? Yes _____ No _____

   b.   If yes, does your homeschooling compete with your
        work time? Yes _____ No _____

   c.   Do you feel competent to immediately "home school"
        your child/children? Yes _____ No_____

   d.   Did homeschooling for your children become better
        once schools closed and online classes became avail-
        able? Yes ___ No ___

   e.   If your employer relocated your work to home, did
        they cover the cost of work-related expenses? Yes _____
        No _____

   f.   If you work for your employer from home, do you put
        in more hours because you are working from home?
        Yes ___ No _____

   g.   If you work from home, do you have access to your
        supervisor and co-workers for work-related business
        interactions? Yes __No __

   h.   Did you have to start your own home internet busi-
        ness? Yes _____ No _____

   i.   What is your home life like with everyone's home
        under quarantine? Please explain.

   _____

16. Are you the only wage earner in your household? If not, are all wage earners currently working? What is this like financially for you? Do you support or monetarily help out family members, sharing a combined household? Explain.

_____

17. Describe how you feel after a year's social distancing, closed businesses, and restricted travel. (Example: feel isolated, miss hugs, other expressions of love and care? Resentment, overwhelmed, etc.) Please Explain.

_____

18. Describe your work, family, social, community activities in which you participated in 2019–2020. Has technology helped you maintain these relationships through 2020–2021? Yes _____ No _____ Please explain.

_____

Personal familiarity with The Bible: its
relevance, daily influences, if any?

19. Do you own a Christian Bible? Yes _____ No _____

20. If you have more than one version, which version do you primarily use?

_____

21. Prior to reading this book, have you ever thought of your relationship to God in terms of a contract (covenant)? Yes _____ No _____ Please Explain.

_____

22. Now that you know/are considering that your relationship with God is on a voluntary contractual basis, does this provide you with more or less peace and assurance that God's promises will never change?

   More _____ Less _____ Not sure _____ Please Explain?

_____

23. Does the inclusion of Jesus Christ as a contracted mediator for you make you think differently about your relationship to Jesus? Yes _____ No _____

   a.   How do you feel about this? Please explain.

_____

24. Do you primarily associate with others who "are under contract" with God and His Son Jesus? Yes _____ No _____

   a.   If not, why not? Please explain.

_____

25. If you have children or in a position to significantly influence children, do your behaviors serve as a role model to these minors? Yes _____ No _____

   Unsure _____

26. In your business relationships, either personal or work-related, do your behaviors innocuously but powerfully establish you are a "child of God"? Yes _____ No _____ Unsure _____

27. Do you have one or more occurrences in your life that you are absolutely certain that something spiritual/angelic/ Jesus/God has intervened, and the intervention significantly saved/changed/made you consciously aware God is real? Yes ___ No___ Just coincidence _____

CORE VALUES ARE TESTED DURING TUMULTUOUS OR CHAOTIC TIMES.

1. Have you ever felt that God betrayed, failed to answer, or does not exist? Explain?

   _____

2. Do you think your core value(s) allow or hinder you, making all the adjustments and changes required during 2020? If so, how? Explain?

   _____

3. Was there a time you had to adapt to changes that were out of your control? If so, did you intentionally consider your core value(s) to deal with the situation? Yes _____ No _____ Never occurred to me _____ Please explain.

   _____

4. What "triggers" stress for you? Please explain.

   _____

5. Are you progressively more irritated as a stressful situation continues? Yes _____ No _____ I never stress out ____ Please explain.

_____

   a. Do you have a primary way to destress? Yes _____ No _____

6. Do you recognize when you are: Circle all that apply, please.
   a. envious,
   b. jealous,
   c. manipulative,
   d. overwhelmed,
   e. vindictive.
   f. Other?

Do your relatives and close friends have
the same or similar core values?

1. "Best friend(s) and I have discussed at times our values, visions, and concerns?

   Yes_____ No _____

2. My family and I have similar core values? Yes_____ No _____

3. Friction in our familial relationship because of different core values? Yes ___No ____

4. Do any of your close relationships have behaviors that are manipulative, devious, scheming, deceitful, or self-centered? Yes _____ No _____

5. These frictions are caused because of your different core values. Yes _____ No _____

6. Do you associate frequently with individuals who are not encouraging you in your walk with God? Yes _____ No _____

    a. If yes, why do you continue to remain affiliated with these individuals? Please DO NOT WRITE THIS ANSWER…just think about this.
    b. Have you considered counseling? Yes ___ No ___

Can you now answer the first three questions presented in this book?

7. Can you now precisely list your core values?

    a. _____

    b. _____

    c. _____

8. Do you now realize/considering…that God's Word, His voice, creates form,

    Yes _____ No _____ Not sure still thinking about this. _____

9. Do you now deliberately incorporate your core values when making decisions?

    Yes _____ No _____ Sometimes when I remember _____

Is there a difference in your core beliefs
and your behaviors, decisions?

1. Is there a noticeable gap between what you say your core values are compared to?
   a. The way you: conduct business? Yes _____ No _____

   b. Do you treat people who you consider "unworthy," unfit, or reprehensible differently? Yes _____ No _____

   c. Do you consider yourself to be undeserving, worthless, pitiful, or ugly?

      1. Yes _____ No _____

   d. Have you ever considered seeking professional counseling regarding any of the previous questions in the affirmative? Yes ___ No_____

2. In your opinion, do you display a gap in any area between what you say, think, your core values are and what your behavior displays? Yes _____ No _____
   a. If so, does this gap bother you? Yes _____ No _____

Has this book been interesting and helpful
to you? Yes _____ No _____

1. What was the most interesting part of this book?

   _____

2. What was the most helpful part of this book?

   _____

3. Is there anything that you wish this book had covered?

_____

4. If you were to write this book, what would you have done differently?

_____

5. Want to chat with others who read this book, The Leadership Voices™ page is; Link http://www.Facebook.com/profile.php?id=100000603619065

_____

I hope this book has been interesting,
informative, and helpful to you.

*Trust in the Lord with all thine heart; and lean
not unto thine own understanding. In all thy ways
acknowledge him, and he shall direct thy paths.
In the name of Jesus Christ, Amen
Proverbs 3:5–6*

ENDNOTES

....

1   Irby, L C. (2002). Leadership Voices ™: Values, proactive Management, and consciousness. Proquest Information and Learning Company, An Arbor, Mi.
2   "Quantum Mechanics: Schrodinger's Cat) https://youtu.be/iVpXrbZ4bnU
3   If you do not understand Quantum Physics,: https://youtu.be/Usu9xZfabPM
4   This YouTube video list an array of Physics Videos by Eugene Khutoryansky for those who have an interest to view additional video addressing various aspects of physics. Physics Videos by Eugene Khutoryansky
5   Technically a black hole is a considered to be a space where gravity is so strong that nothing, no particles or even electromagnetic radiation can escape from it. It devours everything, thus in this case suggesting the ultimate doom for American nation status, leadership, and the demise of its clientship.
6   Margaret Mead Brainy Quotes—BrainyQuote https://www.brainyquote.com/authors/margaret-mead-quotes
7   Pastor Lawson's You Tube video: "Scientist and elite try to hide what really happened at CERN." https://youtu.be/Kk0Ax6Mlw4w
8   There are three video's that help explain the LHC.
     o   First, CERN's supercollider, Brian Cox (Ted Talk) https://youtu.be/_6uKZWnJLCM
     o   Second, How does the large Hadron Collider work? Ars Technica https://youtu.be/oWpy0SAAI6E
     o   Third, Inside the World' Largest Particle Accelerator https://youtu.be/328pw5Taeg0
9   Information for this section has been provided by EartSky. 10 years of Large Hadron Collider discoveries. Posted by EarthSky Voice in Human World. September 16, 2018. 10 years of Large Hadron Collider discoveries | Human World | EarthSky
10   For more basic information discussing the "God particle," see the YouTube video "The "God particle" explained by Bill Nye July 4,2012. https://youtu.be/rbu6IodYAa0\
11   This video in the description segment states that this video may be used for training and/or educational purposes (Copyright "Fair Use" exception. So, here is the link if you are interested in watching. (4) Scientist and the Elite

Try to Hide What Really Happened at CERN, Demonic Entities, Extra Dimensions—YouTube

[12] Nola Taylor Redd. What Are Black holes, Facts, Theory And Definition. https://www.sp, ace.com/15421-black-holes-facts-formation-discovery-sdcmp. html

[13] The history of CERN timeline. https://timeline.web.cern.ch/timeline-header/89

[14] Aggravated Quarks, https://www.britannica.com/science/subatomic-particle/Four-basic-forces

"Four basic forces. Quarks and leptons are the building blocks of matter, but they require some sort of mortar to bind themselves together into more-complex forms, whether in on a nuclear or a universal scale. The particles that provide the mortar are associated with four basic forces that are collectively referred to as the fundamental interactions of matter. These four basic forces are gravity (or the gravitational force) the electromagnetic force, and two forces more familiar to physicists than to laypeople: the strong force and the weak force.

On the larger scales the dominant force is gravity. Gravity governs the aggregation of matter into stars and galaxies and influences the way that the universe has evolved since its origin in the big bang. The best understood force, however, is the electromagnetic force which underlies the related phenomena of electricity and magnetism. The electromagnetic force binds negatively charged electrons to positively charged atomic nuclei and gives rise to the bonding between atoms to form matter in bulk.

Gravity and electromagnetism are well known at the macroscopic level. The other two forces act only on subatomic scales, indeed on subnuclear scales. The strong force binds quarks together within protons, neutrons, and other subatomic particles. Rather as the electromagnetic force is ultimately responsible for holding bulk matter together, so the strong force also keeps protons and neutrons together within atomic nuclei. Unlike the strong force, which acts only between quarks, the weak force acts on both quarks and leptons. This force is responsible for the beta decay of neutron into a proton and for the nuclear reactions that fuel the Sun and other stars.

[15] (Herbert, 1993, p.180)

[16] (Herbert, 1985, pp. 94–98).

[17] (Sztompka, 1993, pp.2–20).

[18] (Samuels et al., 1993, p. 26).

[19] (Samuels et al., 1993, p. 117

[20] (Bucke, 1923).

[21] (Samuels et al., 1993, p. 128).

[22] Jung, 1991, pp. 55–56).

[23] Jung (1991

[24] (Bellah, 1985, 1991; Eisler, 1987; Gwaltney, 1981; Johansen & Swigart, 1994; Peck, 1987; Rubin, 1976; Terkel, 1986, 1995; The New York Times, 1996; Wheatley, 1992, 1996; Wiley, 1991).

[25] (Wheatley & Kellner-Rogers, 1996, p. 51).

[26] (Alder & Towne, 1993; Aziz, 1990; Burke, 1923; Chopra, 1993, 1994; Davidson & Neale, 1990; Gleick, 1987; Jung, 1969, 1977, 1990; Herbert, 1985, 1993; Papadopoulos & Saayman, 1991; Wheatley, 1992; Wheatley & Kellner-Rodgers, 1996; Wolinsky, 1993)

[27] (Alder & Towne, 1993; Jung, 1990, 1991; Wheatley, 1992; Wheatley & Kellner-Rogers, 1996).

[28] (Sztompka, 1993, p. 221).

[29] (Sztompka, 1993, p. 222).

[30] (Herbert, 1985, pp. 94–98).

[31] Quantum Consciousness: The Guide To Experiencing Quantum Psychology. 1993.

[32] (Wolinsky, 1993, p. 7).

[33] (Wolinsky, 1993, p. 17)

[34] Common interpretation of Heisenberg's Uncertainty Principle is Proved False—Scientific American https://www.scientificamerican.com/article/common-interpretation-of-heisenbergs-uncertainty-principle-is-proven-false/ Regarding the uncertainty principle, a state of uncertainty occurs where some possible outcomes have an undesired effect or significant loss, measurement of risk. Students are still taught the uncertainty principle in introductory classes, but it turn out that it's not always true. There seems to be some sort of inner professional stalemate regarding this theory. There is some agreement amongst all that there is no way you can know both quantum states accurately at the same time."

[35] (Sztompka, 1993, p. 222).

[36] (Sztompka, 1993, pp. 222–223).

[37] (Wheatley & Kellner-Rogers, 1996, pp. 47–49)

[38] (Gleick, 1989; Jung, 1973, 1997, 1990; Papadopoulos & Saayman, 1991; Samuels et al., 1986; Wheatley, 1992; Wolinsky, 1993).

[39] (Bucke, 1923; Edelman & Crain, 1993; Gardiner, 1993; Gilbreath, 1993; Gretz & Drozdeck, 1992; Gwaltney, 1981; James, 1996; Naisbitt & Aburdene; 1990; Oakley & Krug, 1991; Peck, 1987; Popcorn, 1991; Terry, 1993; Wiley, 1991).

[40] (Eisler, 1987; Forbes, 1991; Jung, 1990; Kouzes & Posner, 1993),

[41] Eisler, Riane., The Chalice and The Blade: Our History, Our Future. (Harper: San Francisco. 1987). Forbes, Beverly A. (1001). Profile Of the Leader Of the Future: Origin, Premises. Values And Characteristics Of The Theory F Transformational Leadership Mode. Unpublished manuscript. Seattle, WA., October 1993. Jung, Carl. G., The undiscovered Self: With Symbols and the Interpretation of Dreams. In the Revised Translation by R.F.C. Hull with a new

introduction by W. McGuire. From Volume 10 of the Collected Works of C. G. Jung, Civilization in Transition (Second Edition). (Bollingen Series: Princeton University Press. 1990).

[42] Bucke, 1923; Chopra, 1993, 1994; Covey, 1992; DePree, 1972; Eisler, 1987; Herbert, 1985, 1993; Jung, 1973; Watzlawick, 1984).

[43] (Evans, 1992, 1993; Farson, 1996; Greenleaf, 1982; Keisei & Bates, 1984; Lens, 1973; Rubin, 1976, 1994; Simons et al., 1993; Terkel, 1986, 1995; West, 1991).

[44] (Gardner, 1990; Hitt, 1990; Kouzes & Posner, 1987, 1993; Peck, 1993: Rosen, 1991; Weisbord, 1987).

[45] Peck, 1987, p. 118–126; Samuels et al., 1993, pp. 150–151.

[46] Wheatley & Keller-Rogers, 1996, p. 51.

[47] Ford, 1991; Gardiner & Forbes, 1993; Hess et al., 1988; Hollander, 1978; Kouzes & Posner, 1987, 1993; Peck, 1987; Wheatley & Kellner-Rogers, 1996.

[48] Burns, 1978; Ford, 1991: Peck, 1987: Samuels et al., 1993; Wheatley & Kellner-Rogers, 1996.

[49] Irby, L C. (2002). Leadership Voices™ : Values, proactive Management, and consciousness. Proquest Information and Learning Company, An Arbor, Mi.

[50] Peck, 1987, p.102.

[51] Peck, 1987, pp. 60–66.

[52] Peck, 1987, pp. 73–77.

[53] Peck, 1987, p. 75.

[54] Peck, 1987, pp. 83–85.

[55] Tuckman's change plan from MndTols.com. https://www.mindtools.com/pages/article/newLDR_86.htm

[56] Peck, 1987, pp. 64–65.

[57] Wolinsky, 1993, p. 20.

[58] Werner Heisenberg/Biography, Nobel Prize, and Facts/ Britannica https://www.britannica.com/biography/Werner-Heisenberg.

[59] The Guardian, Science https://wwwltheguardian.com/science/2013/nov/10/what-is-heisenbergs-uncertainty-principle.

[60] The term "Self-fulfilling prophecies," was coined in 1940 by Robert K. Merton to describe a false definition of the situation evoking a new behavior which makes the originally false conception come true. For a more in-depth discussion please see: Self-Fulfilling Prophecies, Michael Biggs. The Oxford Handbook of Analytical Sociology. Online Publication Date: June 2017. https://www.oxfordhandbooks.com/view/10.1093/oxfordhb/9780199215362.001.0001/oxfordhb-9780199215362-e-13

[61] Wolinsky, 1993, p. 20.

[62] Herbert, 1985.

[63] Aziz, 1954; Bellah et al., 1995, 1991; Covey, 1989, 1992; Ford, 1991; Jung, 1973; Greenleaf, 1982; Hall & Thompson, 1980; Kouzes & Posner, 1987, 1993; Peck, 1997; Wheatley, 1992.

[64] My definition of entrained cellular memories: an accidental or intended biophysics synchronization, with location and time being irrelevant, of any two or more human body systems to any identified external person, place, or thing (the target event or intention) to determine an action, event, or location.

[65] See the video: 7 New age belief's and how to immediately recognize them. https://youtu.be/weGGxMJbYJw

[66] Aleister Crowley (1875–1947), was a British occultist, writer and a practitioner of "magick" (as he spelled it); he also called himself "the Beast." He founded his own religious order, was a controversial occultist, and his most favorite dictum is: "Do what thou wilt shall be the whole of the law." For more extensive information use the provided following link. https://www.nationaltrust.org.uk/features/the-great-beast-666-who-was-aleister-crowley

[67] Baphomet is a longstanding, pagan idol recognized today by many different occult practices. He represents harmonizes opposites (example: good and bad, male and female...and so forth). The Latin words on the god's arms "solve" (dissolve) and "coagula" (join together). Additionally, this idol is often covered with numerous occultic symbols to indicate the "well rounded," appeal to a wide range of lesser god's followers. An overview of this pagan god is provided at the following link: http://www.theblackwardrobe.com/blogs/news/who-was-baphomet-was-he-satan Another web link, which presents a anti-religion adaptation of some followers is: "Detroit's Satanic Statue Has A Political Point to Make/Time." https://time.com/3972713/detroit-satanic-statue-baphomet/

[68] Host: Ryan Ries, Guest: Steven Bancarz. Former New Age Practitioner Exposes aliens, Demons, Spiritism and the Occult. https://youtu.be/2rUmof6AaVw

[69] Grudem, W. (2020). An Introduction to Biblical Doctrine: Systematic Theology, Second Edition. Inter-Varsity Press, Great Britain. Additionally, in his study guide all Scripture quotations are changed from RSV to ESV (English Standard Version). When exceptions of translations occur they will be independently verified as either: (1) NASAB (New American Standard Bible), (2) NIV (New International Bible), (3) RSV (Revised Standard Version), and (4) CMG (Church Motion Graphics). AND MacArthur, J. (2019). The MacArthur Study Bible. Second Edition. Thomas Nelson Inc.: China. Dr. MacArthur uses the ESV Bible (the English Standard Version of the Bible).

[70] Grudem, (2021) publication

[71] Grudem, (2021) publication

[72] Grudem, page 1048.

[73] Grudem, pages 1048–1049.

[74] Grudem, pages 647–657.

[75] MacAuthur. Matthew 5:1–12, pages 1270–1271.

[76] Grudem, page 647.

[77] Grudem, page 647

[78] Grudem, page 656.

[79] Grudem, page 652.

[80] Grudem, page 656.

[81] Dr. MacArthur, is an established author and conference speaker, an acknowledged prolific author, having published 400 books and study guides; including the MacArthur Study Bible, available in nine languages and has so far sold over one million copies. In 2015, MacArthur completed his 34-volume New Testament commentary, "The MacArthur New Testament Commentary," which takes readers book by book, verse by verse, and word by word through the entire New Testament.

[82] MacAuthur, Matthew 5:1–12. pages 1270–1271

[83] Dr. Barnett is the Senior Pastor Calvary Bible Church. He has been teaching the Word of God for 30+ years—Teacher, bible Expositor, Ministry Coach, Spiritual Mental Health Care Provider and Global Partner: Discover the Book Ministry, International. He has seven publications, and can be contacted on LinkedIn https://www.linkedinlcom/in/pastorjohnbarnett or website https://www.youtube.com/c/DTBMOnlineVideoTraining or on Twitter Discover the Book.

[84] Grudem, pages 638–640.

[85] MacArthur, page 1331.

[86] Jean Piaget (1896–1980), a Swiss psychologist and genetic epistemologist. Most known for his theory of cognitive development, how children develop intellectually. Also known as a pioneer of the constructivist theory, which suggests that people actively construct their knowledge of the world based on the interactions between their ideas and their experiences. Jean Piaget: Life and Theory of Cognitive Development. https://www.verywellmind.com/jean-piaget-biography-1896–1980–2795549

[87] Horowitz. D. (2019). Dark Agenda: The war to Destroy Christian America. pages 63–158.

[88] Obedience to Authority, Stanley Milgram's 1961, experiment begun with an advertisement placed in a local paper asking for volunteers to participate in a learning experiment at nearby Yale University. Since the advertisement response was low invitations to participate were also sent by a direct mail campaign.

  o Once subjects had been selected for the experiment, they were asked to come to Yale to participate in the experiment which would last no more than an hour. In the Laboratory they met what they believed to be another participant like themselves and the "project's scientist/manager." The scientist explained that the experiment was test to the effect of punishment on learning. The test, a memory test, involved the ""learner" volunteer" memorizing and repeating a correct sequence of word pairs.

- Both participants (the volunteer "learner" and the actual study subject the "teacher") were asked draw (the drawing was rigged with both slips of paper saying ""teacher"." The "teacher" being the person who would administer the punishment to the "learner" in response to right or wrong answers. The "learner", who would try to learn the word pairs read out by the "teacher" would receive a punishment for every incorrect answer. The punishment was an electroshock, generated by an impressive (but fake) generator with rows of switches and dials. The "teacher" was instructed by the scientist to give the "learner" increasingly severe shocks each and every time he made a mistake. The shocks started at 15 volts and increased by 15 volts in thirty levels to a maximum of 450 volts.

- The "learner" was taken to an adjoining room, strapped to a chair with an electrode attached on his forearm. The" teacher" was told that the straps were necessary so that the "learner" would not move when shocked. The "learner" was told in front of the "teacher" that the shocks would hurt but would leave no permanent damage to the skin.

- As the experiment begins the "learner" initially, for the first few word pairs, does well. Then he increasingly and consistently makes mistakes-and receives a shock for each mistake. The shocks are administered by the "teacher" who is told by the experimenter to depress the appropriate switch on the shock machine. The scientist has a pre-determined script if the "teacher" objects which restates that in order to conduct the experiment the "teacher" must continue to administer the volts. The "teacher" has been told that he can stop participation in the research at any time.

- At Level Ten-150 volts the "learner" demands to be let out of the room and stop the experiment. As the voltage increases so do the "learner's" (false but perceived as real by the "teacher") cries (which soon turn to agonized screams) and demands that the experiment stop.

- By Level Twenty -300 volts the "learner" is refusing to answer any more questions and screaming in pain. From Level 23–345 volts nothing more is heard of him. Is he alive? Has he had a heart attack?

- The "learner" was very much alive and an actor. The shocks were not real, and the "learner's screams were prerecorded, and broad cast back into the laboratory. The experimenter was also an actor and the selection—where the "learner" apparently randomly selected while in fact his role was fixed.

- Down to the last detail Milgram's experiment was an extraordinary illusion entirely designed to put the real volunteer-the "teacher", in a position where he or she had to decide whether to obey the experimenter carrying on with experiment shocking the "learner". Or refuse to continue with the experimenters instructions, persuaded by the agonized screams of the "learner". Over a period of three years Milgram performed many variations of this experiment.

- The results of the study: Milgram polled 40 psychologists before the experiment asking them at what point they believed the subject-teacher would break off, stop giving shocks and defy the scientist/administrator. The psychologists believed that less than 1% of the hypothetical subjects would administer the maximum 450 volts shock. They gave a figure of one subject in a thousand. In practice 65% of subjects were fully obedient administering the maximum shock until they were told to stop. This percentage did not alter when the group of test subjects were women.

- These statistics are probably some of the most significant in the history of psychology. They show the inadequacy of the profiling models that psychologists were working with at the time, and to a large extent reflect a wider set of assumptions about human nature. The results surprised Milgram as much as the wider psychology community. Ultimately, they force researchers in the field of psychology to entirely reassess the susceptibility of human behavior to conform and respond to authoritative social structures, irrespective of any moral or ethical dilemma that they face.

[89] The Milgram Obedience Experiment this time is recreated in the name of art. Rod Dickinson is a conceptual artist who has previously gained recognition though his re-enactment, using actors and collaborators, of sermons originally given by Jim Jones, the notorious leader of the People's Temple religious cult whose member's mass suicide occurred in Guyana in 1978.

[90] Evans, 1993; James, 1987, 1990; McKay et al., 1983.

[91] Charles Cooley's "Perception is reality: The Looking-glass self," contended that behavior and self-esteem are dictated by a person's predictions of how they will be perceived by others. Today, particularly when applied to the digital age, raises questions about the nature of identity, socialization, and the changing landscape of self. Cooley's theory is notable because it suggests that self-concept is built not in solitude, but rather within social settings. In this way, society and individuals are not separate, but rather two complementary aspects of the same phenomenon. Ultimately, the process of the looking-glass self is one of alignment. People constantly seek to create consistency between their internal and external worlds and, therefore, continue to perceive, adjust, and strive for equilibrium throughout their lives.

[92] Capra (1996), James (1987) and Evans (1992, 1993).

[93] Capra along with Ford (1991), Forbes (1991), Gardiner and Forbes (1993), Gretz and Drozdeck (1992), Johansen and Swigart (1994) and Rubin (1997)

[94] Mapes, (1966), Values and Leadership Within Organizations. p. 56

[95] Irby, *Leadership Voices™: Neutralizing Bullies, Determinedly Difficult People, Bullies, And Predators At Work. pages 80–86*

[96] The description of the movie is from the movie trailer for "Falling Down." 1993, director, Joel Schumacher, Staring Michael Douglas, Robert Duvall, Barbara Hershey, Rachel Ticotin, and Tuesday Weld. Warner Bros. Pictures

[97] Ross, Elisabeth, K. (1997). On Death and Dying. Scribner Classic Edition. Simon and Schuster: New York

[98] MacArthur's Study Bible indicates in the footnotes that "SAMECH," refers to the meaning "I hate the divided heart or mind—and refers us to (Psalms 119:162 I rejoice at Your word). pages 758–769.

BIBLIOGRAPHY

- "Study to shew thyself approved unto God, a workman that needeth not to be ashamed, rightly dividing the word of truth" (2 Timothy 2:15)
- Alder, R. B., & Towne, N. (1993). Looking out/looking in. (7th ed.). Harcourt Brace Jovanovich College Publishers: Florida.
- Alexander, M. (2012). The New Jim Crow: Mass incarceration in the age of colorblindness. The New Press: New York.
- Anderson, C. (2017), White Rage. The unspoken truth of our racial divide. Bloomsbury Publishing: Bloomsbury
- Atlanta Jacobsen, S.E. (1994). Spirituality and leadership in secular settings: A Delhi study. Seattle University.
- Autry, J. A. (1991). Love and profit: The art of caring leadership. Avon Press: New York. Aziz, R. (1990).
- Bass and Stogdill's handbook of leadership: Theory, research and managerial applications. The Free Press: New York. Beauchamp, T. L., & Bowie, N.E. (1988). Third edition: Ethical theory and business. Prentice Hall: New Jersey.
- Beckhard, R., & Pritchard, W. (1992). Changing the essence: The art of creating and leading fundamental changes in organizations. Jossey-Bass Publishers: San Francisco.
- Bellah, R. N., et al. (1985). Habits of the heart: Individualism and commitment in American life. Harper & Row: New York. 223

277

- Bellah, R. N., et al. (1991). The good society. Alfred A. Knopf: New York.
- Bennis, W. (1989). On becoming a leader. Addison-Wesley: Menlo Park.
- Bennis, W., & Nanus, B. (1985). Leaders: The strategies for taking charge. Harper and Row: New York.
- Bernstein, A. J., & Rozen, S. C. (1992). Neanderthals at work: How people and politics can drive you crazy... And what you can do about them. Ballantine Books: New York.
- Billingsley, A. (1968). Black families in white America. Simon & Schuster Inc.: New York.
- Blake, R. R., et al. (1964). Breakthrough in organization development. Harvard Business Review, 42, 133–135.
- Bolman, L. G. (1995). Leading with soul: An uncommon journey of spirit. Jossey-Bass: San Francisco.
- Bolman, L. G., & Deal, T. E. (1991). Reframing organizations: Artistry, choice, and leadership. Jossey-Bass: San Francisco.
- Bouwsma, W. J. (1988). John Calvin: A sixteenth century portrait. Oxford University Press: New York.
- Bridges, W. (1991). Managing transitions: Making the most of change. Addison Wesley: Massachusetts. Bucke, R. M. (1923). Cosmic consciousness: A study in the evolution of the human mind. Penguin Books: New York. Burns J. M. (1978). Leadership. Harper & Row: New York.
- Bridges, W. (1994). Job shift. Addison-Wesley: New York 224
- Brown, S.L. (2009). Women who love psychopaths. Inside the relationships of inevitable harm with psychopaths, sociopaths, and Narcissists. Book Printing Revolution: Minneapolis. Book Summary
- Buchanan, L. (2003). The Seventh Sense: The secrets of remote viewing as told by a "psychic spy" for the U.W. military. Paraview: New York: New York.
- C.G. Jung's psychology of religion and synchronicity. State University of New York Press. Bass, B. M. (1990).

- Capri, F. (1996). The web of life. Doubleday: New York. Chopra, D. (1993). The higher self. Simon and Schuster: New York.
- Chopra, D. (1994). The seven spiritual laws of success: A practical guide to the fulfillment of your dreams. Amber-Allen Publishing: San Rafael, CA.
- Cohen, H. (1993). Negotiating the game: New perspectives on negotiating. Harper Collins Publisher, Inc.: New York. Compilation (A Harvard Business Review Book), (1992). Leaders on leadership: Interviews with top executives. Preference by Warren Bennis. Covey, S. R. (1989). The 7 habits of highly effective people. Simon and Schuster: New York.
- Covey, S. R. (1992). Principled centered leadership: Give a man a fish and you feed him for a day; Teach him how to fish and you feed him for a lifetime. Simon and Schuster: New York. 225
- Cox T. JR. (1993). Cultural diversity in organizations: Theory, research, & practice. Berrett-Koehler Publisher: San Francisco.
- Davison, G. D., & Neil, J. M. (1990). Abnormal psychology: Fifth edition. John Wiley & Sons: New York.
- Deming, W. E. (1986). Drastic changes for western management. Center for Quality and Productivity Improvement: Madison, WI.
- Deming, W. E. (1986b). Out of the crisis. Massachusetts Institute of Technology, Center for Advanced Engineering Study: Cambridge, MA.
- Deming, W. E. (1991). Deming's 14 points applied to services. Marcel Dekker, Inc.: New York.
- DePree, M. (1989). Leadership is an art. Dell Trade: New York.
- DePree, M. (1992). Leadership jazz. Doubleday: New York.

- Deutsche, D. (1998). The fabric of reality: The science of parallel universes-and its implication. Viking Penguin: New York.
- Diangelo, R. (2018). White fragility. Why ist's so hard for white people to talk about racism. Beacon Press: Boston.
- Dickson, J. A. (1973). Holy Bible: New analytical Bible and dictionary of the Bible. Authorized King James Version with comprehensive general index edition. John A. Dickinson Publishing Co.: Chicago.
- Dilenschneider, R. L. (1990). Power and influence: Mastering the art of persuasion. Prentice Hall Press: New York. 226
- Dizdar, R. (2009). The black awakening: Rise of the satanic super soldiers and the coming chaos. Preemption Books and Products: Canton, Ohio.
- Dorsey, D. (1994). The force. Random House: New York. Doyle, W., & Perkins, W. (1994). Smash the pyramid: 100 career secrets from America's fastest-rising executives. Warner Books: New York.
- Drucker, P. (1967). The effective executive. Harper and Row: San Francisco.
- Dutton, K. (2012). The wisdom of psychopaths. What saints, spies, and serial killers can teach us about success. Scientific American: New York.
- E. C. (1996). Leadership IQ: A personal development process based on a scientific study of a new generation of leaders. John Wiley & Sons: New York.
- Ebenstein, W. (1969). Great political thinkers: Plato to the present. (Fourth edition). Holt, Rinehart and Winston, Inc.: New York.
- Edelman, J., & Crain, M. B. (1993). The tao of negotiation: How you can prevent, resolve and transcend conflict in work and everyday life. Harper Business: New York.
- Effler, W.B. (1994). Leadership by God's design: Spirituality for leadership's personal and corporate growth. DIA, 55(6A) 1600.

- Eisler, R. (1987). The chalice and the blade: Our history, our future. Harper: San Francisco.
- English, H. B, & English, A. C. (1966). A comprehensive dictionary of psychological and psychoanalytical terms. A guide to usage, for readers and writers in the fields of psychology, psychoanalysis, psychiatry, education, guidance, and social work. David McKay Company, Inc.: New York.
- Evans, P. (1992). The verbally abusive relationship: How to recognize it and how to respond. Bob Adams, Inc.: Holbrook, Massachusetts. 227
- Evans, P. (1993). Verbal abuse survivors speak out: On relationship and recovery. Bob Adams, Inc. Holbrook, Massachusetts.
- Everett, WA. Gilligan, C. (1993). In a different voice: Psychological theory and women's development. Harvard University Press: Cambridge.
- Farson, R. (1996). Management of the absurd: Paradoxes in leadership. Simon and Schuster: New York.
- Fisher, R., & Ury, W. (1981). Getting to yes: Negotiating agreement without giving in. (Second edition). Penguin Books: New York.
- Forbes, B. A. (1991). Profile of the leader of the future: Origin, premises, values and characteristics of the theory F transformational leadership model. Unpublished manuscript. Seattle, Washington, October 1993.
- Forcese, D. P., & Richer, S. (1970). Stages of social research: Contemporary perspectives. Prentice-Hall: Englewood Cliffs, New Jersey.
- Ford, L. (1991). Transforming leadership: Jesus' way of creating vision, shaping values & empowering change. InterVarsity Press: Downers Grove, Illinois.
- Fruehling, R. T., & Lacombe, J. M. (1966). Communicating for results. EMC Paradigm: St Paul, MN.
- Gardiner, J. J. (1988). Building leadership teams. In M.F. Green (Ed.) Leaders for a new era: Strategies for higher edu-

cation. (pp. 137–153). American Council on Education/ MacMillan Publishing: New York. 228

- Gardiner, J. J. (1993). Beyond leader and community: Creating new metaphors of governance for American higher education. Article. Seattle, Washington.
- Gardiner, J. J., & Forbes, B. A. Preparing effective leaders for an interdependent world: Seattle University's multidisciplinary doctoral cohorts. Paper presented to the National Leadership Group of the American Council on Education, Washington, D.C. December 3, 1993.
- Gardner, W. (1990). On leadership. The Free Press: New York.
- Gilbreath, R. D. (1993). Escape from management hell: 12 tales of horror, humor, and heroism. Berrett-Koehler Publishers: San Francisco.
- Gillespie, R. C. (1992). Managing is everybody's business. Work/Life Books:
- Gleick, J. (1987). Chaos: Making a new science. Penguin Books: New York.
- Goleman, D. (1995). Emotional intelligence: Why it can matter more than IQ. Bantam Books: New York.
- Greenleaf, R. K. (1982). Servant leadership: A journey into the nature of legitimate power and greatness. Paulist Press: New York. 229
- Gretz, K. F., & Drozdeck, S. R. (1992) Empowering innovative people. Prous Publishing Company: Chicago.
- Grudem, W. (2020). An Introduction to Biblical Doctrine: Systematic Theology, Second Edition. Inter-Varsity Press, Great Britain
- Gwaltney, J. L. (1981). Drylongso: A self-portrait of Black America. Vintage Books: New York.
- Hall, B. P., & Thompson, H. (1980). Leadership through values. Paulist Press: New York.
- Hammond, J., & Morrison, J. (1996), Stuff Americans are made of: Seven cultural forces that define Americans—A

new framework for quality, productivity and profitability. Simon and Schuster Macmillan Company: New York.

- Heider, J. (1985). The tao of leadership: Leadership strategies for a new age. Bantam Books: New York.
- Herbert, N. (1985). Quantum reality: Beyond the new physics an excursion into metaphysics and the meaning of reality. Anchor Books, Doubleday: New York.
- Herbert, N. (1993). Elemental mind: Human consciousness and the new physics. Plume: New York.
- Hersey, P., & Blanchard, K. H. (1977). Management of organizational behavior: Utilizing human resources. Prentice-Hall: Englewood Cliffs.
- Hess, B. B., Markson, E. W., & Stein, P. J. (1988). Sociology: Third edition. MacMillan Publishing Company: New York. 230
- Hitt, W. D. (1990). Ethics and leadership: Putting theory into practice. Battelle Press: Columbus, Ohio.
- Hollander, E. P. (1978). Leadership dynamics: A practical guide to effective relationships. The Free Press: New York.
- Holroyd, S. (1977). PSI and the consciousness explosion. Taplinger: New York.
- Hood, B. (2013). The self-illusion: How the social brain creates identity. Oxford University Press: New York.
- Horowitzz, D. (2018). Dark agenda: The war to destroy Christian America. Humanix Books: Florida.
- Irby, L. C. (2002). Leadership Voices™: Values, proactive management, and consciousness. Dissertation. UMI Number 3041369. ProQuest Information and Learning Company. Ann Arbor: MI.
- Irby, L. C. (2006). Leadership Voices™: Neutralizing bullies, determinedly difficult people, and predators at work. University Press of America: New York.
- James, J. (1987). Windows. Expanded edition. Newmarket Press: New York.
- James, J. (1990). You know I wouldn't say this if I didn't love you: How to defend yourself against verbal zaps and

zingers. Revised, expanded edition of The slug manual: The rise and fall of criticism. Newmarket Press: New York.

- James, J. (1996). Thinking in the future tense: Leadership skills for a new age. Simon and Schuster: New York.

- Jamieson, D., & O'Mara, J. (1991). Managing workforce 2000: Gaining the diversity advantage. Forward by Warren Bennis. Jossey-Bass: San Francisco.

- Jaworski, J. (1996). Synchronicity: The inner path of leadership. Introduction by Peter Senge. Berrett-Koehler Inc.: San Francisco.

- Johansen, R., & Swigart, R. (1994). Upsizing the individual in the downsized organization: Managing in the wake of reengineering, globalization, and overwhelming technological change. Doddison-Wesley Publishing: New York. 231

- John Wiley and Sons: New York. McKay, M., et al. (1983). How to communicate: The ultimate guide to improving your personal and professional relationships. MJF Books: New York.

- Jung, C. G. (1969). The psychological foundations of belief in spirits and the soul and death. Extracted from Volume 8, The structure and dynamics of the psyche (2nd ed.). Princeton University Press.

- Jung, C. G. (1973). Synchronicity: An acausal connecting principle. Translation by R. F. C. Hull. From the Collected Works of C. G. Jung, Volume 8. Bollingen Series: Princeton University Press.

- Jung, C. G. (1977). Psychology and the occult. Translation by R. F. C. Hull. From the Collected Works of C. G. Jung, Volumes 1, 8, and 18. Bollingen Series: Princeton University Press.

- Jung, C. G. (1990). The undiscovered self: With symbols and the interpretation of dreams. In the Revised Translation by R. F. C. Hull with a new introduction by W. McGuire. From Volume 10 of the Collected Works of C. G. Jung,

Civilization in transition (Second Edition). Bollingen Series: Princeton University Press.

- Keirsey, D., & Bates, M. (1984). Please understand me: Character and temperament types. Prometheus Nemesis: Del Mar, CA.
- Kotex, J. P. (1995). The new rules: How to succeed in today's post-corporate world. The Free Press: New York.
- Kouzes, J. M., & Posner, B. Z. (1987). The leadership challenge: How to get extraordinary things done in organizations. San Francisco: Jossey-Bass.
- Kouzes, J. M., & Posner, B. Z. (1993). Credibility: How leaders gain and lose it, why people demand it. Jossey-Bass: San Francisco.
- Kreitner, R., & Kinicki, A. (1992). Organizational behavior. Irwin: Homewood, IL.
- Kreuger, R. A. (1988). Focus groups: A practical guide for applied research. Sage: London. 232
- Kubler-Ross, E. (1997). And death and dying. Scribner: New York New York.
- L. R. Pondy, R. J. Boland, Jr. and H. Thomas (Eds.), Managing ambiguity and change. (pp.93–126).
- Labovitz, S., & Hagedorn, R. (1971). Introduction to social research. Mcgraw-Hill Inc: New York.
- Lawler, E., et al. (1980). Organizational assessment, perspectives on the measurement of organizational behavior and the quality of work life. John Wiley and Sons: New York.
- Lens, S. (1973). The labor wars: From the Molly Maguries to the sit-downs. Doubleday & Company, Inc.: New York.
- Lindelöf, T. R. (1955). Qualitative communication research methods. Sage Publications: Thousand Oaks.
- Locke, E. A., et al. (1991). The essence of leadership: The four keys to leading successfully. Lexington Books: New York. 233
- Lutz, G. M. (1983). Understanding social statistics. MacMillan Publishing Co., Inc.: New York.

- MacAuthur, J. (2019). The MacArthur Study Bible. Second Edition. Thomas Nelson Inc.: China
- Machiavelli, N. (1981). The prince. Translated with an introduction by George Bull. Penguin Books: New York.
- Maps, J. J. (1996). Quantum leap thinking: An owner's guide to the mind. Dove Books: Beverly Hills.
- Martin, J., & Meyerson, D. (1988). Organizational cultures and the denial, channeling and acknowledgment of ambiguity.
- McMonegle, J. (1998). The ultimate time machine. A remote viewer's perception of time, and predictions for the new millennium. Hampton Roads Publishing: Newburyport.
- Meehan, M., et al. (1997). Future ain't what it use to be. Penguin Putnam Inc.: New York.
- Miller, D. C. (1983). Handbook of research design and social measurement. Longmont: New York.
- Morgan, D. L. (1988). Focus groups as qualitative research. Sage: London.
- Morgan, D. L., & Kreuger, R. A. (1993). When to use focus groups and why. In D.L. Morgan (Ed.) Successful focus groups. Sage: London. 234
- Morgan, G. (1966). Images of organizations. Sage Publications: Newborn Park.
- Moss. L. (1981). Management stress. Addison-Wesley Publishing Co. Murphy,
- Naisbitt, J., & Aburdene, P. (1990). Megatrends 2000: Ten new directions for the 1990's. William Morrow and Co., Inc.: New York.
- Neave, H. R. (1991). The Deming dimension. SPC Press, Inc.: Knoxville, Tennessee.
- Oakley, E., & Krug, D. (1991). Enlightened leadership: Getting to the heart of change. Fireside: New York.
- oriented team. Prima: Rocklin, CA.

- Ouchi, W. (1981). Theory Z: How American business can meet the Japanese challenge. Addison-Wesley: Menlo Park, CA.
- Papadopoulos, R. K., & Saayman, G. S. (Eds.). (1991). Jung in modern perspective: The master and his legacy. Unity Press: Australia.
- Peck, S. (1987). The different drum: Community-making and peace. Simon and Schuster: New York.
- Peck, S. (1993). A world waiting to be born: Civility rediscovered. Bantam Books: New York. 235
- Peppers, D., & Rogers, M. (1996). The one-to-one future: Building relationships one customer at a time. Currency: New York.
- Peppers, D., & Rogers, M. (1997). Enterprise one to one: Tools for competing in the interactive age. Currency: New York. Peters, T. (1988).
- Peters, T. (1994). The pursuit of wow!: Every person's guide to topsy-turvy times. Random House, Inc.: New York.
- Piantanida, M., & Garman, N. B. (1999). The qualitative dissertation: A guide for students and faculty. Corwin Press: Thousand Oaks.
- Popcorn, F. (1991). The Popcorn report: Faith Popcorn on the future of your company, your world, your life. Doubleday Currency: New York.
- REFERENCES 1993 Parliament of Religions-Chicago, Our religions: The seven world religions introduced by preeminent scholars from each tradition. Arvind Sharma (Ed.) Harper: San Francisco.
- Riplinger, G.A. (1993). New age bible version. Avpublications.com: Arorat Va.
- Ritzer, G. (2000). The McDonaldization of society. Pine Forge Press: Thousand Oaks
- Robbins, S. P. (1988). Management. (second ed.) Prentice Hall: New Jersey.
- Roberts, W. (1990). Leadership secrets of Attila the Hun. Warner Books. New York.

- Rodale, J. I. (1978). The synonym finder: Special deluxe edition. Rodale Press: Emmaus, Pa. 236
- Rosen, R. with Berger, L. (1991). The healthy company: Eight strategies to develop people, productivity and profits. Jeremy P. Tarcher/Perigree: New York.
- Rossi, E. L. (1993). The psychobiology of mind-body healing. Revised edition. W. W. Norton and Company, Inc.: New York.
- Rossi, P. H., et al. (1979). Evaluation: A systematic approach. Sage Publications: Beverly Hills.
- Rubin, H. (1997). The princessa: Machiavelli for women. Currency: New York.
- Rubin, L. B. (1976). Worlds of pain: Life in the working-class family. Basic Books, Inc., Publishers: New York.
- Rubin, L. B. (1994). Families on the fault line: America's working class speaks about the family, the economy, race and ethnicity. Harper Perennial: New York.
- Ruche, K.E. (n.d.) Influencing performance in manufacturing work systems: An examination of causal relationships of organizational structures and situational workplace variables on proactive management behavior. DIA, 54(07).
- Rusk, T. (1993). The power of ethical persuasion: From conflict to partnership at work and in private life. Penguin Books: New York.
- Ryan, K. D., & Oestreich, D. K. (1991). Driving fear out of the workplace: How to overcome the invisible barriers to quality, productivity, and innovation. JosseyBass: San Francisco. 237
- Safari, W. (1993). Safari's new political dictionary: The definitive guide to the new language of politics. Random House: New York.
- Samuels, A., et al. (1993). A critical dictionary of jungian analysis. Routledge and Kegan Paul LTD: New York.
- Sapolsky, R. M. (2017), Behave: The biology of humans at our best and worst. Penguin Books: New York.

- Schellardt, T.D. (1996, August 1). Are layoffs moral? One firm's answer: You ask, we'll sue. The Wall Street Journal.
- Schmidt, J.E. (1993). Transformational leadership: The relationship between consciousness, values and skills (leadership). DIA, 54(11A), 4057.
- Senge, P. (1990). The fifth discipline. Doubleday: New York.
- Sheehy, G. (1995). New passages: Mapping your life across time. Random House, Inc.: New York.
- Simons, G. F., et al. (1993). Transcultural leadership: Empowering the diverse workforce. Gulf Publishing Company: Houston.
- Slusser, G. H. (1986). From Jung to Jesus: Myth and consciousness in the New Testament. John Knox Press:
- Smith, H. (2012). Who stole the American dream. Random House, Inc.: New York.
- Storey, J. (1994). Cultural theory and popular culture: A reader. Harvester/Wheatsheaf: New York 238
- Sundstrom, E., DeMeuse, K. P., & Futrell, D. (1990). Work teams. American Psychologist. 120–133.
- Swann, I. (2018). Everybody's guide to natural ESP: Unlocking the extrasensory power of your mind. Swann-Ryder Production LLC: U.K.
- Sztompka, P. (1993). The sociology of social change. Blackwell, Oxford U.K. and Cambridge U.S.A.
- Tapscott, D. and Tapscott, A. (2016). Blockchain revolution. How the technology behind bitcoin and other cryptocurrencies is changing the world. Portfolio: New York: New York.
- Terkel, S. (1986). Hard times: An oral history of the Great Depression. Pantheon Books: New York.
- Terkel, S. (1995). Coming of age: The story of our century by those who've lived it. The New Press: New York.
- Terry, R. W. (1993). Authentic leadership: Courage in action. Jossey-Bass: San Francisco.

- The New York Times. (1996). Special report: The downsizing of America. millions of Americans are losing good jobs. This is their story. Expanded to include additional reporting and reader responses to the extraordinary series by the reporters of The New York Times.
- Thriving on chaos: Handbook for a management revolution. Alfred A. Knopf: New York.
- Torres, C., & Spiegel, J. (1990). Self-directed work teams: A primer. Pfeiffer and Co.: San Diego.
- Tuckman, B. W. (1965). Developmental sequence in small groups. Psychological Bulletin. 239
- Ury, W. (1991). Getting past no: Negotiating with difficult people. Bantam Doubleday Dell: New York.
- Walding, D. M. (1994). Spirituality and leadership. DIA, 55 (7A), 1783.
- Wall, B., et al. (1992). The visionary leader: From mission statement to a thriving organization, here's your blueprint for building an inspired cohesive, customer
- Walton, C. C. (1988). The moral manager. Harper Business: New York. Ward, L. B. (1965). The ethics of executive selection. Harvard Business Review, 43 (2), 6–28.
- Watzlawick, P. (1984). The invented reality: How do we know what we believe we know? (Contributions to constructivism). W.W. Norton and Company.
- Weber, M. (1995). The Protestant ethic and the spirit of capitalism. Translated by T. Parsons. Introduction by A. Gibbens, Fellow of King's College, Cambridge. Routledge: New York.
- Weisbord, M. R. (1987). Productive workplaces: Organizing and managing for dignity, meaning, and community. Jossey-Bass: San Francisco.
- West, C. (1991). Race matters. Beacon Press: Boston. Wheatley, M. J. (1992). Leadership and the new science: Learning about organization from an orderly universe. Berrett-Koehler: San Francisco. 240

- Wheatley, M. J., & Kellner-Rogers, M. (1996). A simpler way. Berrett-Koehler: San Francisco.
- Wiley, R. (1991). Why Black people tend to shout: Cold facts and wry views from a Black man's world. Penguin Books: New York.
- Williams, F. (19860. Reasoning with statistics: How to read quantitative research. (Third Edition). Holt, Rinehart and Winston: New York.
- Wolcott, H. (1994). Transforming qualitative data: Description, analysis and interpretation. Sage Publications: Thousand Oaks
- Wolin, S.S. (2001). Tocqueville between two worlds: The making of a political and theoretical life. Princeton University Press: Princeton and Oxford.
- Wolinsky, S. (1993). Quantum consciousness: The guide to experiencing quantum psychology. Bramble Books: Northfork, Connecticut.
- Wolinsky, S. (1999a). The way of the human: Volume I Developing multi-dimensional awareness. The quantum psychology notebooks (Special section: Trances people live revised). Quantum Institute: Capitola, California.
- Wolinsky, S. (1999b). The way of the human: Volume II The false core and the false self. The quantum psychology notebooks. Quantum Institute: Capitola, California.
- Wolinsky, S. (1999c). The way of the human: Volume III Beyond quantum psychology. The quantum psychology notebooks. (Special section: Trances people live revised) Quantum Institute: Capitola, California. 241
- Woodward, B. (2018). Fear: Trump in the white house. Simon and Schuster: New York.
- Yankelovich, D. (1981). New rules: Searching for self-fulfillment in a world turned upside down. Random House: New York.
- Yukl, G. A. (1981). Leadership in organizations. Englewood Cliffs, NJ: Prentice Hall.

- Zacharias, R. (2000). Jesus among other gods. The absolute claims of the Christians message. Thomas Nelson. Inc.: Nashville.

APPENDIX A

List Of Tables By Chapter

Chapter 1.
Table 1: Selected array of occult practices contributing to the normalization of occult practices in the U.S.

Chapter 3
Table 2. Man has both a spirit (life force) within earthly body.

Chapter 5
Table 3: Selected array of occult practices contributing to the normalization of occult practices in the U.S.

Chapter 8
Table 4: Selected scriptures that bring comfort, security, and joy.

APPENDIX B

···

Lists Of Internet Links By Chapter

- **Book Summary**
  - https://www.academia.edu/575575/ Dissertation-Leadership-Voices-Values-Proactive Management and consciousness Here is the download for the full 2002 dissertation, "Leadership Voices™: Values, Proactive Management, and Consciousness.
  - Facebook page: Leadership Voices™: for open discussions, thoughts, and questions. (20+) Facebook
  - lindairbybb@outlook.com for direct email contact related to dealing with determinedly difficult people, bullies and predators at work—and other dysfunctional work force group transformation.
  - https://www.linkedin.com/in/linda-irby-ed-d-20026017 for my educational and work profile, awards, and other publications.

- **Chapter 1: Our new norm started in 2001.**
  This book's backstory:
  - "If you do not understand Quantum Physics,: https://youtu.be/Usu9xZfabPM

- **Chapter 2: Change, catastrophic change, and berserk chaos.**
  - Margaret Mead Brainy Quotes—BrainyQuote https://www.brainyquote.com/authors/margaret-mead-quotes
  - See YouTube video Flash point, the Equality Act passes house. This video concisely lists four issues and thoroughly explains why Christians need to know why this bill is imminently important video published Feb. 25, 2021). https://youtu.be/UV63ebFBoe4

- **Chapter 3: Conscious awareness, what is this?**
  - Pastor Lawson's You Tube video: "Scientist and elite try to hide what really happened at CERN." https://youtu.be/Kk0Ax6Mlw4w

Advancements in Quantum Mechanics since 2002
  - For more basic information discussing the "God particle," see the YouTube video "The "God particle" explained by Bill Nye July 4,2012. https://youtu.be/rbu6IodYAa0

There are three video's that help explain the LHC.
  - First, CERN's supercollider, Brian Cox (Ted Talk) https://youtu.be/_6uKZWnJLCM
  - Second, How does the large Hadron Collider work? Ars Technica https://youtu.be/oWpy0SAAI6E
  - Third, Inside the World' Largest Particle Accelerator https://youtu.be/328pw5Taeg0
  - HIGHLY RECOMMENDED TO WATCH: Concerns regarding the attempt to replicate the original Big Bang, video presenters by Pastors Chuck Missler and Charles Lawson. "Scientist and the Elite Try to Hide What Really Happened at CERN, Demonic Entities, Extra Dimensions. Speakers: Pastors Chuck Missler and Charles Lawson. (4) Scientist and the

Elite Try to Hide What Really Happened at CERN, Demonic Entities, Extra Dimensions—YouTube
- Those interested in following CERN on Facebook this is the link: (3) CERN | Facebook

Quantum Mechanics and the large Hadron Collider.
- "What are Black Holes?" By Nola Taylor Redd July 11, 2019, https://www.space.com/15421-black-holes-facts-formation-discovery-sdcmp.html
- "Microscopic Smart Dust'" sensors are set to revolutionise a range of sectors—The New Economy By Courtney Goldsmith | Monday, June 3rd, 2019
- "Programmable Matter." Elliot Hawkes, Byoungkwon (Kwon) An, Nadia Benbernou, Hiroto Tanaka, Sangbae Kim, Erik D. Demaine, Daniela Rus, Robert J. Wood. Proceedings of the National Academy of Sciences 2010.YouTube "AutoDesk" Programmable Matter by Folding (autodesk.com)
- HIGHLY RECOMMENDED TO WATCH: You tube (49) Robot Origami: Robot self-folds, walks, and completes tasks—YouTube

- November 14, 2019. Quantum physics: our study suggests objective reality doesn't exist. https://theconversation.com/quantum-psysics-our-study-suggests-objective-reality-doesn't-exist-125805

- **Chapter 4: Building of community**.
  - Interested in learning more about Tuckman's change plan go to: Forming, Storming, norming, and performing—From MindTols.com https://www.mindtools.com/pages/article/newLDR_86.htm
  - Werner Heisenberg's Uncertainty Principle, The Guardian, Science https://wwwltheguardian.com/science/2013/nov/10/what-is-heisenbergs-uncertainty-principle

- The World Bank organization page: How countries are using EDTECH to support access to remote learning during the COVOD-19 pandemic. For more information contact their website directly at: https://www.worldbank.org/en/topic/edutech/brief/how-countries-are-using-edtech-to-support-remote-learning-during-the-covid-19-pandemic

- **Chapter 5: What facilitated normalization of Occult practices?**
  - Former New Age practitioner exposes aliens, demons, spiritism and the occult. https://youtu.be/2rUmof6AaVw ;
  - See the video: 7 New age belief's and how to immediately recognize them. https://youtu.be/weGGxMJbYJw
  - Barnett's class on what Jesus says is the Unpardonable Sin. https://youtu.be/REdr6ibRGd0
  - The Court's official web page. About the Supreme Court | United States Courts (uscourts.gov)

- **Chapter 6: Leadership. There is always a leader.**
  - Charles Cooley's "Looking Glass" study. https://lesley.edu/article/perception-is-reality-the-looking-glass-self

- **Chapter 8: God: all things were made by Him.**
  - Paster Mike Hoggard's (posted Dec. 27, 2020). The Difference: The King James Bible vs. Modern Translations. https://youtu.be/ZmFmzyPq3Lk

www.ingramcontent.com/pod-product-compliance
Lightning Source LLC
Chambersburg PA
CBHW052047150125
20428CB00045B/1406